S0-ACL-853

SOCIAL STUDIES
Anthology

THE WORLD AROUND US

Art from three of the regions of

the world is shown in the cover

photos. The background is

a Kasii mat from Zaire in

Africa, the rug was made in

the Caucasus region of North

Asia, and the Mixtec mask is

from Mexico in Latin America.

MACMILLAN/McGRAW-HILL SCHOOL PUBLISHING COMPANY
NEW YORK   CHICAGO   COLUMBUS

PROGRAM AUTHORS •

Dr. James A. Banks
Professor of Education and Director of the Center for
    Multicultural Education
University of Washington
Seattle, Washington

Dr. Barry K. Beyer
Professor of Education and American Studies
George Mason University
Fairfax, Virginia

Dr. Gloria Contreras
Professor of Education and Director of the Office of
    Multicultural Affairs
University of North Texas
Denton, Texas

Jean Craven
District Coordinator of Curriculum Development
Albuquerque Public Schools
Albuquerque, New Mexico

Dr. Gloria Ladson-Billings
Assistant Professor of Education
University of Wisconsin
Madison, Wisconsin

Dr. Mary A. McFarland
Director of Staff Development and Instructional
    Coordinator of Social Studies, K-12
Parkway School District
Chesterfield, Missouri

Dr. Walter C. Parker
Associate Professor of Social Studies Education and
    Director of the Center for the Study of Civic
    Intelligence
University of Washington
Seattle, Washington

CONTENT CONSULTANTS •

Yvonne Beamer
Resource Specialist
Native American Education Program
New York, New York

Mario T. Garcia
Professor of History and American Studies
Yale University
New Haven, Connecticut

Héctor Lindo-Fuentes
Associate Professor of History
Fordham University
Bronx, New York

Ruthanne Lum McCunn
Chinese Historical Society of America
San Francisco, California

Valerie Ooka Pang
Associate Professor, School of Teacher Education
San Diego State University
San Diego, California

Clifford E. Trafzer
Professor of Ethnic Studies and Director of Native
    American Studies
University of California
Riverside, California

GRADE-LEVEL CONSULTANTS •

Desiree Allen
Sixth Grade Social Studies Teacher
Shadow Lawn Middle School
Arlington, Tennessee

Marianne Hogan
Core Teacher
Winston Park Junior High School
Palatine, Illinois

Nadine Kauffman
Principal and Seventh Grade Teacher
St. Francis Xavier School
Lake Station, Indiana

Karen Rectanus
Seventh Grade Teacher
Carroll Middle School
Raleigh, North Carolina

ACKNOWLEDGMENTS •

*The publisher gratefully acknowledges permission to reprint
the following copyrighted material:*

"Observations of a 14th Century Traveler" from
AFRICAN CIVILIZATION REVISITED by Basil
Davidson. Copyright © Basil Davidson. First AWP
Edition 1991. Reprinted by permission of Africa World
Press.

"Mali under Mansa Musa" from A GLORIOUS AGE
IN AFRICA by Daniel Chu and Elliot Skinner.
Copyright © Daniel Chu and Elliott Skinner. First
AWP edition 1990. Reprinted by permission of Africa
World Press.

(continued on page 215)

Macmillan/McGraw-Hill School Division
10 Union Square East
New York, New York 10003

Printed in the United States of America
ISBN 0-02-146128-7
1 2 3 4 5 6 7 8 9 POH 99 98 97 96 95 94 93 92

TABLE OF *Contents*

🔲 = audio cassette

USING YOUR *Anthology*

This year you will be reading about many different peoples, places, and times in your Social Studies textbook. This Anthology, or collection of documents created by different people, will make the information in your textbook come to life in a special way. It includes diaries, songs, stories, posters, poems, speeches, and even ancient pictographs and hieroglyphics. As you read and study these primary sources, you will be able to see, feel, and hear what it was like to live in other times and places. The documents in this Anthology will help you to better understand the world around you and the people—famous and non-famous—who have shaped our world.

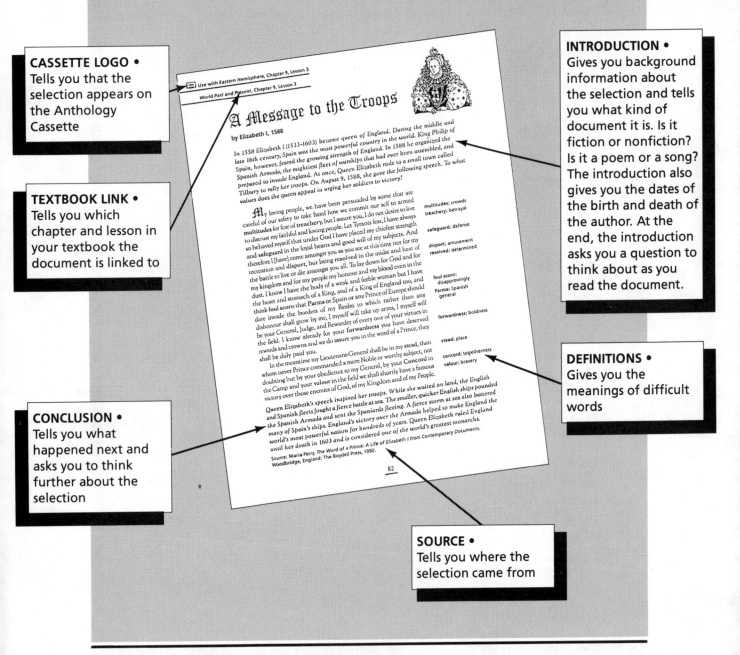

CASSETTE LOGO •
Tells you that the selection appears on the Anthology Cassette

TEXTBOOK LINK •
Tells you which chapter and lesson in your textbook the document is linked to

CONCLUSION •
Tells you what happened next and asks you to think further about the selection

INTRODUCTION •
Gives you background information about the selection and tells you what kind of document it is. Is it fiction or nonfiction? Is it a poem or a song? The introduction also gives you the dates of the birth and death of the author. At the end, the introduction asks you a question to think about as you read the document.

DEFINITIONS •
Gives you the meanings of difficult words

SOURCE •
Tells you where the selection came from

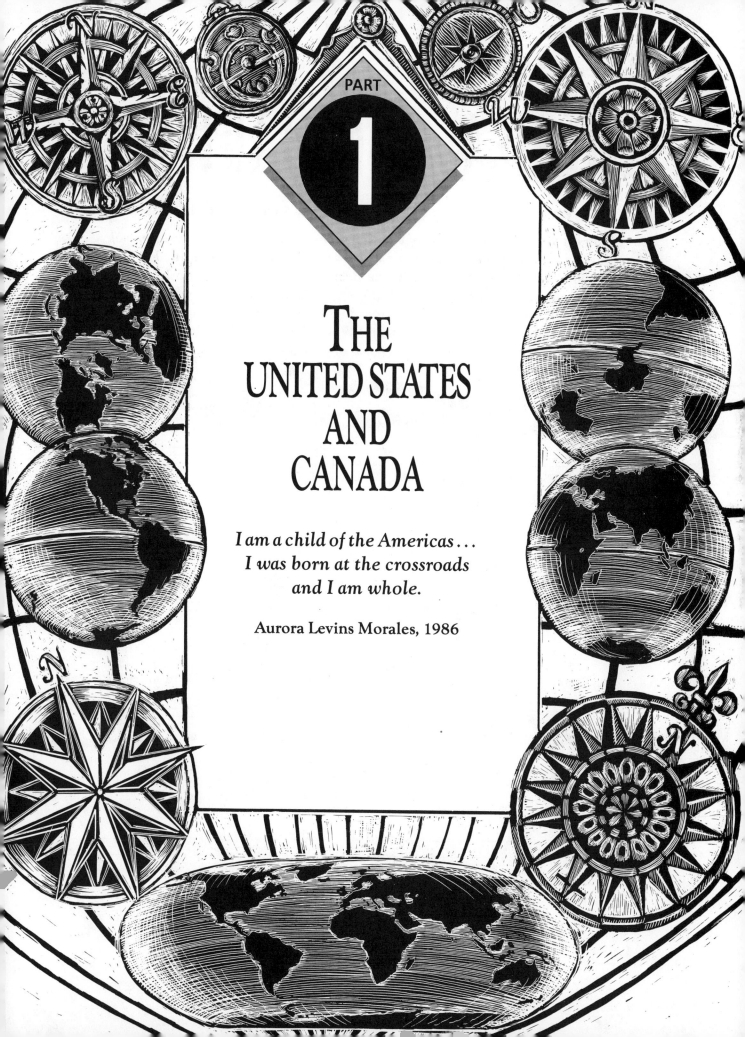

PART

1

THE UNITED STATES AND CANADA

I am a child of the Americas...
I was born at the crossroads
and I am whole.

Aurora Levins Morales, 1986

AMERICA, THE BEAUTIFUL

☆☆☆☆ **Words by Katharine Lee Bates and Music by Samuel Ward, 1893** ☆☆☆☆

Songs can often express the beauty of a nation's land. They can also express some of the values and the heritage of the people who live there. In 1893 Katharine Lee Bates (1859-1929) wrote the poem, "America, the Beautiful," and Samuel Ward later put her words to music. As you read or sing this song, notice the different landforms and geographic features that are mentioned. How does Bates describes these features? How does she want the listener to feel about them? What are some of the values and ideals that she mentions? If you were to write a poem or song about the United States, what images or ideas would you include?

1. O beau-ti-ful for spa-cious skies, For am-ber waves of grain.
2. O beau-ti-ful for pil-grim feet, Whose stern, im-pass-ion'd stress
3. O beau-ti-ful for he-roes proved In lib-er-a-ting strife,
4. O beau-ti-ful for pa-triot dream That sees be-yond the years,

For pur-ple moun-tain maj-es-ties, A-bove the fruit-ed plain,
A thor-ough-fare for free-dom beat A-cross the wil-der-ness.
Who more than self their coun-try loved, And mer-cy more than life.
Thine al-a-bas-ter cit-ies gleam Un-dim'd by hu-man tears.

A-mer-i-ca! A-mer-i-ca! God shed His grace on thee,
A-mer-i-ca! A-mer-i-ca! God mend thine ev-'ry flaw,
A-mer-i-ca! A-mer-i-ca! May God, thy gold re-fine,
A-mer-i-ca! A-mer-i-ca! God shed His grace on thee,

And crown thy good with broth-er-hood, From sea to shin-ing sea.
Con-firm thy soul in self con-trol, Thy lib-er-ty in law.
Till all suc-cess be no-ble-ness, And ev-'ry gain di-vine.
And crown thy good with broth-er-hood, From sea to shin-ing sea.

Stopping by Woods on a Snowy Evening by Robert Frost, 1922

Just like songs, such as the one you read on page 2, poetry can also express the beauty of the land. The American poet Robert Frost (1874-1963) was one of the nation's best-known poets of the twentieth century. In addition to being a poet, Frost also worked as a shoemaker, teacher, editor, and farmer. He lived in New England for much of his life and his poems often captured the flavor and spirit of this region. In the following poem, Frost describes a traveler and his horse traveling through the woods on a winter night. What does the poem tell you about a New England winter?

Whose woods these are I think I know.
His house is in the village though;
He will not see me stopping here
To watch his woods fill up with snow.

My little horse must think it queer
To stop without a farmhouse near
Between the woods and frozen lake
The darkest evening of the year.

He gives his harness bells a shake
To ask if there is some mistake.
The only other sound's the sweep
Of easy wind and downy flake.

The woods are lovely, dark and deep.
But I have promises to keep,
And miles to go before I·sleep,
And miles to go before I sleep.

Robert Frost was one of the most widely appreciated poets in the United States. In 1961 he was asked by John F. Kennedy to read a poem at his Presidential inauguration, the first poet to receive such an honor. Frost's poems remain highly prized, for they capture not only the spirit of New England, but that of America as well. To learn how another poet also captures the spirit of the American land and its people, read the next document on page 4.

Source: Robert Frost, *Selected Poems*. New York: Henry Holt and Company, 1934.

The People, Yes

by Carl Sandburg, 1936

Have you ever exaggerated a story to make it sound more fun? Telling yarns, or tall tales, is an old American tradition. In his poem, "The People, Yes," Carl Sandburg (1878-1967) recalls many of the yarns he heard during his childhood in Illinois and on his many travels across America in the early 1900s. How do these yarns describe the geography, the people, and the culture of the United States? How are they also exaggerations? What yarns could you think of adding to Sandburg's poem?

They have yarns
Of a skyscraper so tall they had to put hinges
On the two top stories so to let the moon go by,
Of one corn crop in Missouri when the roots
Went so deep and drew off so much water
The Mississippi riverbed that year was dry,
Of pancakes so thin they had only one side,
Of "a fog so thick we shingled the barn and six feet out on the fog,"
Of Pecos Pete straddling a cyclone in Texas and riding it to the west
   coast where "it rained out under him,"
Of the man who drove a swarm of bees across the Rocky Mountains
   and the Desert "and didn't lose a bee,"
Of a mountain railroad curve where the engineer in his cab can touch
   the caboose and spit in the conductor's eye,
Of the boy who climbed a cornstalk growing so fast he would have
   starved to death if they hadn't shot biscuits up to him,
Of the old man's whiskers: "When the wind was with him his whiskers
   arrived a day before he did,"
Of the hen laying a square egg and cackling, "Ouch!" and of hens laying
   eggs with the dates printed on them,

Carl Sandburg became one of the leading poets and authors in the United States during the twentieth century. Much of his writing reflected his deep love of America's land and its people. To learn how another American expressed his strong ties to the land, read the next document on pages 5-6.

Source: Carl Sandburg, *The People, Yes.* New York: Harcourt Brace Jovanovich, Inc., 1936.

THE LAKOTA AND NATURE

by Luther Standing Bear, 1933

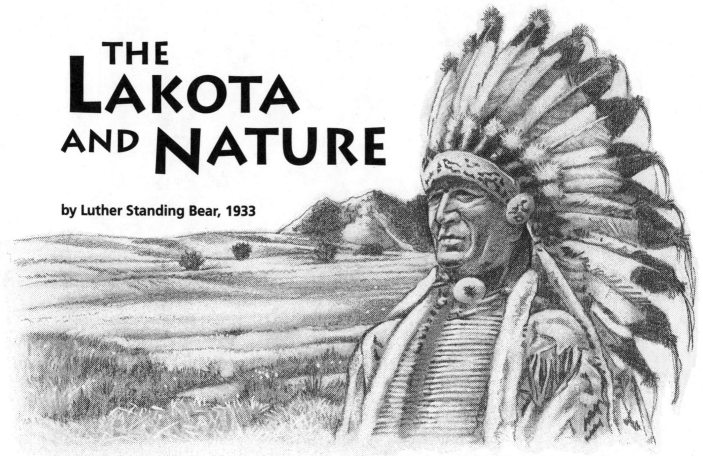

The ways of life of North America's first settlers were as varied as the lands on which they lived. Yet Native American groups all over the continent were united by their deep respect for nature and the environment. In 1933 one Native American leader wrote a book about his people, the Lakota, and their roots in the land. Luther Standing Bear grew up on the grassy plains of what is now South Dakota. In the following excerpt from his book, Land of the Spotted Eagle, *he explains why the Lakota feel such strong ties to the earth. According to Luther Standing Bear, what ties do the Lakota have to the earth and all of its creations?*

The Lakota was a true naturist—a lover of Nature. He loved the earth and all things of the earth, the attachment growing with age. The old people came **literally** to love the soil and they sat or **reclined** on the ground with a feeling of being close to a mothering power. It was good for the skin to touch the earth and the old people liked to remove their moccasins and walk with bare feet on the sacred earth. Their tipis were built upon the earth and their **altars** were made of earth. The birds that flew in the air came to rest upon the earth and it was the final **abiding** place of all things that lived and grew. The soil was soothing, strengthening, cleansing, and healing.

This is why the old Indian still sits upon the earth instead of propping himself up and away from its life-giving forces. For him, to sit or lie upon the ground is to be able to think more deeply and to

literally: actually
reclined: lay down

altars: places where religious services are performed
abiding: dwelling

feel more keenly; he can see more clearly into the mysteries of life and come closer in **kinship** to other lives about him. . . .

From **Wakan Tanka** there came a great unifying life force that flowed in and through all things—the flowers of the plains, blowing winds, rocks, trees, birds, animals—and was the same force that had been breathed into the first man. Thus all things were **kindred** and brought together by the same Great Mystery. . . .

The animals had rights—the right of man's protection, the right to live, the right to multiply, the right to freedom, and the right to man's **indebtedness**—and in recognition of these rights the Lakota never enslaved the animal, and spared all life that was not needed for food and clothing.

This **concept** of life and its relations was humanizing and gave to the Lakota an abiding love. It filled his being with the joy and mystery of living; it gave him **reverence** for all life; it made a place for all things in the **scheme** of existence with equal importance to all. The Lakota could despise no creature, for all were of one blood, made by the same hand, and filled with the **essence** of the Great Mystery. . . .

But the old Lakota was wise. He knew that man's heart, away from nature, becomes hard; he knew that lack of respect for growing, living things soon led to lack of respect for humans too. So he kept his youth close to its softening influence.

kinship: understanding

Wakan Tanka: the Creator

kindred: related

indebtedness: owing something to another

concept: idea

reverence: respect
scheme: plan

essence: heart and soul

The Lakota and many other Indian groups have kept this deep respect for nature. Today many Indians and other Americans are working to help protect the environment.

Source: Luther Standing Bear, *Land of the Spotted Eagle*. Lincoln, NE, and London, England: University of Nebraska Press, 1933.

HEADING WEST

Posters, late 1800s

In one of the greatest waves of immigration in world history, millions of people came to the United States during the late 1800s and early 1900s. They came for freedom and for the chance to build a better life. They also came for cheap land. Railroad companies, which claimed ownership to much of the land west of the Mississippi River, encouraged immigrants to come to the West, where Native Americans had lived for thousands of years. The poster below from the 1800s was aimed at attracting people to move westward. The poster on the next page was designed to attract German immigrants. An English translation appears next to it. How do these posters make the idea of settling in the West seem attractive?

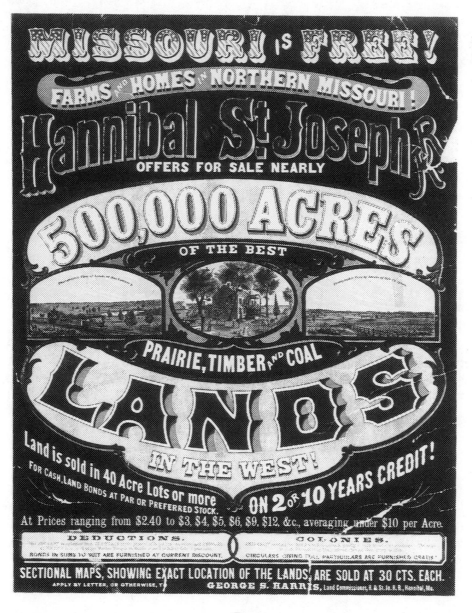

For the westbound immigrant!
Iowa Land
in the area around
the Des Moines Rivers

You can find enough woods to build your own house or farm cheaply!

Everywhere you go in this area, there are open spaces where you can build, on land that you can buy cheaply.

One Million Acres
For a loan get in touch with the Des Moines Navigation Company

Spurred on by the hope of a better life, many immigrants risked everything they owned to buy land and make the West their home. These immigrants, as well as Native Americans who were already living on the land, have helped to make the United States a nation of many cultures.

On the Way Home

by Laura Ingalls Wilder, 1894

The Great Plains of the United States is one of the most beautiful regions in the country. During the 1800s, millions of new settlers came to this region to "break the land" and build farms. Many of them were lured by the posters you saw on pages 7-8. Others had already settled in this region but kept moving from place to place, in the hopes of finding better land. In the summer of 1894, Laura Ingalls Wilder (1867-1957), her husband Almanzo, and their seven-year-old-daughter Rose left their drought-stricken farm in South Dakota in search of new land. A drought is a weather condition that occurs when there is a severe lack of rainfall. During their 650-mile (1,040-km) journey by covered wagon from De Smet, South Dakota to Mansfield, Missouri, Laura Ingalls Wilder kept a diary. This diary was made into a book many years later by her daughter. As you read excerpts from her diary, you can follow her route on the map on page 11. Notice how important the resources of the land are to the Wilders' decision about where to resettle. Notice also the different backgrounds of the many people they meet. How do her diary entries seem to capture the pioneer spirit?

July 27

Started at 8:15. We have gone through Cedar County and nearly through Wayne County, Nebraska. We cannot tell when we come to a county line as we could in Dakota, the roads pay no attention to section lines but wander up and down and around the hills.

The soil in Wayne County is very fine and close, not exactly clay but clayey. The people here claim it is the best soil on earth to **stand drought**.

stand drought: remain fertile without rainfall

Crossed the line into Stanton County at 9. There are large pastures and the grain fields are all fenced. A good many sleek cattle are in sight. Cornfields are 3 miles long and as far back as you can see. There are a few groves. Wind blows hard but cool this morning.

At 10:20 we saw *an orchard with apples.*

The hills are covered with corn as far as [the] eye can see, acres and acres of corn. Lots of groves. Nearly all the people are Germans. One gave **Manly** two large apples off his trees. He has a large orchard and the trees hang full.

Manly: nickname for Almanzo, Laura's husband

Just passed a house where the man owns 540 acres of land and has 300 hogs.

A little farther on, a farm of 500 acres. The owner had 450 hogs and only 50 bushels of old corn. He says if it does not rain within 24 hours the tassels on the new crop will dry and he will not harvest a kernel of corn. The corn looks nice to us but I suppose the farmers here know. Their wheat only sold for 32 cents last year and it is 32 cents now.

We came into the Elkhorn valley at 1:45 and it is pretty, very level, with many groves and nice houses and natural timber along the river.

An **emigrant** team is behind us and every minute I expect to hear the usual, Where did you come from? Where are you going? How are the crops up your way? This never-hardly ever-fails.

Found an ear of corn 10 inches long, 7 1/2 inches around.

Arrived at **Stanton** at 3 P.M. It is a good looking town, large pretty buildings, clean big houses with trees. People mostly Germans. German signs on the stores and German texts on the churches. Wheat is [growing] 16 to 20 bushels to the acre. Corn is killed by the hot wind. Yesterday it was 126°[dg] in the shade here in Stanton.

Crossed the Elkhorn river on a bridge. A few miles farther on we camped by the side of the road in the shade of some trees. There was a gang of horse traders on the river and we did not want to camp near them.

August 4

On the road at 7:45, a nice level road and good farms fenced with board fences. We are following the telegraph wires to **Beatrice**, then do not follow the railroad but go across country.

We have crossed Little Salt Creek and Big Salt Creek. Orchards are as common here as houses. Manly traded one **fire mat** for a whole bushel of large ripe apples. Plums are nearly ripe. Crops look splendid to us but everyone tells Manly that they are very poor and will make no grain to mention. We passed the best field of oats that Manly ever saw.

Made a hard long drive to get to a good camp, and when we got there we found the creek dry and no grass but plenty of **sand burs**. Camped in the edge of a town.

August 22

A good start at 7:15 and this morning we are driving through pretty country. Crops look good. Oats are [growing] 30 to 60 bushels to the acre, wheat from 10 to 30. All the wood you want can be had for the hauling and coal is delivered at the house for $1.25 a ton. Land is worth from $10. an acre up, unimproved, and $15. to $25. when well improved, 12 miles from **Fort Scott**.

Exactly at 2:24 3/4 P.M. we crossed the line into Missouri. And the very first cornfield we saw beat even those Kansas cornfields.

We met 7 emigrant wagons leaving Missouri. One family had a red bird, a mocking bird, and a lot of canaries in cages hung under the canvas in the wagon with them. We had quite a chat and heard the mockingbird sing. We camped by a house in the woods.

August 30, 1894

Hitched up and going at 7:10. The road is rough and rocky through the **ravines** but not so bad between them and there are trees all the way.

emigrant: person who moves from one country to another

Stanton: town in northeastern Nebraska

Beatrice: town in southeastern Nebraska

fire mat: nonflammable metal sheets placed under cooking fires to help food cook evenly

sand burs: rough, prickly plants

Fort Scott: town in southeastern Kansas

ravines: deep, narrow valleys

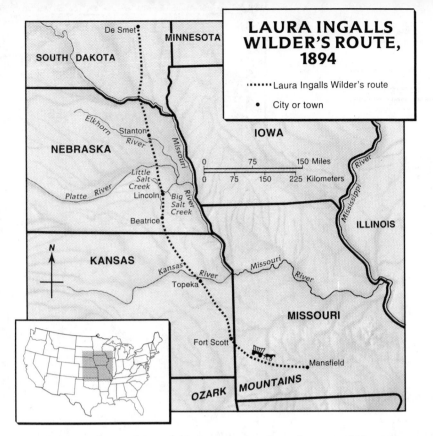

LAURA INGALLS
WILDER'S ROUTE,
1894

········· Laura Ingalls Wilder's route
•   City or town

We are passing through the Memphis fruit farms, 1,500 acres, part of the way on both sides of the road. It is a young orchard, rows upon rows of little trees, apple and peach, curving over the plowed hills.

Some covered wagons came up behind us and we came up behind some ahead, all the teams going slowly, holding back down hill and pulling up hill. At 11:30 we came into **Mansfield** in a long line of 10 emigrant wagons.

Mansfield: town in Southern Missouri

Mansfield is a good town of 300 or 400 inhabitants in a good central location where it should grow fast. The railroad runs on one side of the square and two stagecoach lines go from the depot, one south to the County seat of Douglas County, the other north to the County seat of Wright County. There is everything here already that one could want though we must do our worshipping without a Congregational church. There is a Methodist church and a Presbyterian. There is a good school. Around the Square, two general stores, two drug stores, the bank, a Boston Racket store, livery stable, blacksmith shop near. There are several nice large houses in big yards with trees. South of the tracks is as good as north of them; two or three big houses, and a flour mill is there by a mill pond.

Camped in the woods in the western edge of town and this afternoon Manly looked over one place for sale but was not exactly suited.

After arriving in Mansfield, Missouri, the Wilder family bought a farm and spent the rest of their lives there. It was in this town that Laura Ingalls Wilder began to write stories about her childhood on the prairie. In such stories as The Little House on the Prairie *and many others, Laura Ingalls Wilder captured the hardships and joys of life on the Great Plains in the 1800s.*

Source: Laura Ingalls Wilder, *On the Way Home.* New York: Harper & Row, Publishers, Inc., 1962.

An Immigrant to the United States

by Celestino Fernández, 1990

Today most immigrants to the United States come from countries in Asia and Latin America, especially Mexico. Many Mexicans call the United States el norte, *which is Spanish for "the north." Each year about 3 to 4 million Mexicans head to* el norte *to find better jobs and the chance for a better life. One of these immigrants is Celestino Fernández, who was born in Santa Inez, a small town in Mexico. As a young boy in 1957, he and his family immigrated to Santa Rosa, California. Today Fernández is a vice president at the University of Arizona in Tucson. In the following oral history excerpt, Fernández tells the story of his family's move from Mexico and their adjustment to the United States. What kinds of changes did he and his family have to go through? How did they cope with these changes?*

The change was so dramatic. It was complete culture shock. We went from a small town in Mexico with a population of about 700 to a community of about 48,000 in California. The traffic seemed like it never stopped in Santa Rosa, whereas in Santa Inez we'd see a bus or a truck go by only once in a while. There we had the cobblestone streets, here it was all pavement. Santa Rosa is almost rural, but coming from a community of 700 people, it looked like a **megalopolis**. . . .

Yes, the size was different, but there was much more than that. Everything and anything, all the way from hot running water to electricity, at any time of the day. In Mexico we had electricity maybe a couple of hours a day, but we didn't know when, so one never depended on it. No refrigerators, no stoves, no washing machines, and we moved into a home with all those things. . . .

We knew everybody in Santa Inez and everybody knew us, not only in that little town, but in all the towns and ranches around. Everybody was family in that respect. In the evening we would go to my grandmother's and sit around the fire and chat. Even when I visit now,

megalopolis: a crowded area of cities and suburbs

that's what we do; we sit around the kitchen and talk. We moved from that to Santa Rosa, California, where we didn't know anyone.

My dad knew his boss before our coming. He had worked several seasons with this particular gentleman and his family. He helped us obtain our **documents** when we all came up in 1957. My sister and I didn't know anyone, and we couldn't communicate. That fall my sister entered the fourth grade and I entered second. . . .

During that first year I never said a word. The teacher wouldn't have known if I was **mute** or not. I never said a word. It was after that summer, coming back, that I remember speaking. I could do mathematics. That was it. . . .

My parents always stressed the importance of education, but they themselves never really had that much opportunity. My dad had a sixth grade education and my mom a third grade education in the Catholic school in Santa Inez.

From elementary school on I worked after school and weekends. In the winter, picking up **brush** in the apple orchard after they **prune**, and in the summer picking apples off the ground, then later in the packing house. In high school I worked at a golf course and in a bakery. I always had a job, so I never had the opportunity for sports or anything like that. I'd just rush off from school to work.

So, it wasn't easy. My dad owed a good deal of money in simply bringing us here. He used to work in the apple orchards, but in the winter it rained and there was no work. So he would save up in the summers and we'd use it up in the winter, and it went around like that. But we all worked to help. . . .

I feel Mexican and I behave American. Inside, my feelings, my values, my attitudes, my beliefs are based in Mexican culture, but my behavior is very American. I feel very comfortable here. I understand the system and I can work it. My wife says when I'm in Mexico I'm Mexican. I know that system as well and can fit in and behave Mexican. I'm the only one in my family who is a **naturalized** American citizen. . . .

My dad just retired last year and they still maintain a home in Santa Inez. . . . They were saying they're going to go back and retire there. I think they'll go back for some months there and some months here, but they'll never go back to live there. What happens is you become **binational** and **bicultural**. You're comfortable in both countries but never fully **integrated** in either. You don't want to be, because you know the best world is in the margins, in between, where you can choose and take what is best from each culture.

documents: official papers allowing people to come to the United States to work

mute: unable to speak

brush: fallen branches

prune: cut off unwanted branches

naturalized: legalized

binational: of two nations

bicultural: of two cultures

integrated: blended

Like Celestino Fernández, immigrants live in two cultures—the culture of their native land and the culture of the United States. By bringing their traditions and beliefs to the United States, immigrants have shaped and continue to shape our country's culture. Their contributions have helped to make the United States a nation of many cultures.

Source: Marilyn P. Davis, *Mexican Voices/American Dreams: An Oral History of Mexican Immigration to the United States.* New York: Henry Holt and Company, Inc., 1990.

THE AMERICAN ☆DREAM☆

by Martin Luther King, Jr., 1961

Until the mid-1900s, segregation, or the separation of people by color, remained legal in some parts of the United States. Under this system, blacks were not allowed to attend the same schools or use the same public facilities as whites. In an attempt to end these unfair practices, African Americans launched the civil rights movement in the 1950s. The main goal of the civil rights movement was equal rights and equal opportunities for all Americans. In 1961 Martin Luther King, Jr. (1929-1968), a leader of the civil rights movement, gave the following speech at a graduation ceremony at Lincoln University in Pennsylvania. As you read excerpts from this speech, think of what King means by the American dream. What ways does he suggest for Americans to fulfill this dream? Which of King's ideas do you think are most important and why?

As you go out today to enter the **clamorous** highways of life, I should like to discuss with you some aspects of the American dream. For in a real sense, America is essentially a dream, a dream as yet unfulfilled. It is a dream of a land where men of all races, of all nationalities and of all **creeds** can live together as brothers. The substance of the dream is expressed in these **sublime** words, words lifted to cosmic proportions: "We hold these truths to be self-evident, that all men are created equal, that they are endowed by their Creator with certain **unalienable** rights, that among these are life, liberty, and the pursuit of happiness." This is the dream.

One of the first things we notice in this dream is an amazing **universalism**. It does not say some men, but it says all men. It does not say all white men, but it says all men, which includes black men. It does not say all Gentiles, but it says all men, which includes Jews. It does not say all Protestants, but it says all men, which includes Catholics.

Now may I suggest some of the things we must do if we are to make the American dream a reality. First I think all of us must develop a world perspective if we are to survive. The American dream will not become a reality **devoid** of the larger dream of a world of brotherhood and peace and good will. The world in which we live is a world of geographical oneness and we are challenged now to make it spiritually one. . . .

All this is simply to say that all life is interrelated. We are caught in an inescapable network of **mutuality**; tied in a single **garment of destiny**. Whatever affects one directly, affects all indirectly. As long as there is poverty in this world, no man can be totally rich even if he has a billion dollars. As long as diseases are **rampant** and millions of

clamorous: noisy

creeds: beliefs
sublime: splendid

unalienable: unable to be taken away

universalism: quality that relates to all peoples

devoid: empty

mutuality: dependence
garment of destiny: fate
rampant: widespread

people cannot expect to live more than twenty or thirty years, no man can be totally healthy, even if he just got a clean bill of health from the finest clinic in America. Strangely enough, I can never be what I ought to be until you are what you ought to be. This is the way the world is made. . . .

If we are to **implement** the American dream we must get rid of the notion once and for all that there are superior and inferior races. This means that members of minority groups must make it clear that they can use their resources even under **adverse** circumstances. We must make full and **constructive** use of the freedom we already possess. . . .

There is another myth, that . . . leads one to think that you can't solve this problem through legislation; you can't solve this problem through **judicial decree**; you can't solve this problem through executive orders on the part of the president of the United States. It must be solved by education. Now I agree that education plays a great role, and it must continue to play a great role in changing attitudes, in getting people ready for the new order. And we must also see the importance of legislation.

It is not a question either of education or of legislation. Both legislation and education are required. Now, people will say, "You can't legislate **morals**." Well, that may be true. Even though morality may not be legislated, behavior can be regulated. And this is very important. We need religion and education to change attitudes and to change the hearts of men. We need legislation and federal action to control behavior. It may be true that the law can't make a man love me, but it can keep him from **lynching** me, and I think that's pretty important also. . . .

I know sometimes we get discouraged and sometimes disappointed with the slow pace of things. At times we begin to talk about racial separation instead of racial integration, feeling that there is no other way out. My only answer is that the problem never will be solved by substituting one **tyranny** for another. Black supremacy is as dangerous as white supremacy, and God is not interested merely in the freedom of black men and brown men and yellow men. God is interested in the freedom of the whole human race and in the creation of a society where all men can live together as brothers, where every man will respect the dignity and the worth of human personality. . . . And so, as you go out today, I call upon you not to be **detached spectators**, but involved participants, in this great drama that is taking place in our nation and around the world.

implement: put in place

adverse: difficult
constructive: positive

judicial decree: a judge's order

morals: right behavior

lynching: hanging

tyranny: unjust government

detached spectators: uninvolved observers

Martin Luther King, Jr., spent his entire adult life fighting for freedom and equal rights. For his efforts King received the Nobel Peace Prize in 1964. Four years later King was assassinated. The civil rights movement, however, succeeded in ending legal segregation in the United States. Part of the American dream has been fulfilled but Americans, inspired by King's example, still struggle to establish justice and equality for all.

Source: James Melvin Washington, ed., *A Testament of Hope*. San Francisco: Harper & Row, Publishers, Inc., 1986.

Child OF THE Americas

by Aurora Levins Morales, 1986

Puerto Rico is a commonwealth of the United States. Poet Aurora Levins Morales was born on the island of Puerto Rico in 1954. She is the daughter of a Christian mother from the mainland of the United States and a Jewish father of Russian heritage. In the poem "Child of the Americas," Morales discusses her unique heritage. What do you think she means when she says that "history made me"?

I am a child of the Americas,
a light-skinned **mestiza** of the Caribbean,
a child of many **diaspora**, born into this continent at a crossroads.

mestizas: people of mixed Indian and European ancestry

diaspora: migrations

I am a U.S. Puerto Rican Jew,
a product of the **ghettos** of New York I have never known.
An immigrant and the daughter and granddaughter of immigrants.
I speak English with passion: it's the tongue of my consciousness,
a flashing knife blade of crystal, my tool, my craft.

ghettos: poor neighborhoods

I am Caribeña, island grown. Spanish is in my flesh,
ripples from my tongue, lodges in my hips:
the language of garlic and mangoes,
the singing in my poetry, the flying gestures of my hands.
I am of Latinoamerica, rooted in the history of my continent:
I speak from that body.

I am not african. Africa is in me, but I cannot return.
I am not **taina**. Taíno is in me, but there is no way back.
I am not european. Europe lives in me, but I have no home there.

taína: of the Taíno, the Native American group who first lived in Puerto Rico

I am new. History made me. My first language was **spanglish.**
I was born at the crossroads
and I am whole.

spanglish: a mixture of Spanish and English

Like Aurora Levins Morales, many Puerto Ricans take pride in their diverse cultural background. They also retain a deep love for the beautiful island of Puerto Rico.

Source: Aurora Levins Morales and Rosario Morales, *Getting Home Alive*. Ithaca, NY: Firebrand Books, 1986.

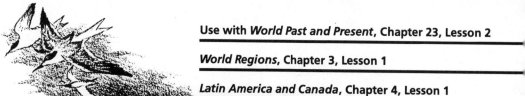

ICY REACHES OF THE NORTH

by Thomas O'Neill, 1991

With its vast, snowy lands, Canada's frozen tundra is a harsh and challenging place to live. Temperatures often plummet to -80°F. (-27°C), and in winter it is dark for many weeks in a row. Despite this severe climate, the Inuit people have thrived in this Arctic region for centuries. One explanation for the Inuit's success is their belief that nature influences all of life and that they must work with nature to survive. This means using materials of the earth to build houses and cutting holes in thick ice to find fish. In the following travel account from 1991, an Inuit named Elijah Panipakoocho takes a walk with author Thomas O'Neill. How does Panipakoocho's knowledge of his environment enable him to live in harmony with nature? What does it mean to live in harmony with nature?

"I love seal meat." Elijah Panipakoocho, an Inuit villager, spoke as if the words themselves tasted good. "Seal meat makes me warm inside," he said, "so warm that sometimes I can't sleep." Elijah had seal on the mind; he and I were standing on a shelf of sea ice five feet [1.5 m] thick, looking down on a watery hole out of which minutes earlier a ringed seal had popped for a breath of Arctic air.

We couldn't move. A single **footfall**, even from far off, would scare the seal beneath the ice. Only the polar bear, with soundproofing fur between its footpads, can confidently sneak up to a seal's breathing hole. We could talk, though. Elijah must be hungry, I figured, as he proceeded to tell me how delicious caribou is, and eider duck, and arctic hare, and Greenland shark. . . . "I tell my sons," Elijah said **paternally**, "to eat fox and polar bear—it gives you good eyes."

In the Inuit **worldview**, animals are created for people to hunt and to eat. Elijah Panipakoocho is a hunter, and as such takes what the land gives. He lives on the **remote** northern end of Baffin Island in the native community of Pond Inlet, one of the northernmost settlements in the Canadian Arctic. From where we stood on the ice, at 72 degrees north latitude, the North Pole is 1,200 miles [1,920 km] to the north, and the **tree line** is 1,000 miles [1,600 km] to the south. Even in late June, with the flush of 24-hour daylight, we were bundled up against a piercing wind. Elijah, in his 40s, and short and powerfully built like most Inuit

footfall: sound of a footstep

paternally: fatherly

worldview: belief about the world

remote: distant

tree line: place above which trees do not grow

men, wore a homemade down parka with a hood **ruff** fashioned from wolf hair. As I listened to Elijah's roll call of **edible** animals, I remembered his telling me of ancestors who died of starvation on Devon Island, and of a great-grandmother who survived only by eating sealskin **thongs.** Hunger was not a lighthearted subject.

For 15 minutes we waited without success at the breathing hole, or *uglo* in Elijah's native language, Inuktitut. This was nothing. Elijah, who learned English on an oil-drilling rig, said that in the past he has stood for two hours in bitter cold at an uglo. Polar bears may lie in wait for up to four hours. But Elijah was not hunting today. He was showing me his home territory on the frozen inlet between Bylot Island and Baffin Island—at 195,930 square miles [509,418 sq km] the largest island in Canada. What had drawn me to this distant coast was the chance to see how the Inuit **sustain** their threatened culture by living, as their ancestors did, off the land and sea—and ice—and to observe the spectacular migrations of wildlife during the Arctic spring. . . .

I scanned my surroundings at the seal hole and saw a desert. Everything looked **formidably stark**—the sea of ice, the bare granite mountains on shore, the awesome blankness of glaciers in the high valleys. . . . Elijah gave up on the seal and went to rev up his snowmobile. I jumped aboard the long wooden sled [Elijah] was pulling, and off we raced over the frozen sea.

Before long we ran out of ice. The abrupt edge was flat and ragged like a torn piece of paper. It was unwise to stand too close to the rim lest a cake of ice break off and drop us in water so chilling we could survive in its grip only a few minutes. By craning my neck I could see the full measure of what we stood on—a chunky reef of greenish, **pockmarked** ice extending several feet below the waterline. Farther out, rafts of pack ice, having split apart in the warming weather, were floating like pieces of wreckage on the **metallic** gray waters of Baffin Bay. . . .

For hours I held **vigil** on the ice edge, watching animals appear from sky and water. . . . Arctic terns, white blurs in the air, dropped like stones into the sea to catch fish. They had flown a **marathon** from Antarctica. A **frenzied** splashing announced a group of harp seals that had surfaced and was now skimming across the water like a startled school of fish. . . .

I shivered with pleasure at the sights and sounds before me. . . . Elijah said that when you listen through a **hydrophone** lowered beneath the ice, the sounds of creatures, large and small, are as noisy as those in a rain forest must be.

By mixing ancient skills, such as ice-fishing, and modern inventions, such as snowmobiles, Inuits like Elijah Panipakoocho have continued to thrive in their icy, Arctic environment. With its clean, cold water and fresh, cool air, this region of northern Canada remains one of the most unspoiled environments in the world.

Source: Thomas O'Neill, "Icy Reaches of the North" from *Canada's Incredible Coasts*. Washington, DC: National Geographic Society, 1991.

---

ruff: collar
edible: safe to eat

thongs: sandals

sustain: keep alive

formidably: awesomely
stark: empty

pockmarked: scarred

metallic: resembling metal
vigil: watch

marathon: long journey
frenzied: frantic

hydrophone: listening device

KOKOOM

**Cree Tale Retold by
Garry Gregory J. Ladouceur, 1982**

For thousands of years, the Cree Indians have lived in Canada's north country, passing down tales from one generation to the next. Many of these tales describe the Cree's closeness to nature and try to explain the origins of the natural world. A Cree named Garry Gregory J. Ladouceur heard the tale called Kokoom from his father as a boy and later wrote it down. "Kokoom" refers to a kind grandmother who loves children. What does this folktale say about the Cree's feelings toward their elders?

In the old days before the world was as it is now, there was only the sun. Once the sun disappeared, however, the night was in blackness. There was no moon. Night was a particularly trying time for children who were **cowed** by the dark. In the community there lived [one] grandmother or "Kokoom" whom the children . . . loved and adored. They spent a great deal of time with her because she was kind and so interesting to be with. Gradually though, with the forces of time "Kokoom" became older, and . . . the children and "Kokoom" realized that she must soon leave. The children became very **distraught** as they came to realize the **inevitability** of "Kokoom's" death. "Kokoom" herself was also pained, not because she feared her own **mortality**, but because of the sorrow she knew the children would feel on her **passing**.

cowed: scared

distraught: upset
inevitability: certainty
mortality: certainty of death
passing: dying

Before she died therefore, she gathered all the children of the village about her and she made a promise. Because of her great love for the children, "Kokoom" promised them that she would continue to protect and give them comfort even if she died.

When "Kokoom" finally died, the children were **disheartened** nonetheless. On the night of her death, however, "Kokoom" rose into the night skies and became the moon. It was obvious that the moon was "Kokoom" as she had a round face (My father explained that older Indian women generally have round faces), and a smile that one could see as shadows on the moon's features. "Kokoom" had kept her promise and is still keeping it today. Where the nights had previously been black and fearful and the "Cheepeyes" (fearful spirits of the forest) had had **free rein** and forced the children to hide in fear, night was now lit by "Kokoom." She always watches over her children.

disheartened: saddened

free rein: complete freedom of movement

By writing down tales such as Kokoom, Garry Gregory J. Ladouceur helps preserve his Cree culture. He also enables other people to learn about Cree traditions and beliefs.

Source: Herbert Halpert, ed., *A Folklore Sampler from the Maritimes*. St. John's, Newfoundland, Canada: Memorial University of Newfoundland, 1982.

THE LUMBER CAMP SONG

Traditional Song, 1840s

Canada's thousands of square miles of forests have been home to the logging industry for more than 200 years. They have also been home to the hardy lumberjacks who cut the timber. These loggers worked from dawn to dusk and often lived in cramped shacks in isolated camps. After a hard week in the forests, they gathered on Saturday nights to tell stories, and to sing and dance to fiddle music. "The Lumber Camp Song" is a famous lumberjack's song, dating back to at least the 1840s. It was probably first sung in the eastern woods of Maine and Canada, until the shanty boys, as the loggers were called, took it westward. What picture does this song give you of Canada's loggers?

1. Come all you jol - ly fel - lows and
2. At four o' - clock each morn - ing the
3. At six o' - clock it's break - fast, and

list - en to my song; It's all a - bout the
boss be - gins to shout: "Heave out, my jol - ly
ev' - ry man is out, For ev' - ry man who

shan - ty boys and how they get a - long. We're the
team - sters; it's time to start the route." The
is not sick will sure be on the route. There's

jol - liest bunch of fel - lows that
team - sters they will all jump up in
saw - yers and there's chop - pers to

e - ver you could find; The way we spend our
a most fret - ful way: "Where is me boots? Where
lay the tim - ber low; There's swam - pers and there's

win - ter months is hurl - ing down the pine._____
is me pants? Me socks is gone a - stray!"_____
log - gers to drag it to and fro._____

4. And then comes up the logger, all at the break of day:
   "Load up my slide, five hundred feet; to the river drive away."
   You can hear those axes ringing until the sun goes down.
   "Hurrah, my boys! The day is spent. To the shanty we are bound."

5. And when we reach the shanty, with cold hands and wet feet,
   We there pull off our larrigans, our supper for to eat.
   We sing and dance till nine o'clock; then to our bunks we climb.
   Those winter months they won't be long in hurling down the pine.

6. The springtime rolls around at last, and then the boss will say:
   "Heave down your saws and axes, boys, and help to clear away."
   And when the floating ice goes out, in business we will thrive:
   Two hundred able-bodied men are wanted on the drive.

Source: Edith Fowke and Alan Mills, *Canada's Story in Song*. Toronto: W. J. Gage, 1965.

BUILDING THE TRANSCONTINENTAL RAILROAD

by Wong Hau-hon, 1926

As Canadians pushed westward in the late 1800s, some dreamed of building a railroad across the huge country. In 1881 construction began on a transcontinental railroad to link Halifax on the east coast to Vancouver on the west coast. Much of the labor to build this railroad was provided by thousands of Chinese immigrants. One of these immigrants was Wong Hau-hon, a teenager from China who worked for two years on a rugged mountainous stretch through British Columbia. More than 40 years later, in 1926, Wong spoke about the many dangers that he and others had faced in helping to build the railroad. As you read his oral history, notice the different skills railroad workers had to have to construct the Canadian Pacific Railway. How does Wong feel about the contributions he has made to Canada?

I first came to Canada in 1882 . . . on a sailing vessel. There were 90 or so fellow Chinese on the same ship. We **debarked** at Westminster in mid-March of that year. After a few days ashore, I set out on foot with a group of about 400 Chinese to join railroad construction crews at **Yale**. . . .

After our arrival at Yale, we had worked only two days when the white foreman ordered the [work] gang to which I was assigned to move to [the settlement of] North Bend. We started on our way at 7 in the morning; there were many Chinese in our traveling group. The weather was bad, for it rained all day, and we were all wet and cold. Among our traveling companions there were some arrivals who were unaccustomed to the exposure of the Canadian climate and sickened. Some died as they rested beneath the trees or laid on the ground. . . .

When we arrived at North Bend, we pitched our tents by the river. But the river level rose because of the recent rains and within a week we had to move our camp 3 times. The floods also **severed** the road from Vancouver to North Bend in several places so that pack trains could not come through. Our food supply was cut off and our store of **provisions** dwindled.

Our foreman then ordered us to pack up and return to Yale. So, although already suffering **pangs** of hunger, we had to start on our way immediately. When we were passing [the settlement of] China Bar on

debarked: went ashore

Yale: a town in British Columbia

severed: cut off

provisions: food

pangs: sharp feelings

the way, many of the Chinese died from an **epidemic**. As there were no coffins to bury the dead, the bodies were stuffed into rock **crevices** or beneath the trees to await their arrival. Those whose burials could not wait, were buried on the spot in boxes made of crude thin planks hastily fastened together. There were even some who were buried in the ground wrapped only in blankets or grass mats. . . .

epidemic: widescale outbreak of disease

crevices: narrow cracks

When we returned to Yale, we worked there for awhile. Then the foreman ordered us to move to Hope. At that time I belonged to [work] gang No. 161. At that time each gang consisted of about 30 workers and I heard that there were more than 380 gangs.

The work at Hope was very dangerous. On one occasion, there was a huge rock on the slope of the mountain which stood in [the] railroad's path and must be removed by blasting before the tracks could go through. However, the sides of the rock were nearly **perpendicular** all around and there was no easy way to reach the top. The workers had to scramble to the top by use of timber **scaffolding** and by ropes fastened to the rock. After they reached the top they drilled holes in the rock to hold the dynamite **charges**.

perpendicular: straight up and down

scaffolding: platform built above ground

charges: loads of dynamite

I was one of the workers who was assigned the task of drilling. Each morning I climbed the rock and after I had finished the day's work I was lowered again by rope. I remembered that in blasting this rock more than 300 barrels of explosives were used. . . .

[One] incident occurred about 10-15 miles [16-24 km] west of Yale. Dynamite was used to blast a rock cave. Twenty charges were placed and ignited but only 18 blasts went off. However, the white foreman, thinking that all of the dynamite had [gone] off, ordered the Chinese workers to enter the cave to resume work. Just at that moment the remaining two charges suddenly exploded, and Chinese bodies flew from the cave as if shot from a cannon. Blood and flesh were mixed in a horrible mess. On this occasion, about 10 or 20 workers were killed.

In 1883 I moved from Hope to Thompson River and worked there for a month. Fortunately I suffered no accidents. Later I moved again to work in a **barren** wilderness for more than a year. There more than a thousand Chinese laborers **perished** from epidemics. In all, more than 3,000 Chinese died during the building of the railroad from diseases and accidents.

barren: empty

perished: died

I am now 62 and I have experienced much hardships and difficulties in my life. I am proud of the fact that we Chinese contributed much to the development of transportation in Canada.

In 1885 workers finished building the Canadian Pacific Railway. The project was completed thanks largely to a great number of Chinese workers—many of whom lost their lives. Thousands of Chinese immigrants, including Wong Hau-hon, stayed and settled in Canada. Today the Chinese are one of the many groups that help make Canada a nation of many cultures.

Source: Joe Huang and Sharon Quan Wong, *Chinese Americans: Realities and Myths Anthology.* San Francisco: The Association of Chinese Teachers, 1977.

THE CANOE IN THE RAPIDS

French-Canadian Tale Retold by Natalie Savage Carlson, 1952

Ever since French explorers first settled in present-day Canada in the early 1600s, French Canadians have created a separate and distinct culture. One feature of French-Canadian culture is storytelling. For hundreds of years, French Canadians have passed down tales orally from one generation to the next. These tales were often the main form of entertainment for early French settlers, who would gather around the cooking stove in someone's kitchen on cold winter evenings to swap stories and keep warm. In 1952 Natalie Savage Carlson gathered many of these tales into a book. The tale below, about an exciting canoe ride, is still a favorite among French Canadians. What lesson do you think the story teaches about the meaning of friendship?

O nce in another time, François Ecrette [frän swä′ e kret′] was an adventurer in the woods. Every winter he went north with Sylvain Gagnon [sēl′ van ga nyon′]. They trapped foxes, beavers, minks and any furred creature that would step into their traps.

When spring came and the ice in the river melted, the two men would load their furs into a canoe and paddle down the swift current to sell their winter's catch to the trader.

It was one such spring that François and Sylvain headed south with the finest catch that they had ever made. If only they could beat the other trappers to the trading post, they could make a fine bargain.

"A-ah, we will be rich men," said Sylvain, who already could hear the tintin of coins in his deep pockets.

"Yes," answered François, "if we get through the Devil's Jaws safely."

Nowhere on any of the rivers of Canada was there such a fearsome place. In the Devil's Jaws, there were waterfalls that roared and

24

whirlpools that spun a boat about like a dry leaf. It was as if the river fell into a panic itself when squeezed into the Devil's Jaws and tried to run away in every direction. . . .

They loaded the canoe with their bundles of furs and their **provisions**. For days they paddled down the river, singing gay songs to pass away the long hours.

provisions: food and
other supplies

One late afternoon they beached their boat on the bank and made for a clearing on the hill. . . .

"We must eat well," said Sylvain, "for we are close to the Devil's Jaws. We will need all our strength for that pull and push."

"But it will soon be dark," François reminded him. "Shouldn't we camp here all night so we can go through the rapids in daylight?"

"Pou, pou," laughed Sylvain, "what a scared rabbit you are! I can paddle at night as well as by day. I could shoot the Devil's Jaws with my eyes closed and a beaver riding on my paddle."

François rubbed his stubbly chin.

"My faith," he exclaimed, "I am the luckiest man in the world to have you for a partner, Sylvain Gagnon. I don't believe you have fear of anything."

As if to test the truth of this, an angry growl came from behind the bushes. Both men jumped to their feet, François seizing his rifle as he did so. The bushes broke open and a big brown bear came through them. He walked slowly on all fours, shuffling from this paw to that paw, and from that paw to this paw. Straight toward the two trappers he came.

François lifted his rifle to his shoulder and took careful aim. He pulled the trigger. Plink! Nothing happened. There was no bullet in the rifle because it had been used on [a] rabbit.

The bear gave another angry growl. He rose on his hind legs and walked toward François like a man, shuffling from this paw to that paw.

François dropped the gun and ran for his life. Already Sylvain Gagnon was far ahead of him, his fur coat making him look like a bear that ran too fast to shuffle from this paw to that paw. François made for a big tree, but he didn't have time to climb it as the bear was almost on him. So around the tree he ran. And behind him followed the bear. Round and round and round the tree ran François and the bear. . . .

Around and around and around went the man and the beast. The bear got dizzy first. He ran slower and slower. Finally he broke away from the tree and went staggering away, first to this side and then to that side. And as he reeled and stumbled, he knocked his head into one tree trunk after another. Bump—bump—bump.

François lost no time in finding another tree to climb, for the tree they had been running around had been stripped of its bark as far up as a bear could reach. As he climbed, he could hear the bump, bump, bump of the bear's head as he stumbled into tree trunks.

Panting and dizzy himself, François settled into a crotch of the tree. Now where was that false friend, Sylvain Gagnon, who had left him

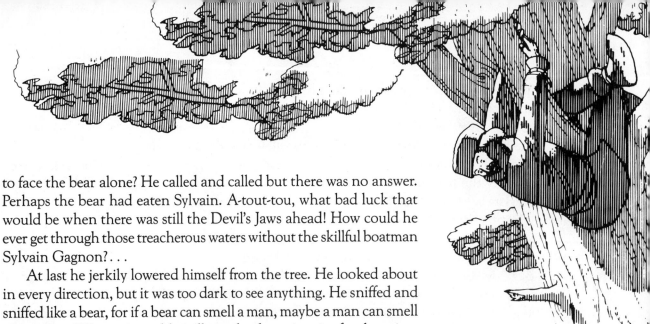

to face the bear alone? He called and called but there was no answer. Perhaps the bear had eaten Sylvain. A-tout-tou, what bad luck that would be when there was still the Devil's Jaws ahead! How could he ever get through those treacherous waters without the skillful boatman Sylvain Gagnon? . . .

At last he jerkily lowered himself from the tree. He looked about in every direction, but it was too dark to see anything. He sniffed and sniffed like a bear, for if a bear can smell a man, maybe a man can smell a bear. But all François could smell was the sharp, icy air of early spring. Slowly he made his way down the hill toward the place they had left the canoe.

Then great joy filled the heart of François Ecrette. Although the trees blackened the river, a faint moonlight glimmered through them. Its pale light fell upon a figure hunched in the **bow** of the canoe with the fur coat pulled up over its ears.

bow: front end of a boat

"Sylvain," cried François, "you are safe after all. Why didn't you come back to me?"

But Sylvain must have felt a deep shame, for he only put his head down between his arms and made a sad, apologetic sound.

"Believe me, my friend," said François, "I'm certainly glad you escaped, for we have a terrible ride ahead of us this night. Do you think we better try the rapids after all?"

But his companion **resolutely** straightened up and squared his shoulders in the fur coat. François pushed the boat into the stream, leaped aboard and grabbed a paddle. Silently they floated into the current; then the slender canoe headed for the dangers ahead.

resolutely: with determination

"My faith, it is good to have you in this boat with me," cried François. "This current is like a bolt of lightning."

The boat raced faster and faster. Instead of paddling for speed, François had to spend his strength flattening the paddle like a brake. The trees made a dark tunnel of the river course so that François could barely see his companion's stout back.

On, on they went. The frail canoe sped in a zigzag flight like a swallow. François Ecrette's sharp ear caught the distant roar of the rapids.

"Brace yourself, Sylvain," he cried, "for the boat is now in your hands. I will help you as much as I can."

So he **plied** his paddle from this side to that side and from that side to this side. The river had become like an angry, **writhing** eel. He heard the waterfall ahead and began paddling like mad so the canoe would shoot straight and true. The least slant of the boat and the churning current would turn it over and over, and swallow them both.

plied: used
writhing: twisting

François felt the icy wind and the cold spray on his face as they plunged over the waterfall and bobbed in the whirlpool below. He fought the churning, **frothing** waters that he could hear more than see. His muscles tightened like iron and the air blew up his lungs.

frothing: foaming

"My faith, but it's a good thing to have such a boatman as Sylvain Gagnon guiding this canoe," rejoiced François. "In such a current as this, no other man could bring a boat through safely. I will forget the way he deserted me when that big brown bear attacked us."

All danger was not over yet, for the **stern** of the canoe was sucked into the outer rim of a whirlpool. . . . The canoe spun around completely. For fully ten minutes, there was such a battle with the churning waters as François had never known before. Around and around, up and down rocked the canoe, with François fiercely wielding his paddle. If it hadn't been for the soothing figure in front of him, he would have given up in fright.

stern: rear part of a boat

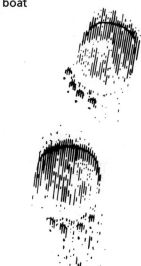

Finally the canoe straightened out and leaped straight ahead. The roar of the rapids grew fainter. François let his paddle drag and relaxed.

"My faith," he gasped. "I thought that was the last of us for sure. You have saved us both, Sylvain Gagnon. No boatman in all Canada but you could have gotten us out of that Devil's trap."

But his modest companion only shrugged his shoulders and humped lower into the bow.

Then because François was worn out from his paddling, he decided to take a little nap. With no other partner but Sylvain would he have dared doze off. But Sylvain had proved his **mettle** in getting them through the rapids, and the waters ahead were slow and peaceful. So François rested his paddle, closed his eyes and fell into a deep sleep.

mettle: courage

When he awoke, it was morning. The sun had chased the shadows out from under the trees, and the river sparkled in the friendliest kind of way.

François rubbed the sleep out of his eyes.

"Ah, Sylvain," he yawned, "what a night we had in the rapids. If it hadn't been for you — a-tou-tou-tou-tou!"

For François Ecrette's partner in the canoe was not Sylvain Gagnon, the great boatman, but a big brown bear.

François jumped up and gave a bloodcurdling shriek. The bear slowly turned around and looked at him. He shook his great furry head as if to shake his brains back into their right place after they had been knocked apart by the tree trunks. He gave a low threatening growl.

François didn't wait any longer. He dived into the river and furiously swam through the icy water. After what seemed a . . . lifetime, he reached the frosty shore. When he looked back at the river, he had a last glance of the canoe, full of furs, disappearing among the trees with the big brown bear standing in the bow.

Now this was a fine how-does-it-make of trouble. Here was François all alone in the wilderness without Sylvain, furs, provisions or even a dry match.

Luckily the trading post couldn't be too far away now....

It was late afternoon by the time he reached the trader's village. Everyone seemed surprised to see him alive.

"Your canoe was found caught in a log jam below here, with bear tracks on the shore," said the trader. "We thought a bear had carried you off."

"But the furs," cried François. "What happened to them? Were they lost?"

"They are all safe," said the trader. "Your friend Sylvain Gagnon arrived only a little while ago. He helped me check through them."

Then a familiar face appeared in the crowd.

"François, my good friend," cried Sylvain. "I got a ride back with a **party** of Indians. But how did you ever get the canoe through the rapids all by yourself?"

party: group

"Sylvain, my false friend," retorted the trapper, "I was not alone. The big brown bear was with me."

Then François Ecrette shivered and shook in a way that had nothing to do with the cold spring afternoon or his damp clothing.

So all turned out well for François Ecrette in the end. But he never went on any more trapping trips with Sylvain Gagnon. You see, my friends, one who turns into a big brown bear when you need him most is not a true friend.

French Canadians have worked hard to preserve their French heritage. Today the province of Quebec in eastern Canada remains largely French.

Source: Natalie Savage Carlson, *The Talking Cat and Other Stories of French Canada*. New York: Harper & Row, Publishers, Inc., 1952.

A Voice for WOMEN'S RIGHTS

by Nellie McClung, 1916

For many years, Canadian women were denied the right to vote. Unfair practices also prevented them from holding certain jobs or having the same rights as men. In the late 1800s Canadian women began demanding more rights. The leader of this movement was Nellie McClung (1873-1951), an Ontario-born woman who grew up in the province of Manitoba. In the following excerpt from an essay that appeared in a Canadian magazine in 1916, McClung examines some of the reasons Canadian women were still being denied the right to vote. What are some of those reasons? How does McClung respond?

Men **held to** slavery for long years, **condoning** and justifying it, because they were afraid that without slave labor life would not be comfortable. Certain men have opposed the advancement of women for the same reason; their hearts have been **beset** with the old . . . fear that, if women were allowed equal rights with men, some day some man would go home and find the dinner not ready, and the potatoes not even peeled! But not many give expression to this fear, as a reason for their opposition. They say they oppose the **enfranchisement** of women because they are too frail, weak and sweet to mingle in the **hurly burly** of life; that women have far more influence now than if they could vote, and besides, God never intended them to vote, and it would break up the home, and make life a howling wilderness; the world would be full of neglected children (or none at all) and the **homely** joys of the fireside would vanish from the earth.

I remember once hearing an eloquent speaker cry out in alarm, "If women ever get the vote, who will teach us to say our prayers?"

Surely his experience of the **franchised** class had been an unfortunate one when he could not believe that anyone could both vote and pray!

held to: continued to practice
condoning: excusing

beset: troubled

enfranchisement: right to vote

hurly-burly: uproar

homely: simple

franchised: voting

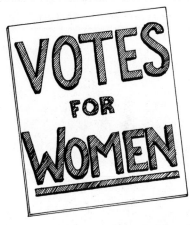

That women are physically **inferior** to men is a strange reason for placing them under a further handicap, and we are surprised to find it **advanced** in all seriousness as an argument against women's suffrage. The **exercising of the ballot** does not require physical strength or endurance. Surely the opponents of women's suffrage do not mean to advocate that a strong fist should rule; just now we are a bit sensitive about this, and such **doctrine** is not popular. Might is not right; with our heart's blood we declare it is not!

No man has the right to citizenship on [account of] his weight, height, or lifting power; he exercises this right because he is a human being, with hands to work, brain to think, and a life to live.

It is to save women from toil and fatigue and all unpleasantness that the **chivalrous** ones would deny her the right of exercising the privileges of citizenship; though just how this could be brought about is not stated. Women are already in the battle of life; 30 percent of the adult women of Canada and the United States are wage earners, and the percentage grows every day. How does the lack of the ballot help them? Is it any comfort to the woman who feels the sting of social injustice to reflect that she, at least, had no part in making such a law? Or do the homes, alone and unprotected after their hard night's work at office-cleaning, ever proudly reflect that at least they never had to drag their skirts in the **mire** of the polls, or be stared at by rude men as they approach the ballot box? . . .

Women will make mistakes of course—and pay for them. That will be nothing new—they have always paid for men's mistakes. It will be a change to pay for their own. Democracy has its failures—it falls down utterly sometimes, we know, but not so often, or so hopelessly, as any other form of government . . . .

Democracy has its faults; the people may run the country to the dogs, but they will run it back again. People, including women, will make mistakes, but in paying for them they will learn wisdom.

inferior: weaker

advanced: proposed

exercising of the ballot: voting

doctrine: set of beliefs

chivalrous: honorable, courteous

mire: deep mud

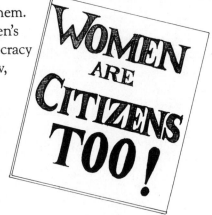

During World War I, as men joined the armed forces, women took their places in factories and on farms. Women's rights leaders such as Nellie McClung pointed out that women shared the burden equally during the war and deserved equality at the ballot box also. Thanks to Nellie McClung and the efforts of thousands of other women, Canadian women gained the right to vote in 1918. For the rest of her life, McClung continued to work for expanded opportunities for women.

Source: Jean Cochrane and Pat Kincaid, eds., *Women in Canadian Politics*. Toronto: Fitzhenry & Whiteside Limited, 1977.

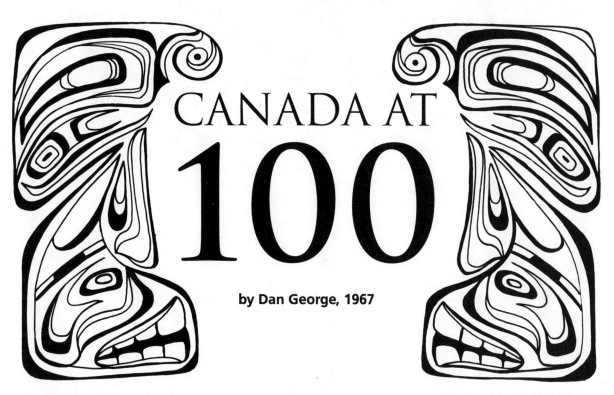

CANADA AT 100

by Dan George, 1967

In the large, beautiful land of Canada, Indians established villages thousands of years before European settlers came. They fished, farmed, and hunted, using the earth's resources with care. When European settlers began to arrive in large numbers, they gradually forced many Indians off their lands and changed—even destroyed—some Indian groups' ways of life. In 1967 Canada celebrated the 100th anniversary of its independence. On this occasion, Dan George, a chief of the Coast Salish tribe in western Canada, gave a speech about Indian culture. How does Dan George view the past and what changes does he recommend for his people? Do you think he is hopeful or fearful about the future?

How long have I known you, oh Canada? A hundred years? Yes, a hundred years and many many years more. And today, when you celebrate your hundred years, oh Canada, I am sad for all the Indian people throughout the land.

For I have known you when your forests were mine; when they gave me my meat and my clothing. I have known you in your streams and rivers where your fish flashed and danced in the sun, where the waters said come, come and eat of my abundance. I have known you in the freedom of your winds. And my spirit, like the winds, once roamed your good lands.

But in the long hundred years since the white man came, I have seen my freedom disappear like the salmon going mysteriously out to sea. The white man's strange customs which I could not understand, pressed down upon me until I could no longer breathe.

When I fought to protect my land and my home, I was called a savage. When I neither understood nor welcomed this way of life, I was called lazy. When I tried to rule my people, I was stripped of my **authority**.

My nation was ignored in your history textbooks—they were little more important in the history of Canada than the buffalo that ranged the plains. I was ridiculed in your plays and motion pictures.

Oh Canada, how can I celebrate with you this Centenary, this hundred years? Shall I thank you for the reserves that are left to me of my beautiful forests? For the canned fish of my rivers? For the loss of my pride and authority, even among my own people? For the lack of my will to fight back? No! I must forget what's past and gone.

Oh, God in Heaven! Give me back the courage of the olden Chiefs. Let me wrestle with my surroundings. Let me again, as in the days of old, dominate my environment. Let me humbly accept this new culture and through it rise up and go on.

Oh, God! Like the Thunderbird of old I shall rise again out of the sea; I shall grab the instruments of the white man's success—his education, his skills, and with these new tools I shall build my race into the proudest segment of your society. Before I follow the great Chiefs who have gone before us, oh Canada, I shall see these things come to pass.

I shall see our young braves and our chiefs sitting in the houses of law and government, ruling and being ruled by the knowledge and freedom of our great land. So shall we shatter the barriers of our isolation. So shall the next hundred years be the greatest in the proud history of our tribes and nations.

Today many of Canada's Indians live on about 2,200 reserves, which are like reservations in the United States. Many others live in cities and towns throughout the country. In recent years Canadian Indians have organized to protect their rights and beliefs, and they have won greater control over the resources on their lands.

Source: T. C. McLuhan, *Touch the Earth: A Self-Portrait of Indian Existence.* New York: Promontory Press, 1971.

authority: power to govern

2

LATIN AMERICA

*We have already seen the
light.... The chains have
been broken;
we have been freed.*

Simón Bolívar, 1815

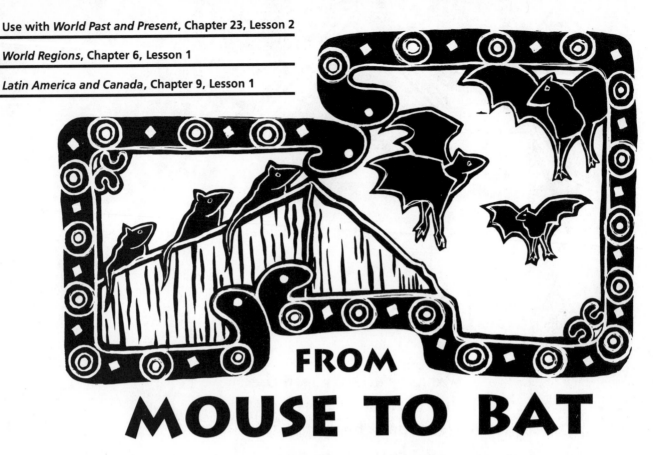

FROM
MOUSE TO BAT

Mayan Fable Retold by Victor Montejo, 1991

Between 500 B.C. and A.D. 900, the ancient Mayas had a rich civilization in what are today the countries of Mexico, Guatemala, Honduras, and El Salvador. They left many written records of their civilization in the form of books and temples carved with hieroglyphs and other pictures. They also left oral records such as fables, stories, and tales that have been passed down from one generation to the next. This practice of using fables to teach a lesson has continued to the present day. Victor Montejo (mon tā' hō), a Maya born in 1952, recently collected some of the fables and stories that he heard while growing up in Guatemala. As you read this Mayan fable, try to determine the moral of the story.

When the Creator and Shaper made all the animals, each **species** was eager to know where they would live, and he assigned their **habitats** to them.

species: category of animals

habitats: places to live

The happiest were the birds who flew singing to the trees to build their nests. Only *Tx'ow* [tshō], the mouse, didn't move. He stood there open-mouthed **contemplating** the marvelous flight of the birds.

contemplating: thinking about

"Go on," the Creator told him. "Go eat the kernels of corn, seeds, and all the forgotten pieces of food."

But *Tx'ow* wouldn't move. His body shook with resentment.

The Creator, very angry, picked him up by the tail and threw him in the bush. *Tx'ow* still could not say a word. He only stared at the flight of the singing birds with his eyes popping out. Then he looked at himself and became very sad. He could make little jumps, but fly? No, he could never achieve that.

Now is the time to act, he said to himself. He decided to call together all the members of his species. There weren't many in those times. Well, he thought, they must be as discontented as I am.

Tx'ow easily convinced his brothers and sisters that they deserved more. One afternoon the **delegation** of mice came before the god, as he rested from the work of creation.

delegation: group

"What do you want? Speak up," he ordered them.

The delegation tried to speak but it could not. All they could say was, *witz'itz'i, witz'itz'i* [wēts ēts ē'].

The wise god understood what they had come for and he said to them, "You want to fly like the birds?"

The delegation broke out in a big racket of *witz'itz'i, witz'itz'i* nodding their heads yes.

"Very good," the Creator said, "Tomorrow you should appear at *tx'eqwob'al* [tshā kwō bäl'], the place for jumping, and I will give you your opportunity."

The mice went away satisfied, believing that a favorable **resolution** was at hand. To celebrate, there was a great rejoicing among the [tree] roots that night.

resolution: outcome

When the sun came up, the Creator was waiting at the place he had chosen to meet the unhappy mice. "Ready for the test?" he asked. "Those who can jump over this **ravine** will instantly receive wings and go flying away. And those who do not succeed will remain as they are."

ravine: steep valley

The discontented mice filed up one by one and launched out on the grand adventure. Those whose efforts carried them to the other side received wings and went flying off to the caverns, looking still like mice except for their wings. Those who did not succeed resigned themselves to their fate.

When the great test was over, the Creator warned them, "I don't want you returning to bother me anymore. You who are mice will continue eating grain and seeds. If you want, you can climb the trees and make your nests there. On the other hand those who now have wings will from now on be called *Sotz'* [sōts], the bats. For them day will be night. They will feed on mosquitoes and blood, and sleep hanging upside down from the walls of *nhach'en* [nä chān'], the caverns, today and forever."

So it was that *Tx'ow*, the mouse, learned to accept himself and understood that his relatives, the bats, had not found happiness in their new condition either. They lost their tails and their toes grew long in order to cling to the rocks.

Today more than 6 million Mayas live in Mexico and the countries of Central America. The oral tradition—the passing down of stories, beliefs, and history—remains a central part of Mayan culture.

Source: Victor Montejo, *The Bird Who Cleans the World and Other Mayan Fables*. Willimantic, CT: Curbstone Press, 1991.

BATTLE OF TENOCHTITLÁN

by Aztec Historians, 1521

Beginning around 1325, the Aztecs ruled a powerful empire in the Central Valley of Mexico. In 1519, however, Hernando Cortés and his army of Spanish soldiers arrived in the Aztec capital of Tenochtitlán. At first the Aztec ruler Moctezuma permitted the Spaniards to enter the city peacefully. The Spaniards, however, were not interested in peace but rather in the vast quantities of Aztec gold and silver stored at Tenochtitlán. The Spaniards attacked the Aztecs and, in 1521, laid siege to the city for 85 days. Aztec historians recorded these events in pictographs, a form of writing in which pictures are used to represent events and ideas. Aztec pictographs were written on amatl (ä mät′ əl), a type of paper that was made by pounding the inner bark of a wild fig tree. The pictograph on the next page, based on the Aztec calendar, tells the history of the Spanish conquest. The three boxes at the top of the pictograph contain Aztec symbols that stand for three different years. Study the other images, and try to determine what they mean. Then compare your ideas to the explanation below.

On the left side of the pictograph, the soldier on a horse carrying a sword, shield, and cross represents the Spaniards landing in Mexico in the Aztec year of 1-Reed. It is believed that the event in this picture took place in 1519, because a reed, which is pictured in the box above the soldier, is one of the symbols used by Aztecs in naming that year. The Aztecs used a calendar year fixed at 365 days, much as the United States and many other countries do today.

Beside the Spanish soldier is an Aztec official who is greeting him. The official is shown offering the soldier a gift, which indicates that at first the Aztecs welcomed the Spaniards. The faces in the row of images at the bottom of the pictograph show the different Indian groups allied with the Aztecs.

The next scene shows that during the year of 2-Flint, or 1520, a fight took place in the Aztec capital. The pictograph shows Aztec priests being cut down in battle by the Spaniards' steel swords on the steps of the city's main pyramid. This pyramid—the most important building in Tenochtitlán—housed the two main temples dedicated to Aztec gods. These are shown by the two sets of steps leading up the pyramid. Try to find the image of the cactus and stone joined to a temple, which was another symbol for Tenochtitlán. Although the Spaniards' first attempt to capture Tenochtitlán was unsuccessful, they later conquered the city on the day 1-Serpent of the year 3-House, or 1521.

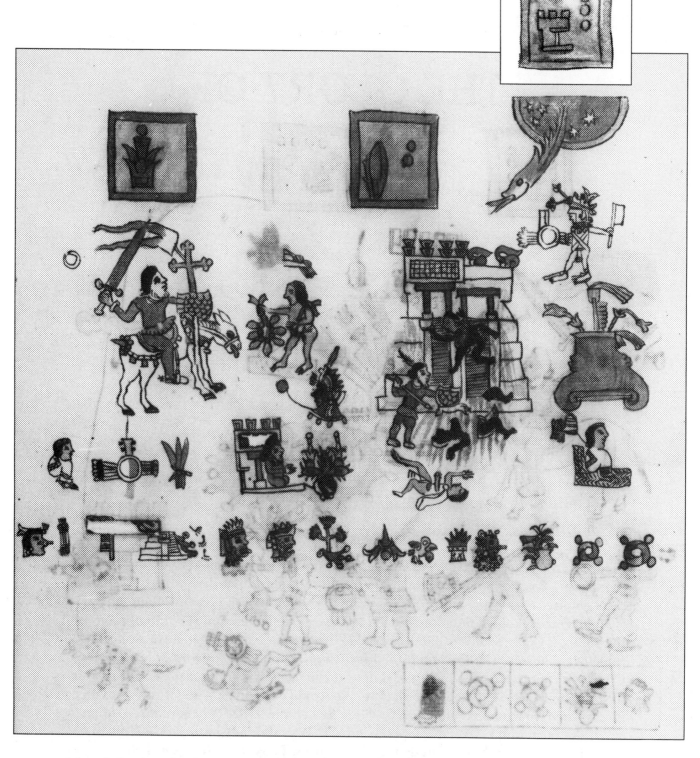

After defeating the Aztecs at Tenochtitlán, the Spaniards built a new city, called Mexico City, on top of the Aztec ruins. Today this modern, bustling city is the capital of Mexico. This pictograph preserves the memory of Tenochtitlán and helps us to understand the Spanish conquest from an Aztec point of view. Suppose you were asked to make a pictograph of an event in your life or that of your classroom or country. What symbols might you use?

THE GLORY OF

THE INCAS

by Pedro de Cieza de León, 1553

Five hundred years ago, the Incas ruled a vast empire that stretched 2,500 miles along the western coast of South America. They built thousands of miles of roads to connect their empire. They also built terraces on the steep slopes of the Andes Mountains. These terraces enabled them to grow crops that yielded abundant supplies of food. In the 1530s, a young Spanish soldier named Pedro de Cieza de León (dā syä′ sä dā lā ôn′) traveled on horseback throughout the Incan empire and kept a record of his journey. Cieza de León was impressed by the skill of Incan carvers. He was also amazed at how well the Incas distributed food so that no one would go hungry. The following excerpt is translated from a book published by Cieza de León in 1553. What are three things about the Incas that most impressed the author? Why did they impress him? When you are finished reading the text, study the illustrations. They were drawn by Felipe Guamán Poma de Ayala, a seventeenth-century Incan nobleman from the Andes Mountains. How do his drawings help illustrate Cieza de León's account?

There is no disputing the fact that when one sees the fine handicraft they have produced, it arouses the admiration of all who have knowledge of it. The most amazing thing is how few tools and instruments they have for their work, and how easily they produce things of finest quality. At the time the Spaniards conquered this kingdom, articles of gold, clay, and silver were discovered, the parts joined one to the other as though they had been created that way. The most amazing examples of silverwork, **statuettes**, and other larger things were seen, . . . I have seen dinner **services** made with the use of pieces of copper and two or three stones, so finely worked, and the goblets, platters, and **candelabra** all **embossed** with leaves and designs, that master workmen would have their work cut out for them to do as well with all the instruments and tools they have. Aside from the articles of silver, many of them make **medallions**, chains, and other things of gold. And little boys, who if you saw them you would not think knew how to talk yet, understand how to do these things. . . .

The *Orejones* [ôr ā hō′ nās] of **Cuzco** who supplied me with information are in agreement that in olden times, in the days of the Lord-Incas, all the villages and provinces of Peru were notified that a report should be given to the rulers and their representatives each year of the men and women who had died, and all who had been born, for this was necessary for the **levying** of the **tributes** as well as to know how many were available for war and those who could assume the defense of the villages. This was an easy matter, for each province at the end of the year had a list by the knots of the **quipus** [ke püz] of all the people who had died there during the year and how many deaths. This was reported with all truth and accuracy, without any **fraud** or **deceit**. In this way the **Inca** and the governors knew which of the Indians were poor, the women who had been widowed, whether they were able to pay their taxes, and how many men they could count on in the event of war, and many other things they considered highly important.

As this kingdom was so vast, as I have repeatedly mentioned, in each of the many provinces there were many storehouses filled with

statuettes: small statues

services: table settings

candelabra: branched candlesticks

embossed: decorated

medallions: large medals

Orejones: Incan nobles

Cuzco: capital of the Incan empire

levying: raising

tributes: payments to a ruler

quipus: special cords used for counting

fraud: cheating

deceit: trickery

Inca: title for the Incan emperor

supplies and other needful things; thus, in times of war, wherever the armies went they [drew] upon the contents of these storehouses, without ever touching the supplies of their **confederates** or laying a finger on what they had in their settlements. And when there was no war, all this stock of supplies and food was divided up among the poor and the widows. These poor were the aged, or the lame, crippled, or paralyzed, or those **afflicted** with some other disease; if they were in good health, they received nothing. Then the storehouses were filled up once more with the tributes paid the Inca. If there came a lean year, the storehouses were opened and the provinces were lent what they needed in the way of supplies; then, in a year of abundance, they paid back all they had received. . . .

No one who was lazy or tried to live by the work of others was **tolerated**; everyone had to work. Thus on certain days each lord went to his lands and took the plow in hand and cultivated the earth, and did other things. Even the Incas themselves did this to set an example, for everybody was to know that there should be nobody so rich that, on this account, he might **disdain** or **affront** the poor. And under their system there was none such in all the kingdom, for, if he had his health, he worked and lacked for nothing; and if he was ill, he received what he needed from the storehouses. And no rich man could deck himself out in more **finery** than the poor, or wear different clothing, except the rulers and headmen, who, to maintain their dignity, were allowed great freedom and privilege, as well as the *Orejones*, who held a place apart among all the peoples.

confederates: allies

afflicted: suffering

tolerated: permitted

disdain: look down on
affront: insult

finery: fancy clothing

At the time Cieza de León was traveling through the Incan empire, Spanish troops set out to conquer the Incas and seize their treasures of gold and silver. Led by Francisco Pizarro, the Spaniards surprised the Incas and defeated them in 1532. Today Cieza de León's writings survive as one of the finest personal accounts of the once-mighty Incan empire.

Source: Victor Wolfgang von Hagen, ed., *The Incas of Pedro de Cieza de León*. Norman, OK: University of Oklahoma Press, 1959.

TEARS OF THE INDIANS

by Bartolomé de Las Casas, 1542

When Spanish colonists arrived in Latin America, they set up the encomienda system, which used enslaved Indians as forced labor. This system, as well as the diseases brought by Europeans, caused the deaths of many Native Americans in the early 1500s. Bartolomé de Las Casas (1474-1566) was a Spanish priest who supported the encomienda system at first but then turned against it. In fact, Las Casas was so upset about the behavior of the Spanish colonists that he wrote letters to Spain's rulers, protesting the mistreatment of Indians. In the excerpt below, translated from a book about the colonies he wrote in 1542, Las Casas presents his views about how the Spaniards' actions were destroying the Indians and their civilization. According to Las Casas, what effect did Spanish colonization have on the Indians? What evidence does he give to support his claim?

There were ten kingdoms [on the continent of North America] as large as the kingdom of Spain, Aragon, and Portugal, **encompassing** over a thousand square miles [2,600 sq km]. Of all this the inhumane and **abominable** villainies of the Spaniards have made a wilderness, for though it was formerly occupied by vast and **infinite** numbers of men [women and children] it is stripped of all people. And we dare assert with confidence that in those forty years during which the Spaniards have exercised their abominable cruelties and detestable **tyrannies** in those parts, over twelve million souls innocently **perished**, women and children being included in the sad and fatal list. Moreover I truly believe that I should be speaking within the truth if I were to say that over fifty millions were **consumed** in this massacre.

encompassing: including

abominable: terrible

infinite: endless

tyrannies: abuses of power

perished: died

consumed: killed

41

As for those that came out of Spain, boasting themselves to be Christians, they had two ways of **extirpating** the Indian nation from the face of the earth: the first was by making bloody, unjust, and cruel wars against them, the second was by killing all those that so much as sought to recover their liberty, as some of the braver sort did. And as for the women and children that were left alive, the Spaniards laid so heavy and **grievous** a **yoke of servitude** upon them that the condition of beasts was much more tolerable.

All the various other torments and inhumanities which they **employed** to the ruin of these poor nations may be included under these two headings.

What led the Spaniards to these **unsanctified impieties** was the desire for gold to make themselves suddenly rich, in order to obtain dignities and honors that were in no way fit for them. In a word their **covetousness**, their ambition which could not be exceeded by any people under heaven, the riches of the country, and the patience of the people gave occasion for this devilish **barbarism**. For the Spaniards so despised them (I now speak what I have seen without the least untruth) that they used them not like beasts, for that would have been tolerable, but looked upon them as if they had been but the **dung** and filth of the earth, and so little did they regard the health of their souls that they permitted this great **multitude** to die without the least light of religion. Nor is this less true than what I have said before and what those tyrants and hangmen themselves do not deny . . . namely, that the Indians never gave them the least cause for such violence but received them as angels sent from heaven, until the excessive cruelties and torments and slaughters moved them to take arms against the Spaniards. . . .

extirpating: wiping out

grievous: painful
yoke of servitude: state of slavery

employed: used

unsanctified impieties: wicked deeds

covetousness: greed

barbarism: uncivilized acts

dung: manure

multitude: large number

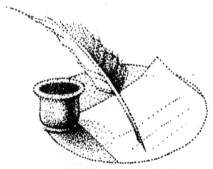

During the early 1500s, Bartolomé de Las Casas's voice of protest was heard by the Spanish king. In 1516 Las Casas was appointed "Protector of the Indians." He made the cause of protecting the rights of Indians his lifelong crusade. Due to Las Casas's efforts, the New Laws— royal decrees prohibiting forced labor of the Indians—were issued in 1542, the same year his book appeared. But the Spaniards soon replaced the Indians with enslaved people from Africa. To learn about the first slaves in Latin America who rebelled and gained their freedom, read the next document on page 43.

Source: Adapted from the translation by John Phillips, from Bartolomé de Las Casas, *The Tears of the Indians, Being an Historical and True Account of the Cruel Massacres and Slaughters of above Twenty Millions of Innocent People* (London, 1656), in Charles Gibson, ed., *The Spanish Tradition in America.* New York: Harper, 1968.

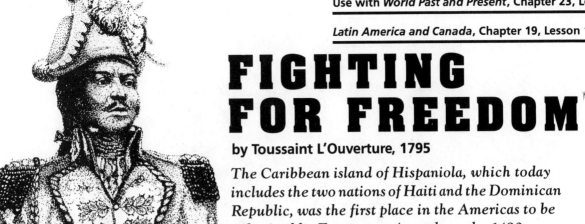

FIGHTING FOR FREEDOM

by Toussaint L'Ouverture, 1795

The Caribbean island of Hispaniola, which today includes the two nations of Haiti and the Dominican Republic, was the first place in the Americas to be colonized by Europeans. As early as the 1490s, Spaniards began enslaving the island's original people. When they died out, Europeans brought millions of Africans across the Atlantic Ocean by force over the next 300 years to work as slaves. Life under slavery was harsh and brutal. In 1791 enslaved Haitians began an uprising against their white rulers. The leader of this revolt was Toussaint L'Ouverture (1744-1803). Toussaint fought both the French who controlled Haiti and the Spanish and British who controlled the eastern part of Hispaniola. In 1795 Toussaint gave the following speech to rally fellow Haitians against the British. How does Toussaint defend the Haitians' struggle for freedom?

That my hopes for you, my friends, will not prove to be in vain, show yourselves to be men who know what liberty means and are prepared to defend it. The army is about to march, take, my friends, the **resolution** not to return home until you have chased from the Colony the English and the **Emigrés**, only then can you enjoy the sweetness of liberty, the justice of the republic and of our country, which you know cannot be possible if your enemies still occupy this land of freedom. Let not **fatigue**, the mountains nor the cliffs prevent you, we must conquer and it is now the time. . . .

resolution: vow

Emigrés: French allies of the British

fatigue: tiredness

It is not for fortune or for riches that we fight, there will be time to think of that when we have chased these enemies from our shores, it is for liberty which is the most precious of all earthly possessions, which we must preserve for our children, our brothers, and our comrades. God, who created all to be free has made it clear that it is our duty to preserve it for all who come after us.

It is my intention and my **resolve** not to cease the fight until I have driven the English and the Emigrés entirely from our shores. Let us leave them nothing which they once possessed. We will make our land flourish once more for this is the foundation and the structure of our liberty.

resolve: firm purpose

After many years of fighting against British, French, and Spanish troops, General Toussaint L' Ouverture led his army to victory and ended slavery in Haiti. As a result of this 13-year revolution, Haiti became an independent nation in 1804. Haiti was the first European-controlled area in Latin America to regain independence. To learn about how other Latin Americans fought for independence in the early 1800s, read the next document on pages 44-45.

Source: Wenda Parkinson, *"This Gilded African": Toussaint L'Ouverture*. London: Quartet Books, 1978.

Letter from Jamaica

by Simón Bolívar, 1815

In the early 1800s Spain still ruled most of Latin America and many people were poor or enslaved. After the revolution in Haiti, which was described in the document on page 43, the desire for independence swept across the region. Simón Bolívar (1783-1830), who as a boy had learned about the ideas of freedom around the world, rallied Latin Americans to fight for independence from Spain. At first Bolívar's efforts were unsuccessful and he was forced to retreat to the island of Jamaica in 1815. While there, he wrote the following letter to an English friend, in which he predicted that South America would succeed in winning its independence. What do you think Bolívar meant by destiny?

September 6, 1815

Success will crown our efforts, because the destiny of America has been **irrevocably** decided; the tie that bound her to Spain has been **severed**. Only a **concept** maintained that tie and kept the parts of that immense monarchy together. That which formerly bound them now divides them. The hatred that the peninsula [of Spain] has inspired in us is greater than the ocean between us. It would be easier to have the two continents meet than to **reconcile** the spirits of the two countries. The habit of obedience; a community of interest, of understanding, of religion; mutual goodwill; a tender regard for the birthplace and good name of our forefathers; in short, all that gave rise to our hopes, came to us from Spain.... At present the **contrary** attitude persists: we are threatened with the fear of death, dishonor, and every harm; there is nothing we have not suffered at the hands of that unnatural step-mother—Spain. The veil has been torn **asunder**. We have already seen the light, and it is not our desire to be thrust back into darkness. The chains have been broken; we have been freed, and now our enemies seek to

irrevocably: impossible to change
severed: broken
concept: idea

reconcile: bring together

contrary: opposite

asunder: apart

enslave us anew. For this reason America fights desperately, and seldom has desperation failed to achieve victory. . . .

With respect to heroic and **hapless** Venezuela, events there have moved so rapidly and the **devastation** has been such that. . . [a] few women, children, and old men are all that remain. Most of the men have perished rather than be slaves; those who survive continue to fight furiously on the fields and in the inland towns, until they **expire** or hurl into the sea those who, **insatiable** in their thirst for blood and crimes, rival those first monsters who wiped out America's. . . [earliest people]. . . .

16,000,000 Americans either defend their rights or suffer **repression** at the hands of Spain, which although once the world's greatest empire, is now too weak, with what little is left her, to rule the new hemisphere or even to maintain herself in the old. . . . What madness for our enemy to hope to reconquer America when she has no navy, no funds, and almost no soldiers! . . .

Americans today, and perhaps to a greater extent than ever before, who live within the Spanish system occupy a position in society no better than that of serfs destined for labor, or at best they have no more status than that of mere consumers. . . . In short, do you wish to know what our future held?— simply the cultivation of the fields of indigo, grain, coffee, sugar cane, cacao, and cotton; cattle raising on the broad plains; hunting wild game in the jungles; digging in the earth to mine its gold— but even these limitations could never satisfy the greed of Spain.

So negative was our existence that I can find nothing comparable in any other civilized society, examine as I may the entire history of time and the politics of all nations. Is it not an outrage and a violation of human rights to expect a land so splendidly **endowed**, so vast, rich, and populous, to remain merely passive?. . .

More than anyone, I desire to see America **fashioned** into the greatest nation in the world, greatest not so much by virtue of her area and wealth as by her freedom and glory. . . .

From the **foregoing**, we can draw these conclusions: The American provinces are fighting for their freedom, and they will ultimately succeed.

hapless: unlucky
devastation: ruin

expire: die
insatiable: unable to be satisfied

repression: mistreatment

endowed: plentiful in resources

fashioned: shaped

foregoing: points stated before

After returning to South America, Bolívar led his troops on a difficult march across the steep, snow-covered Andes Mountains. His forces surprised the Spanish army in Colombia and defeated them in a battle that was the turning point in the struggle for independence. By 1824, with Bolívar's help, the Spanish colonies in South America had broken free from the Spanish empire. For his bold and heroic actions, South Americans remember Simón Bolívar as "The Liberator."

Source: Harold A. Bierck, Jr., ed., *Selected Writings of Bolívar.* New York: The Colonial Press, Inc., 1951.

Guantanamera

Based on a Poem by José Martí, 1890s

Long after most regions in Latin America had gained their independence, which was described on pages 43-45, Cuba remained a colony of Spain. By the late 1800s, however, many Cubans began fighting in hopes of gaining their independence. These hopes found a voice in José Martí (1853-1895), a Cuban poet and patriot. Imprisoned at the age of 16 and forced to leave Cuba in 1879 because of his revolutionary activities, Martí believed his words could keep alive the ideal of "Cuba libre"—free Cuba. While in exile, he organized an independence movement. The song "Guantanamera" (gwän tä nä mâr′ə) is based on the verses Martí wrote while in exile, expressing his love for the people of his island homeland. Years later, José Fernandez Dias rewrote these verses and set them to music. Guantanamera refers to a woman who comes from Guantánamo, a city in Cuba. The guajira (gwä hîr′ə) is a dance rhythm named for a Cuban Indian group. How can songs like "Guantanamera" help to unite people in a common effort?

Words and Music by José Fernandez Dias
Lyrics adapted by Julian Orbon
Music adapted by Hector Angulo and Pete Seeger

¡Guan-ta-na-me-ra, gua-ji-ra Guan-ta-na-me-ra,

Guan-ta-na-me-ra,__ gua-ji-ra Guan-ta-na-me-ra!

Verse

1. Yo soy un hom-bre sin-ce-ro, De don-de cre-ce la pal-ma,

Yo soy un hom-bre sin-ce-ro de don-de cre-ce la pal-ma,

D.C. al Fine

Y an-tes de mo-rir-me quie-ro, ___ E-char mis ver-sos del al - ma.

English Translation of First Verse

I am an honest man from a place where palm trees grow,
I am an honest man from a place where palm trees grow,
And before I die I want to send these verses out from my soul.

Second Verse

Mi verso es de un verde claro
y de un carmín encendido.
Mi verso es de un verde claro
y de un carmín encendido.
Mi verso es un cierro herido
que busca en el monte amparo.

My verse is of clear green
and flaming red.
My verse is of clear green
and flaming red.
My verse is of a wounded fawn
seeking the refuge of the forest.

Third Verse

Con los pobres de la tierra
quiero yo mi suerte echar.
Con los pobres de la tierra
quiero yo mi suerte echar.
El arroyo de la sierra
me complace más que el mar.

With the poor of the earth
I would cast my lot.
With the poor of the earth
I would cast my lot.
The mountain stream fulfills
me more than the sea.

Source: *Music and You*. New York: Macmillan Publishing Company, 1991.

THE GOLD COIN

by Alma Flor Ada, 1991

Latin America has a rich tradition of folktales. Many of these folktales capture the spirit, culture, and values of its people. The folktale below was written by Alma Flor Ada, who was born in Cuba and now lives in the United States. In this tale, set in Central America, a thief sets out to steal gold that he sees a woman holding. How does the thief end up with something far more valuable than gold?

Juan had been a thief for many years. Because he did his stealing by night, his skin had become pale and sickly. Because he spent his time either hiding or sneaking about, his body had become shriveled and bent. And because he had neither friend nor relative to make him smile, his face was always twisted into an angry frown.

One night, drawn by a light shining through the trees, Juan came upon a hut. He crept up to the door and through a crack saw an old woman sitting at a plain, wooden table.

What was that shining in her hand? Juan wondered. He could not believe his eyes: It was a gold coin. Then he heard the woman say to herself, "I must be the richest person in the world."

Juan decided instantly that all the woman's gold must be his. He thought that the easiest thing to do was to watch until the woman left. Juan hid in the bushes and huddled under his **poncho**, waiting for the right moment to enter the hut.

poncho: raincoat

Juan was half asleep when he heard knocking at the door and the sound of **insistent** voices. A few minutes later, he saw the woman, wrapped in a black cloak, leave the hut with two men at her side.

insistent: pleading

Here's my chance! Juan thought. And, forcing open a window, he climbed into the empty hut.

He looked about eagerly for the gold. He looked under the bed. It wasn't there. He looked in the cupboard. It wasn't there, either. Where could it be? Close to despair, Juan tore away some beams supporting the thatch roof.

Finally, he gave up. There was simply no gold in the hut.

All I can do, he thought, is to find the old woman and make her tell me where she's hidden it.

So he set out along the path that she and her two companions had taken.

It was daylight by the time Juan reached the river. The countryside had been deserted, but here, along the riverbank, were two huts. Nearby, a man and his son were hard at work, hoeing potatoes.

It had been a long, long time since Juan had spoken to another human being. Yet his desire to find the woman was so strong that he went up to the farmers and asked, in a hoarse, raspy voice, "Have you seen a short, gray-haired woman, wearing a black cloak?"

"Oh, you must be looking for Doña Josefa," the young boy said. "Yes, we've seen her. We went to fetch her this morning, because my grandfather had another attack of—"

"Where is she now?" Juan broke in.

"She is long gone," said the father with a smile. "Some people from across the river came looking for her, because someone in their family is sick."

"How can I get across the river?" Juan asked anxiously.

"Only by boat," the boy answered. "We'll row you across later, if you'd like." Then turning back to his work, he added, "But first we must finish digging up the potatoes."

The thief muttered, "Thanks." But he quickly grew impatient. He grabbed a hoe and began to help the pair of farmers. The sooner we finish, the sooner we'll get across the river, he thought. And the sooner I'll get to my gold!

It was dusk when they finally laid down their hoes. The soil had been turned, and the wicker baskets were brimming with potatoes.

"Now can you row me across?" Juan asked the father anxiously.

"Certainly," the man said. "But let's eat supper first."

Juan had forgotten the taste of a home-cooked meal and the pleasure that comes from sharing it with others. As he sopped up the last of the stew with a chunk of dark bread, memories of other meals came back to him from far away and long ago.

By the light of the moon, father and son guided their boat across the river.

"What a wonderful healer Doña Josefa is!" the boy told Juan. "All she had to do to make Abuelo better was give him a cup of her special tea."

"Yes, and not only that," his father added, "she brought him a gold coin."

Juan was stunned. It was one thing for Doña Josefa to go around helping people. But how could she go around handing out gold coins— his gold coins?

When the threesome finally reached the other side of the river, they saw a young man sitting outside his hut.

"This fellow is looking for Doña Josefa," the father said, pointing to Juan.

"Oh, she left some time ago," the young man said.

"Where to?" Juan asked tensely.

"Over to the other side of the mountain," the young man replied, pointing to the vague outline of mountains in the night sky.

"How did she get there?" Juan asked, trying to hide his impatience.

"By horse," the young man answered. "They came on horseback to get her because someone had broken his leg."

"Well, then, I need a horse, too," Juan said urgently.

"Tomorrow," the young man replied softly. "Perhaps I can take you tomorrow, maybe the next day. First I must finish harvesting the corn."

So Juan spent the next day in the fields, bathed in sweat from sunup to sundown.

Yet each ear of corn that he picked seemed to bring him closer to his treasure. And later that evening, when he helped the young man husk several ears so they could boil them for supper, the yellow kernels glittered like gold coins.

While they were eating, Juan thought about Doña Josefa. Why, he wondered, would someone who said she was the world's richest woman spend her time taking care of every sick person for miles around?

The following day, the two set off at dawn. Juan could not recall when he last had noticed the beauty of the sunrise. He felt strangely moved by the sight of the mountains, barely lit by the faint rays of the morning sun.

As they neared the foothills, the young man said, "I'm not surprised you're looking for Doña Josefa. The whole countryside needs her. I went for her because my wife had been running a high fever. In no time at all, Doña Josefa had her on the road to recovery. And what's more my friend, she brought her a gold coin!"

Juan groaned inwardly. To think that someone could hand out gold so freely! What a strange woman Doña Josefa is, Juan thought. Not only is she willing to help one person after another, but she doesn't mind traveling all over the countryside to do it!

"Well my friend," said the young man finally, "this is where I must leave you. But you don't have far to walk. See that house over there? It belongs to the man who broke his leg."

The young man stretched out his hand to say goodbye. Juan stared at it for a moment. It had been a long, long time since the thief had shaken hands with anyone. Slowly, he pulled out a hand from under his poncho. When his companion grasped it firmly in his own, Juan felt suddenly warmed, as if by the rays of the sun.

But after he thanked the young man, Juan ran down the road. He was still eager to catch up with Doña Josefa. When he reached the house, a woman and a child were stepping down from a wagon.

"Have you seen Doña Josefa?" Juan asked.

"We've just taken her to Don Teodosio's" the woman said. "His wife is sick, you know—"

"How do I get there?" Juan broke in. "I've got to see her."

"It's too far to walk," the woman said **amiably**. "If you'd like, I'll take you there tomorrow. But first I must gather my squash and beans."

So Juan spent yet another long day in the fields. Working beneath the summer sun, Juan noticed that his skin had begun to tan. And although he had to stoop down to pick the squash, he found that he could now stretch his body. His back had begun to straighten, too.

Later, when the little girl took him by the hand to show him a family of rabbits **burrowed** under a fallen tree, Juan's face broke into a smile. It had been a long, long time since Juan had smiled.

Yet his thoughts kept coming back to the gold.

The following day, the wagon carrying Juan and the woman lumbered along a road lined with coffee fields.

The woman said, "I don't know what we would have done without Doña Josefa. I sent my daughter to our neighbor's house, who then brought Doña Josefa on horseback. She set my husband's leg and then showed me how to brew a special tea to lessen the pain."

Getting no reply, she went on, "And, as if that weren't enough, she brought him a gold coin. Can you imagine such a thing?"

Juan could only sigh. No doubt about it, he thought, Doña Josefa is someone special. But Juan didn't know whether to be happy that Doña Josefa had so much gold she could freely hand it out, or angry for her having already given so much of it away.

When they finally reached Don Teodosio's house, Doña Josefa was already gone. But here, too, there was work that needed to be done. . . .

Juan stayed to help with the coffee harvest. As he picked the red berries, he gazed up from time to time at the trees that grew, row upon row, along the hillsides. What a calm, peaceful place this is! he thought.

The next morning, Juan was up at daybreak. Bathed in the soft, dawn light, the mountains seemed to smile at him. When Don Teodosio offered him a lift on horseback, Juan found it difficult to have to say good-bye.

"What a good woman Doña Josefa is!" Don Teodosio said, as they rode down the hill toward the sugarcane fields. "The minute she heard about my wife being sick, she came with her special herbs. And as if that weren't enough, she brought my wife a gold coin!"

In the **stifling** heat, the kind that often signals the approach of a storm, Juan simply sighed and mopped his brow. The pair continued riding for several hours in silence.

stifling: unbearable

Juan then realized he was back in familiar territory, for they were now on the stretch of road he had traveled only a week ago—though how much longer it now seemed to him. He jumped off Don Teodosio's horse and broke into a run.

This time the gold would not escape him! But he had to move quickly, so he could find shelter before the storm broke.

Out of breath, Juan finally reached Doña Josefa's hut. She was standing by the door, shaking her head slowly as she surveyed the **ransacked** house.

ransacked: destroyed

"So I've caught up with you at last!" Juan shouted, startling the old woman. "Where's the gold?"

"The gold coin?" Doña Josefa said, surprised and looking at Juan intently. "Have you come for the gold coin? I've been trying hard to give it to someone who might need it," Doña Josefa said. "First to an old man who had just gotten over a bad attack. Then to a young woman who had been running a fever. Then to a man with a broken leg. And finally to Don Teodosio's wife. But none of them would take it. They all said, 'Keep it. There must be someone who needs it more.' "

Juan did not say a word.

"You must be the one who needs it," Doña Josefa said.

She took the coin out of her pocket and handed it to him. Juan stared at the coin, speechless.

At that moment a young girl appeared, her long braid bouncing as she ran. "Hurry, Doña Josefa, please!" she said breathlessly. "My mother is all alone, and the baby is due any minute."

"Of course, dear," Doña Josefa replied. But as she glanced up at the sky, she saw nothing but black clouds. The storm was nearly upon them. Doña Josefa sighed deeply.

"But how can I leave now? Look at my house! I don't know what has happened to the roof. The storm will wash the whole place away!"

And there was a deep sadness in her voice.

Juan **took in** the child's frightened eyes, Doña Josefa's sad, **distressed** face, and the ransacked hut.

took in: noticed
distressed: worried

"Go ahead, Doña Josefa," he said. "Don't worry about your house. I'll see that the roof is back in shape, good as new."

The woman nodded gratefully, drew her cloak about her shoulders, and took the child by the hand. As she turned to leave, Juan held out his hand.

"Here, take this," he said, giving her the gold coin. "I'm sure the newborn will need it more than I."

Doña Josefa is a kind and highly skilled woman. What did the thief—and the reader—learn from her and the people she helps in this folktale?

Source: Alma Flor Ada, *The Gold Coin*. New York: Macmillan Publishing Company, 1991.

Saving the Rain Forest

by Paiakan, 1988

The Amazon region of South America contains the largest rain forest in the world, home to thousands of different kinds of plants and animals. In recent years, new settlers have moved in and destroyed large portions of the forest. Careless development also threatens the way of life of Indians who have lived in the rain forest for many hundreds of years. A Kayapó (kä yə pō') Indian leader named Paiakan (pī ə kän') has met with world leaders and urged them to listen to the people who have long made the rain forest their home. In the following excerpt from a speech given in 1988, Paiakan describes how all forms of life in the rain forest depend upon one another. What is the main point that the author is trying to make? What reasons and evidence does he give to support his claims?

The forest is one big thing: it has people, animals, and plants. There is no point saving the forest if the people and animals who live in it are killed or driven away. The groups trying to save the race of animals cannot win if the people trying to save the forest lose; the people trying to save the Indians cannot win if either of the others lose; the Indians cannot win without the support of these groups; but the groups cannot win without the help of the Indians, who know the forest and the animals and can tell what is happening to them. No one of us is strong enough to win alone; together, we can be strong enough to win.

In 1988 the Brazilian government filed criminal charges against Paiakan, saying that his work trying to save the rain forest interfered with the government. Many groups protested, and a court dismissed the charges. Like Paiakan, many people are presently working to preserve the people, the plant life, and the animals of the rain forest.

Source: Susanna Hecht and Alexander Cockburn, *The Fate of the Forest: Developers, Destroyers, and Defenders of the Amazon*. London and New York: Verso, 1989.

Ode to an Artichoke by Pablo Neruda, 1958

Pablo Neruda is widely considered Chile's greatest poet. In the following poem about an artichoke, a vegetable with coarse leaves, Neruda describes how it is grown and then sold at the marketplace. How does Neruda use the character of the artichoke to write about peace?

La alcachofa
de tierno corazoń
se vistió de guerrero,
erecta, construyó
una pequeña cúpula,
se mantuvo
impermeable
bajo
sus escamas
a su lado
los vegetales locos
se encresparon
se hicieron
zarcillos, espadañas,
bulbos commovodores,
en el subsuelo
durmió la zanahoría
de bigotes rojos,
la viña
resecó los sarmientos
por donde sube el vino,
la col
se dedicó
a probarse faldas,
el orégano
a perfumar el mundo,
y la dulce
alcachofa
allí en el huerto,
vestida de guerrero,
bruñida
como una granada,
orgullosa;
y un día
una con otra
en grandes cestos
de mimbre, caminó
por el mercado
a realizar su sueño:

The soft-hearted
artichoke
put on armor,
stood at attention, raised
a small **turret**   turret: little tower
and kept itself
watertight
under
its scales.
Beside it,
the **fertile** plants   fertile: growing
tangled,
turned into
tendrils, cattails,   tendrils: stems
moving bulbs.
In the **subsoil**   subsoil: dirt below
the red-whiskered
carrot slept,
the grapevine
parched the shoots   parched: dried
that wine climbs up,
the cabbage
busied itself
with trying on skirts,
the **marjoram**   marjoram: a spice
with making the world smell sweet,
and the gentle
artichoke
in the kitchen garden,
equipped like a soldier,
burnished   burnished: polished
like a grenade,
was full of itself.
And one day,
packed with others,
in big willow
baskets, it marched
through the market
to act out its dream—

la milicia.
En hileras
nunca fue tan marcial
como en la feria,
los hombres
entre las legumbres
con sus camisas blancas
eran
mariscales
de las alcachofas,
las filas apretadas,
las voces de comando,
y la detonación
de una caja que cae;
pero
entonces
viene
María
con su cesto,
escoge
una alcachofa,
no le teme,
la examina, la observa
contra la luz
como si fuera un huevo,
la compra,
la confunde en su bolsa
con un par de zapatos,
con un repollo y una
botella
de vinagre
hasta
que entrando a la cocina
la sumerge en la olla.
Así termina
en paz
esta carrera
del vegetal armado
que se llama alcachofa,
luego
escama por escama,
desvestimos
la delicia
y comemos
la pacífica pasta
de su corazón verde.

the **militia**.
It was never as **martial**
in rows
as at the fair.
Among the vegetables,
men in white shirts
were
the artichokes'
marshals,
closed ranks,
commands,
the explosion
of a falling crate;
but
then
Maria
shows up
with her basket,
fearlessly
chooses
an artichoke,
studies it, squints at it
against the light
like an egg,
buys it,
dumps it into her bag
with a pair of shoes,
a white cabbage and
a bottle
of vinegar
till
she enters the kitchen
and drowns it
in the pot.
And so
this armored vegetable
men call an artichoke
ends its career
in peace.
Later,
scale by scale,
we strip
this delight
and dine on
the peaceful **pulp**
of its green heart.

militia: army
martial: warlike

marshals: officers

pulp: soft, juicy part

In recognition of his achievements, Neruda was awarded the Nobel Prize for Literature in 1971. His works have had a continuing influence on poetry throughout the world.

Source: Pablo Neruda, *Odas Elementales*. Buenos Aires: Editorial Losada, S.A., 1958. English translation by Cheli Durán, *The Yellow Canary Whose Eye Is So Black*. New York: Macmillan Publishing Co., Inc., 1977.

CHILD OF THE DARK

by Carolina Maria de Jesus, 1962

On the edges of cities in Brazil, thousands of poor people live in slums known as favelas (fä vel' əz). Children play on muddy streets and many go hungry. In the 1950s Carolina Maria de Jesus (dā hā süs') lived there with her three children—Vera, Joao, and Jose Carlos—in a cardboard shack that she had built. She supported her family by collecting scrap paper and selling it for money to buy food. Carolina Maria de Jesus wrote about the terrible living conditions of the favelas in a diary, which she recorded in notebooks saved from the trash. A newspaper reporter met Carolina Maria de Jesus and helped her publish the diary in 1962. Read parts of the diary below to learn what life is like in favelas and what has happened to Carolina Maria de Jesus and her family. What seem to be the major concerns of Carolina Maria de Jesus, and why? How does she feel about living in a favela?

May 11

Today is Mother's Day. The sky is blue and white. It seems that even nature wants to pay **homage** to the mothers who feel unhappy because they can't realize the desires of their children. . . .

homage: honor

Yesterday I got half a pig's head at the **slaughterhouse**. We ate the meat and saved the bones. Today I put the bones on to boil and into the broth I put some potatoes. My children are always hungry. When they are starving they aren't so fussy about what they eat.

slaughterhouse: place in which animals are killed for food

Night came. The stars are hidden. The shack is filled with mosquitoes. I lit a page from a newspaper and ran it over the walls. This is the way the favela dwellers kill mosquitoes.

May 13

It continued to rain and I only have beans and salt. The rain is strong but even so I sent the boys to school. I'm writing until the rain goes away so I can go to Senhor Manuel and sell scrap. With that money I'm going to buy rice and sausage. . . .

I feel so sorry for my children. When they see the things to eat that I come home with they shout:

56

"*Viva Mama!*"

viva: long live

Their outbursts please me. But I've lost the habit of smiling. Ten minutes later they want more food. . . .

May 16

I awoke upset. I wanted to stay at home but didn't have anything to eat.

I'm not going to eat because there is very little bread. I wonder if I'm the only one who leads this kind of life. What can I hope for the future? I wonder if the poor of other countries suffer like the poor of Brazil. . . .

A truck came to the favela. The driver and his helper threw away some cans. It was canned sausage. I thought: this is what these hardhearted businessmen do. They stay waiting for the prices to go up so they can earn more. And when it rots they throw it to the buzzards and the unhappy *favelados.*

favelados: dwellers of the favela

There wasn't any fighting. Even I found it dull. I watched the children open the cans of sausages and exclaim:

"Ummm! Delicious!". . .

May 19

I left the bed at 5 A.M. The sparrows have just begun their morning symphony. The birds must be happier than we are. Perhaps happiness and equality reigns among them. The world of the birds must be better than that of the *favelados*, who lie down but don't sleep because they go to bed hungry. . . .

I broke my train of thought when I heard the voice of the baker: "Here you go! Fresh bread, and right on time for breakfast!"

How little he knows that in the favela there are only a few who have breakfast. The *favelados* eat only when they have something to eat. . . .

August 22

I passed the slaughterhouse to get some bones. In the beginning they used to give us meat. Now they give us bones. I am always shocked with the patience of the poor woman who is happy with any old thing.

The children were content because they got a sausage. . . .

September 18

Today I'm happy. I'm trying to learn how to live with a calm spirit because for these last few days I've had enough to eat. . . .

Thousands of copies of Carolina Maria de Jesus's book were sold in the early 1960s, and it became a bestseller in Brazil. The book introduced many people to the horrible poverty of the favelas. The profits from sales of her book allowed Carolina Maria de Jesus to buy a brick home and move her family out of the favela. Although the author and her family were able to escape from poverty, many other Brazilians still live in favelas.

Source: Carolina Maria de Jesus, *Child of the Dark*. London and New York: E. P. Dutton & Co., Inc., 1962.

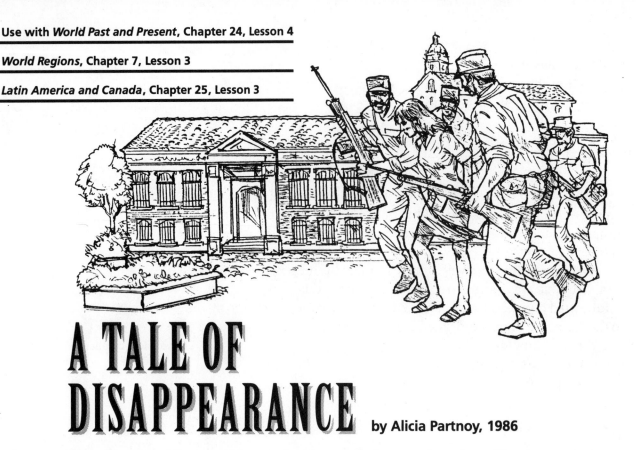

A TALE OF DISAPPEARANCE

by Alicia Partnoy, 1986

Throughout its history Argentina has been ruled many times by military governments. When the Argentine military seized control of power in 1976, violence in the country increased dramatically. In the next four years, the military kidnapped and tortured many Argentines. Alicia Partnoy was one of these desaparecidos— *"disappeared ones." Born in 1955, Alicia Partnoy was a college student at the time of her arrest in 1976. While in prison, she fought back by smuggling stories about her ordeal to the outside world. From her account of imprisonment and torture, what role do you think writers can play when governments take away people's rights? Read Partnoy's account to learn of her struggle and of what has become of her.*

After the Argentine military seized power in 1976, attending school became **hazardous**. I had to pass between two soldiers who were sitting with machine guns at the entrance of the building. A highly ranked officer would request my I.D., check it against a list of "wanted" activists and search my belongings. I did not know when my name was going to appear on that list. [Out of fear,] I stopped going to classes. But the **coup** triggered my rage, and I decided to become more **militant**. That decision meant risking my life. My daughter, Ruth, was nine months old. My answer to my own fears was that I had to work for a better society for the sake of my child's future. For almost a year I did so. I **clandestinely** reproduced and distributed information on the economic situation, the workers' strikes, and the [government's] **repression**.

I learned about "disappearance": the kidnapping of an individual followed by torture and secret detention, which meant that the military denied the fact that the prisoner was in their hands. I did not know that very soon I would become a disappeared person.

hazardous: dangerous

coup: military overthrow

militant: aggressive, determined

clandestinely: secretly

repression: unjust use of force

On January 12, 1977, at noon, I was **detained** by uniformed Army **personnel** at my home, Canadá Street 240, Apt. 2, Bahía Blanca; minutes later the same military personnel detained my husband at his place of work. I was taken to the headquarters of the 5th Army Corps and from there to a concentration camp, which the military **ironically** named the Little School (*La Escuelita*). We had no knowledge of the fate of Ruth, our daughter. From that moment on, for the next five months, my husband and I became two more names on the endless list of disappeared people.

The old house of the Little School was located . . . near a railroad; one could hear trains, the shots fired at the army command's firing range, and the mooing of cows. I stepped off the Army truck, handcuffed and blindfolded. . . .

In the Little School there were two rooms where an average of fifteen prisoners remained **prone**, our hands bound. The floors were wood, the walls yellowing with high windows and dark green shutters and Colonial wrought iron bars. Separating these rooms was a tiled hall where the presence of a guard insured that we neither moved nor spoke. At the end of the hall were the guards' room, a kitchen and a bathroom. A door opened on the patio, where the "torture room," **latrine** and water tank were located. There was also a trailer where the guards slept; and later they added one or two trailers for more "disappeared" people.

When it rained, the water streamed into the rooms and soaked us. When the temperature fell below zero, we were covered with only dirty blankets; when the heat was unbearable, we were obligated to **blanket** even our heads. We were forced to remain silent and prone, often **immobile** or face down for many hours, our eyes blindfolded and our wrists tightly bound.

Lunch was at 1:00 P.M. and dinner at 7:00 P.M.; we went without food for eighteen **consecutive** hours daily. We were constantly hungry. I lost 20 pounds [7kg], going down to 95 pounds [43 kg]. . . . Added to the **meager** food, the lack of sugar or fruits, was the constant state of stress that made our bodies **consume** calories rapidly. We ate our meals blindfolded, sitting on the bed, plate in lap. When we had soup or watery stew, the blows were constant because the guards insisted that we keep our plates straight. When we were thirsty, we asked for water, receiving only threats or blows in response. For talking, we were punished with blows from a **billy jack**, punches, or removal of our mattresses. The atmosphere of violence was constant. The guards put guns to our heads or mouths and pretended to pull the trigger.

On April 25, after three and a half months, the guards told me they were taking me "to see how the radishes grow"—a **euphemism** for death and burial. Instead, I was transferred from the Little School to another place where I remained disappeared for fifty-two more days. The living conditions were better: no blindfold, no blows, better food, a clean cell, daily showers. The **isolation** was complete and the risk of being killed

detained: held
personnel: employees

ironically: with unintended humor

prone: lying face down

latrine: toilet

blanket: cover

immobile: not moving

consecutive: in a row

meager: skimpy
consume: use up

billy jack: club

euphemism: mild expression replacing a harsh one

isolation: separation from others

the same. By June 1977, my family was informed of my **whereabouts**. I "reappeared" but remained a political prisoner for two and a half more years. I could see my daughter [who was being cared for by relatives], and I knew that my husband had also survived.

whereabouts: location

I never discovered why the military had spared my life. My parents, who knocked at every [government official's] door looking for me, might have knocked at the correct door. Yet it is also true that some of the most **influential** people in the country were not able to rescue their own children. My degree of involvement was not the reason for my luck either. People who participated less in politics did not survive. We were **hostages** and, as such, our lives were disposed of according to the needs of our captors.

influential: powerful

hostages: prisoners

While I was imprisoned, no charges were brought against me. Like the majority of the 7,000 political prisoners, I was held **indefinitely** and considered to be a threat to national security. It is estimated that over 30,000 people "disappeared" to detention centers like the Little School. Among them were over 400 children who were either kidnapped with their parents or. . . born in captivity. All but a few of the disappeared still remain unaccounted for.

indefinitely: without time limit

Human rights groups launched an international campaign denouncing the repression in Argentina. One of these was the Mothers of Plaza de Mayo movement, an organization of mothers of disappeared people that demanded answers from the government on the whereabouts of their children. These women soon became targets of repression, and several members disappeared.

Domestic and international pressure forced the **junta** to free a number of political prisoners. In 1979, after the Organization of American States sent a fact-finding mission to Argentina, I was released and forced to leave the country. [United States] President [Jimmy] Carter's human rights policy had also helped. Since some of us were granted U.S. visas and refugee status, the junta knew the United States wanted the release of prisoners.

junta: military leaders

By Christmas 1979, I was taken directly from jail to the airport, where I was reunited with my daughter. Some hours later we flew to the United States. My husband had come two months before.

A short time after my arrival, I started to work on behalf of the remaining prisoners and the disappeared ones. I soon learned more about the widespread use of disappearance as a tool for repression in Latin America. As a survivor, I felt my duty was to help those suffering injustice.

After Alicia Partnoy was released, she continued to work for the freedom of other disappeared ones. In 1982 her testimony before a special Argentine panel led to the conviction of several military officials responsible for the disappearances. In recent years Argentina has become a democracy, and many Argentines are working to ensure that people's rights are never taken away again.

Source: Alicia Partnoy, *The Little School*. Pittsburgh: Cleis Press, 1986.

Living In Mexico Today

by Louis B. Casagrande and Sylvia A. Johnson, 1986

Mexico is home to more than 80 million people. Most Mexicans speak Spanish. But about 8 million speak an Indian language and follow an Indian way of life. Maruch Hernandez Vasquez is a 14-year-old Mayan girl who lives with her family in southern Mexico near the border with Guatemala. From about 500 B.C. to A.D. 900, the Mayas dominated this region, and many Mayas still live here today. The authors of the following selection spent time visiting and talking to Maruch and her family. As you read this excerpt from their book, notice how Maruch follows many traditional Mayan practices. In what ways does Maruch feel comfortable with her life? In what ways do other parts of Mexico interest her?

Maruch Hernandez Vasquez is a Maya Indian girl who lives in the mountainous state of Chiapas, on Mexico's southern border. There are 400,000 Maya in Chiapas, making it the most "Indian" of Mexico's states. Maruch and her family are Tzotzil [zät sil] Maya, speaking that **dialect** of the ancient Maya language.

dialect: local language

Fourteen-year-old Maruch lives with her parents, her two sisters, and her brother in one of the small villages of Zinacantan, a Maya community located in the cool, pine-covered Chiapas highlands. Like most Mexican Indians, the people of Zinacantan are poor, but the Hernandez family is better off than most of their neighbors. They own a large one-room house cut into a mountainside overlooking a lush valley. . . .

Like their other Maya neighbors, the Hernandezes are farmers who produce most of their own food. . . .

The Hernandez family lives in the traditional Maya way, and all the members share in the work of producing and preparing food and of keeping the family supplied with clothing. Maruch's 18-year-old brother, Antun, helps his father in the family **milpa**, which is located in the valley a half day's walk from the house. . . .

milpa: plot of land

While their father and brother labor in the fields, Maruch and her sisters work with their mother at home, cleaning, weaving, and cooking. Fixing food in the traditional Maya way takes a lot of time and effort. Each day, Maruch, her mother, and her sisters have to get up at dawn to make the day's supply of **tortillas**. . . .

tortillas: thin, flat cakes made from flour or corn

Then Señora Hernandez and her two oldest daughters get out their looms and prepare them for weaving.

To make these traditional garments, Señora Hernandez and her daughters use backstrap looms, the same kind that were used by their Maya ancestors. One end of the loom is tied to a post, while the other goes around the hips of the weaver, who kneels in front and controls the tension of the threads with movements of her body. . . .

Her mother made her a small loom when she was 6, but Maruch had great difficulty keeping the threads straight, and she thought that she would never learn this important skill of her people.

By the time she was 10, however, she was able to weave belts. At 12, she could make her own skirts and blouses, and now, at 14, she is an accomplished weaver. . . .

Maruch has such a good reputation as a weaver that she even sells some of her belts and shawls. At first she sold them to other Zinacantecos, who admired the fine workmanship. Now, however, she and her sister are selling their work in the nearby city of San Cristóbal. . . .

On her monthly trips to San Cristóbal to take in her weaving and to pick up the money she has earned, Maruch sometimes goes to visit an Indian nurse who works at the government hospital. She met the nurse last winter when she gave Maruch a shot of penicillin for a bad chest cold. . . .

Maruch enjoys talking to her friend at the hospital, and she listens intently when the Indian nurse tells her what a good nurse's aid she would make. She is very good with her hands and smart, even though she has had only two years of formal education and cannot read or write.

Maruch knows that Indian girls her age work at the hospital, but she also knows that her own parents would disapprove of that kind of life for her. . . .

Maruch is not unhappy with her life in Zinacantan. She is a good weaver and proud of her skill, and she loves her family and her home on the hillside.

Sometimes, however, Maruch thinks that it wouldn't be so bad to live in San Cristóbal and work as a nurse's aid. She would never disobey her parents, but she doesn't really understand why they would not want her to try this new way of living. It wouldn't change her—would it?—to wear shoes and store-bought clothes and to live with other Indian girls in a **dormitory**. She would still be Maruch of Zinacantan no matter where or how she lived.

dormitory: building with many bedrooms, usually for students or workers

Over half the population of Mexico is under the age of 17. Like Maruch, many other young Mexicans must decide whether to remain in rural areas or move to a city. Because there is not enough work for everyone living in rural areas, many people have moved to Mexico's fast-growing cities in search of greater opportunity. Whichever path Maruch decides to follow, however, she realizes that her Mayan heritage will always remain an important part of her identity.

Source: Louis B. Casagrande and Sylvia A. Johnson, *Focus on Mexico*. Minneapolis: Lerner Publications Company, 1986.

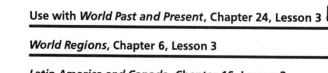

Leave Us in Peace

by Oscar Arias Sánchez, 1987

Central America has had a troubled recent history of violence, civil wars, and military dictatorships. Thousands have died as a result of these conflicts, and many people remain poor and uneducated. In 1987, the president of Costa Rica, Oscar Arias Sánchez, brought together the leaders of Central America to work out a peace plan for the region. After lengthy discussions, the leaders of Costa Rica, Guatemala, Honduras, El Salvador, and Nicaragua signed the peace plan. Arias won the Nobel Peace Prize in 1987 for his efforts. Below is an excerpt from the acceptance speech Arias delivered upon receiving the prize. How does he define the role of Central America as compared with that of other major powers in solving the region's problems?

When you decided to honor me with this prize, you decided to honor a country of peace, you decided to honor Costa Rica. When in this year, 1987, you carried out the will of **Alfred B. Nobel** to encourage peace efforts in the world, you decided to encourage the efforts to secure peace in Central America. I am grateful for the recognition of our search for peace. We are all grateful in Central America. . . .

Alfred B. Nobel: founder of the Nobel Prize

Peace is not a matter of prizes or trophies. It is not the product of a victory or command, it has no finishing line, no final deadline, no fixed definition of achievement.

Peace is a never-ending process, the work of many decisions by many people in many countries. It is an attitude, a way of life, a way of solving problems and resolving conflicts. It cannot be forced on the smallest nation or enforced by the largest. It cannot ignore our differences or overlook our common interests. It requires us to work and live together.

Peace is not only a matter of **noble** words and Nobel lectures. We have **ample** words, glorious words, **inscribed** in the charters of the

noble: splendid

ample: more than enough

inscribed: written

63

United Nations, the World Court, the Organization of American States and a network of international treaties and laws. We need deeds that will respect those words, honor those **commitments, abide by** those laws. We need to strengthen our institutions of peace like the United Nations, making certain they are fully used by the weak as well as the strong. . . .

commitments: pledges
abide by: obey

We seek in Central America not peace alone, not peace to be followed someday by political progress, but peace and democracy, together, **indivisible**, an end to the shedding of human blood, which is inseparable from an end to the **suppression** of human rights.

indivisible: unable to be divided
suppression: putting down

We do not judge, much less condemn, any other nation's political or **ideological** system, freely chosen and never exported. We cannot require **sovereign** states to conform to patterns of government not of their own choosing.

ideological: belief
sovereign: independent

But we can and do insist that every government respect those universal rights of man that have meaning beyond national boundaries and ideological labels. We believe that justice and peace can only thrive together, never apart. A nation that mistreats its own citizens is more likely to mistreat its neighbors.

To receive this Nobel Prize on the 10th of December is for me a marvelous coincidence. My son Oscar Felipe, here present, is 8 years old today. I say to him, and through him to all the children of my country, that we shall never resort to violence, we shall never support military solutions to the problems of Central America.

It is for the new generation that we must understand more than ever that peace can only be achieved through its own **instruments:** dialogue and understanding, **tolerance** and forgiveness, freedom and democracy.

instruments: tools
tolerance: acceptance

I know well you share what we say to all members of the international community, and particularly to those both in the East and the West, with far greater power and resources than my small nation could ever hope to possess.

I say to them, with the utmost urgency: Let Central Americans decide the future of Central America. Leave the **interpretation** and **implementation** of our plan to us. Support the efforts for peace instead of the forces of war in our region.

interpretation: explanation
implementation: carrying out

Send our people **plowshares** instead of swords, **pruning hooks** instead of spears. If they, for their own purposes, cannot refrain from **amassing** the weapons of war, then, in the name of God, at least they should leave us in peace.

plowshares: blades of a plow
pruning hooks: tools for trimming trees
amassing: gathering

The peace plan brought some progress to Central America's conflict-torn nations. In 1990 democratic elections were held in Nicaragua as called for under the plan. The plan also contributed to the decision by the people of El Salvador in January 1992 to end their 12-year civil war. Many people of Central America, such as Oscar Arias Sánchez, continue to devote themselves to working for lasting peace.

Source: "Arias Talk on Getting the Nobel," *The New York Times,* December 11, 1987.

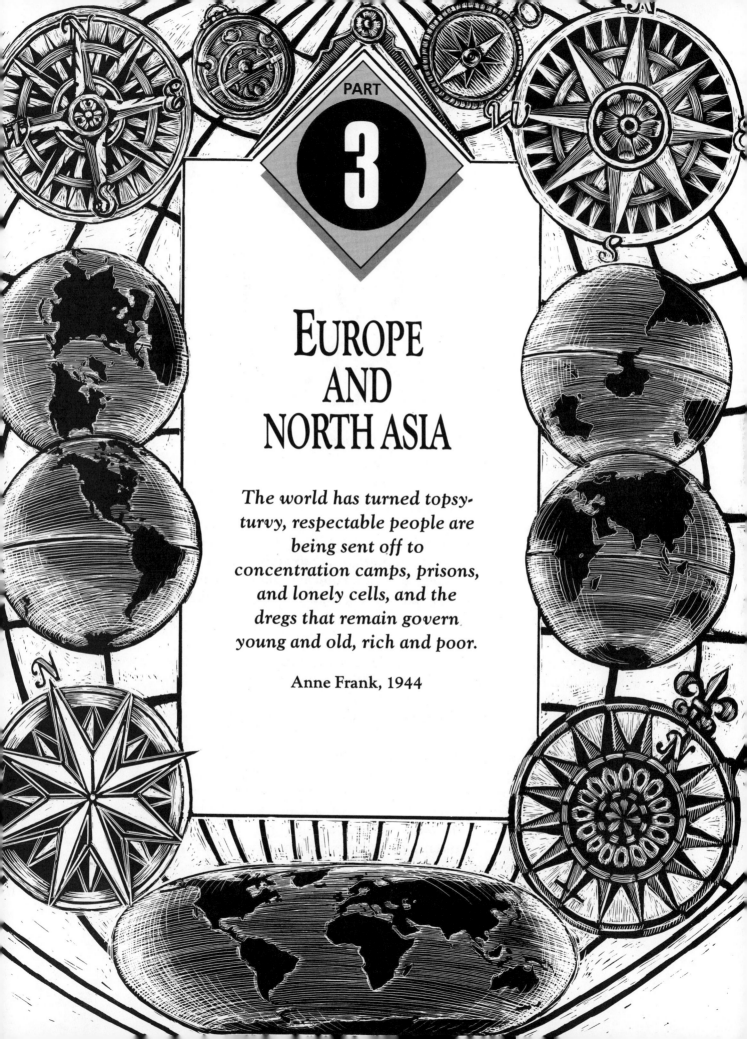

PART

3

EUROPE AND NORTH ASIA

The world has turned topsy-turvy, respectable people are being sent off to concentration camps, prisons, and lonely cells, and the dregs that remain govern young and old, rich and poor.

Anne Frank, 1944

THE FROST GIANT

by Snorri Sturluson, 1220

More than 1,000 years ago, Vikings from Scandinavia sailed the seas attacking towns and villages throughout Europe. Like many early people, the Vikings told long epic poems describing their life. Some of these tales, collected into books known as Eddas, were told by the Vikings to explain their origins, their gods, and the world itself. The story below is part of an Edda that was written down by Snorri Sturluson (1179-1241), an Icelandic historian and poet. What does this Edda tell you about the nature and values of Viking society?

In the beginning, there were two **realms.** Muspell was in the south, and it was full of fire and blinding light. Niflheim, the home of fog, ice, and snow, lay in the north.

Between the two realms was a vast stretch of empty space called Gin-nun-ga-gap, or Yawning Gap. Warm air drifted from Muspell and mixed with the cold from Niflheim, the north realm. The breath of summer and winter met in a thaw above the middle realm of Yawning Gap. The drips and drops started life growing. And life took the form of a great giant. His name was Imir. And from the beginning, he was evil.

Imir was a frost giant. He lay down to sleep in Yawning Gap and sweated through the night. A woman and a man grew from his armpit. A son came forth from his leg. From Imir came the first family of ice-crusted frost giants.

Melting ice from the middle realm of Yawning Gap formed into a giant cow. Imir drank the rivers of milk from the cow. The cow lived off the ice itself. She licked and licked blocks of it.

realms: kingdoms

A man's head appeared from one block. For three days and nights the cow fed on the ice block. And finally a whole man was born from it. He was called Buri, so tall and strong.

Soon Buri had a son he called Bor. Bor married a daughter of a frost giant, and they had three sons. These were the gods Odin, Vili, and Ve.

The god brothers hated the evil Imir and the ever-growing number of brutal frost giants. They attacked Imir and they killed him. Imir bled, and the blood drowned all of the frost giants except two. The two got in a hollow tree trunk and rode away on a blood tide.

Odin, Vili, and Ve carried the dead Imir to the middle of Yawning Gap. They made the world from his body. The earth was shaped from his flesh. Mountains were formed from his bones. Rocks, stones, and boulders came from his teeth and jaws.

After they had formed the earth, Odin, Vili, and Ve took the blood that was left from Imir and made the ocean in a ring.

The three brothers lifted the skull of Imir and made the dome of the sky. . . .

Then the gods went to the southern realm of Muspell and took sparks and embers. From these they made the sun, moon, and stars. They placed the sun, moon, and stars way up over Yawning Gap to light up both heaven and earth.

Odin and Vili and Ve were walking one time at land's edge where it met the sea. They saw an ash tree and an elm tree, both fallen down. The three brothers lifted them and created from them a new man and woman. Odin breathed life into the man and woman. Vili gave them wit and feelings. Ve brought them hearing and sight.

The man's name was Ask, and the woman was Embla. The brothers gave them the land of Midgard as their home. Midgard was protected from the giants' world by a wall made from the eyebrows of Imir.

So it is that all nations and all families and every race of human beings came from Ask and Embla. They were the first of their kind in the new world created by Odin, Vili, and Ve, the sons of Bor.

Like many of the Eddas and sagas written hundreds of years ago, this story captures the ruggedness and violence of Viking life. Other Viking epics from long ago tell of adventures and journeys, which help us to better understand Viking culture.

Source: Virginia Hamilton, *In the Beginning*. San Diego, New York, London: Harcourt Brace Jovanovich, 1988.

The Iliad

by Homer, about the 8th century B.C.

More than 3,000 years ago, a rich civilization flourished in ancient Greece. Theater and poetry played an important role in Greek life. The Greeks often gathered at festivals to watch plays and to hear epics, or long poems, that celebrated their history and their many gods and goddesses. The earliest of the Greek poets whose works still survive is Homer, who probably lived between the 9th and 7th centuries B.C. One of Homer's greatest epics, The Iliad, tells about the Trojan War, which Greece fought against Troy in the 12th century B.C. In the excerpt below, the Greek hero Achilles has just learned that his best friend Patroklos has died in battle. What role do Greek gods and goddesses play in The Iliad?

Achilles' goddess-mother heard the sound of his grief as she sat within the depths of the Ocean. She came to him as he was still moaning terribly. She took his hand and clasped it and said, "My child, **why weep'st thou**?" Achilles ceased his moaning and answered, "Patroklos, my dear friend, has been **slain**. Now I shall have no joy in my life save the joy of **slaying** Hector who slew my friend."

Thetis, his goddess-mother, wept when she heard such speech from Achilles. "Shortlived you will be, my son," she said, "for it is **appointed** by the gods that after the death of Hector your death will come."

"**Straightway** then let me die," said Achilles, "since I let my friend die without giving him help. . . . Here I stayed, a useless **burthen** on the earth, while my comrades and my own dear friend fought for their country—here I stayed, I who am the best of all the Greeks. But now let me go into the battle and let the Trojans know that Achilles has come back, although he **tarried** long."

why weep'st thou: why do you cry?

slain: killed
slaying: killing

appointed: decided

straightway: immediately
burthen: burden

tarried: waited

"But **thine** armor, my son," said Thetis. "Thou hast no armor now to protect thee in the battle. Go not into it until thou seest me again. In the morning I shall return and I shall bring thee armor that **Hephaistos**, the **smith** of the gods, shall make for thee."

So she spoke, and she turned from her son, and she went to Olympus where the gods have their **dwellings**. . . .

Now Thetis, the mother of Achilles, went to Olympus where the gods have their dwellings and to the house of Hephaistos, the smith of the gods. That house shone above all the houses on Olympus because Hephaistos himself had made it of shining bronze. . . .

Hephaistos was lame and crooked of foot and went limping. He and Thetis were friends from of old time, for, when his mother would have **forsaken** him because of his crooked foot, Thetis and her sister **reared** him within one of the Ocean's caves and it was while he was with them that he began to work in metals. So the lame god was pleased to see Thetis in his dwelling and he welcomed her and clasped her hand and asked of her what she would have him do for her.

Then Thetis, weeping, told him of her son Achilles, how he had lost his dear friend and how he was moved to go into the battle to fight with Hector, and how he was without armor to protect his life, seeing that the armor that the gods had once given his father was now in the hands of his foe. And Thetis **besought** Hephaistos to make new armor for her son that he might go into the battle.

She no sooner finished speaking than Hephaistos went to his workbench. . . .

For the armor of Achilles he made first a shield and then a **corselet** that gleamed like fire. And he made a strong helmet to go on the head and shining **greaves** to wear on the ankles. The shield was made with five folds, one fold of metal upon the other, so that it was so strong and thick that no spear or arrow could pierce it. And upon this shield he hammered out images that were a wonder to men. . . .

Not long was he in making the shield and the other wonderful pieces of armor. As soon as the armor was ready Thetis put her hands upon it, and flying down from Olympus like a hawk, brought it to the feet of Achilles, her son. . . .

Then Achilles put his shining armor upon him and it fitted him as though it were wings; he put the wonderful shield before him and he took in his hands the great spear that Cheiron the **Centaur** had given to Peleus his father—that spear that no one else but Achilles could wield. He bade his **charioteer** harness the **immortal** horses Xanthos and Balios. Then as he mounted his chariot Achilles spoke to the horses. "Xanthos and Balios," he said, "this time bring the hero that goes with you back safely to the ships, and do not leave him dead on the plain as **ye** left the hero Patroklos."

Then Xanthos the immortal **steed** spoke, answering for himself and his comrade. "Achilles," he said, with his head bowed and his mane touching the ground, "Achilles, for this time we will bring thee safely

thine: your

Hephaistos: Greek god of fire
smith: one who makes metal objects
dwellings: homes

forsaken: abandoned
reared: raised

besought: begged

corselet: armor for the upper body

greaves: armor for the leg below the knee

centaur: creature that is half-human, half-horse
charioteer: driver of a chariot, or carriage
immortal: godlike

ye: you
steed: horse

back from the battle. But a day will come when we shall not bring thee back, when thou too shalt lie with the dead before the walls of Troy."

Then was Achilles troubled and he said, "Xanthos, my steed, why dost thou remind me by thy **prophecies** of what I know already — that my death too is appointed, and that I am to **perish** here, far from my father and my mother and my own land."

prophecies: predictions

perish: die

Then he drove his immortal horses into the battle. The Trojans were **affrighted** when they saw Achilles himself in the fight, blazing in the armor that Hephaistos had made for him. They went backward before his **onset**. And Achilles shouted to the captains of the Greeks, "No longer stand apart from the men of Troy, but go with me into the battle and let each man throw his whole soul into the fight."

affrighted: frightened

onset: attack

And on the Trojan side Hector cried to his captains and said, "Do not let Achilles drive you before him. Even though his hands are as irresistible as fire and his fierceness as terrible as flashing steel, I shall go against him and face him with my spear." . . .

And when Achilles saw Hector before him he cried out, "Here is the man who most deeply wounded my soul, who slew my dear friend Patroklos. Now shall we two fight each other and Patroklos shall be **avenged** by me." And he shouted to Hector, "Now Hector, the day of thy triumph and the day of thy life is at its end."

avenged: revenged

But Hector answered him without fear, "Not with words, Achilles, can you affright me. Yet I know that thou art a man of might and a stronger man than I. But the fight between us depends upon the will of the gods. I shall do my best against thee, and my spear before this has been found to have a dangerous edge."

He spoke and lifted up his spear and flung it at Achilles. Then the breath of a god turned Hector's spear aside, for it was not appointed that either he or Achilles should be then slain. Achilles darted at Hector to slay him with his spear. But a god hid Hector from Achilles in a thick mist. . . .

Then on toward the City, [Achilles] went like a fire raging through a **glen** that had been **parched** with heat. Now on a tower of the walls of Troy, Priam the old King stood, and he saw the Trojans coming in a **rout** toward the City, and he saw Achilles in his armor blazing like a star — like that star that is seen at harvest time and is called Orion's Dog; the star that is the brightest of all stars, but yet is a sign of evil. And the old man Priam sorrowed greatly as he stood upon the tower and watched Achilles, because he knew in his heart whom this man would slay — Hector, his son, the protector of his City.

glen: valley

parched: burned dry

rout: retreat

In a later battle Achilles killed the Trojan leader Hector. But, just as the gods had predicted, Achilles was also killed in battle, the result of a wound from a Trojan arrow. After many long years of warfare, the Greeks finally defeated the Trojans. For hundreds of years, the Greeks retold the story of the battles, gods, and heroes described in The Iliad. *Today this epic poem remains one of the greatest works of literature ever written.*

Source: Padraic Colum, *The Children's Homer*. New York: Macmillan Publishing Company, 1982.

THE AENEID by Virgil, 19 B.C.

The Roman Empire left many great monuments, such as the Colosseum, giant aqueducts, and stone roads. But one of Rome's greatest monuments is not a building at all. It is an exciting epic called the Aeneid *(i nē′ id). This epic, written by the poet Virgil around 19* B.C., *is a grand adventure story about the history of Rome. The* Aeneid *is based on a mythical Trojan character called Aeneas who is half-god and half-man. After the Trojan War, which Homer described in* The Iliad *on pages 68-70, Aeneas sees a star in the sky and begins a long journey at sea, in hopes of founding a new kingdom. In the excerpt below, Aeneas arrives in Sicily, an island located in the Mediterrenean Sea in southern Italy. What do the sporting events that Aeneas orders upon his arrival reveal about some of the values held by people in ancient Rome?*

So they shifted their course, and let their ships run before the wind, and came in a very short time to the island of Sicily. Now Acestes, the king of the country, was the son of a Trojan woman. He had before entertained Aeneas and his people very kindly, and now, when he saw their ships coming toward the land, for he happened to be standing on the top of a hill, he was very glad, and he **made haste** to meet them. He came to the shore, having a lion's skin about his shoulders, and carrying a spear in his hand. He greeted them with many words of kindness, and sent a supply of food and drink to the ships.

made haste: hurried

The next day, early in the morning, Aeneas called all the Trojans to an assembly, and said to them: "My friends, it is a full year since we buried my dear father in this land of Sicily; yes, if I remember right, this is the very day. Let us keep it holy therefore. . . . And if the ninth day from this be fair, then we will have great games in honor of my dear father. There shall be a contest of ships, and running in a race, and games of throwing the **javelin**, and of shooting with the bow, and of boxing. . . ."

javelin: spear

And now the ninth day came, and the weather was fine. There came great crowds of people to see the games. . . . Many came to see the Trojans, and many for the sake of the games, desiring to win the prizes if they might. First the prizes were put **in the midst** for all to see. There were crowns of palm, and swords, and spears, and purple garments, and **talents** of gold and silver. . . .

in the midst: in plain view

talents: coins

For [the foot race] there came many, both Trojans and men of Sicily. . . . Aeneas said: "I will give gifts to all who run; none shall go away empty. To the first three I will give crowns of olive. The first also shall have a horse with its **trappings**; the second a **quiver** full of arrows, and a belt with which to fasten it; the third must be content with a Greek helmet."

trappings: saddle and harness

quiver: case for holding arrows

Then all the men stood in a line, and when the signal was given they started. For a short time they were all close together. Then Nisus outran the rest. Next to him came Salius, but there was a long space between them; and next to Salius was Euryalus. The fourth was one of the king's **courtiers**, Helymus by name, and close behind him the Trojan Diores. When they had nearly come to the end of the course, by bad luck Nisus slipped in the blood of an ox which had been **slain** in the place, and fell. But as he lay on the ground he did not forget his friend Euryalus, for he lifted himself from the ground just as Salius came running in, and tripped him up. So Euryalus had the first place, Helymus was second, and Diores third. But Salius loudly complained that he had been cheated. "I had won the first prize," he cried, "had not this Nisus tripped me up." But the people favored Euryalus, for he was a **comely lad**; Diores also was on the same side, for otherwise he had not won the third prize. "Then," said Aeneas, "I will not change the order; let them take the prizes as they come—Euryalus the first, Helymus the second, and Diores the third. Nevertheless I will have pity on the man who suffered not from his own fault." And he gave to Salius a lion's skin, of which the **mane** and the claws were covered with gold. . . .

courtiers: attendants

slain: killed

comely lad: handsome boy

mane: long hair on the neck

Next to this came the trial of shooting with the bow. Aeneas set up the mast of a ship, and to the top of the mast he tied a dove by a cord. This was the mark at which all were to shoot. The first hit the mast, and shook it, and all could see how the bird fluttered his wings. Then the second shot. He did not touch the bird, but he cut the string by which it was fastened to the mast, and the bird flew away. Then the third, a man of Lycia, aimed at the bird itself, and struck it as it flew, and the dove fell dead to the earth with the arrow through it. Last of all King Acestes shot his arrow. And he, having nothing at which to aim, shot it high into the air, to show how strong a bow he had and how he could draw it. Then there happened a strange thing to see. The arrow, as it went higher and higher in the air, was seen to catch fire, and leave a line of flame behind it, till it was burned up. When Aeneas saw this, he said to himself: "This is a sign of good to come," for he thought how the fire had burned on the head of his son Ascanius, and how a star had shot through the air when he was about to fly from Troy. And as this had been a sign of good at the beginning of his wanderings, so was this a sign of good at the end.

After many more adventures, Aeneas helps to unite the people of Italy and Troy. This union, according to the Aeneid, gave birth to the civilization of Rome. Many people consider the Aeneid to be the greatest work of Roman literature.

Source: Alfred J. Church, *The Aeneid for Boys and Girls.* New York: The Macmillan Company, 1962.

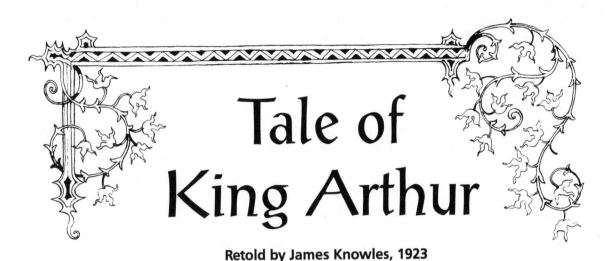

Tale of King Arthur

Retold by James Knowles, 1923

One of the best-known tales of the Middle Ages, a period in Europe from about A.D. 500 to 1500, involves a king of England named Arthur. According to legend, King Arthur lived in the 5th century. The tale of King Arthur, which has been told over and over again for hundreds of years, concerns heroic deeds, tragic love stories, and magical powers. In the excerpt below, a wizard named Merlin has cast a magic spell and taken young Arthur away from his father, King Uther. A knight named Sir Ector has then raised Arthur as his own son. As you read this excerpt, notice the amazing feat that Arthur performs to become king. According to the storyteller, what were the qualities that made a great leader in the Middle Ages?

Now Arthur the prince had all this time been nourished in Sir Ector's house as his own son, and was fair and tall and **comely**, being of the age of fifteen years, great in strength, gentle in manner, and accomplished in all exercises proper for the training of a knight.

comely: attractive

But as yet he knew not of his father; for Merlin [the magician] had so dealt, that none save Uther and himself knew **aught** about [Arthur]. Wherefore it **befell**, that many of the knights and barons who heard King Uther speak before his death, and call his son Arthur his successor, were in great amazement; and some doubted, and others were displeased.

aught: anything
befell: happened

Anon the chief lords and princes set forth each to his own land, and, raising armed men and **multitudes** of followers, determined every one to gain the crown for himself; for they said in their hearts, "If there be any such a son at all as he of whom this wizard forced the king to speak, who are we that a beardless boy should have rule over us?"

anon: soon
multitudes: crowds

So the land stood long in great peril, for every lord and baron sought but his own advantage; and the **Saxons**, growing ever more adventurous, wasted and overran the towns and villages in every part.

Saxons: Germanic tribe that conquered parts of England in the fifth century

Then Merlin went to Brice, the **Archbishop of Canterbury**, and advised him to require all the earls and barons of the **realm** and all knights and gentlemen-at-arms to come to him at London, before Christmas, that they might learn the will of Heaven who should be king. This, therefore, the archbishop did, and upon Christmas Eve were met together in London all the greatest princes, lords, and barons; and . . . the archbishop **besought** Heaven for a sign who should be lawful king of all the realm.

And as they prayed, there was seen in the churchyard, set straight before the doorways of the church, a huge square stone having a naked sword stuck in the midst of it. And on the sword was written in letters of gold, "Whoso pulleth out the sword from this stone is born the rightful King of Britain."

At this all the people wondered greatly; and, when [the religious service] was over, the nobles, knights, and princes ran out eagerly from the church to see the stone and sword; and a law was **forthwith** made that whoso should pull out the sword should be **acknowledged straightway** King of Britain.

Then many knights and barons pulled at the sword with all their might, and some of them tried many times, but none could stir or move it.

When all had tried in vain, the archbishop declared the man whom Heaven had chosen was not yet here. "But God," said he, "will doubtless make him known **ere** many days."

So ten knights were chosen, being men of **high renown**, to watch and keep the sword; and there was proclamation made through all the land that whosoever would, had leave and liberty to try and pull it from the stone. But though great multitudes of people came, both gentle and simple, for many days, no man could ever move the sword a hair's **breadth** from its place.

Now, at the New Year's Eve a great tournament was to be held in London....To which tournament there came, with many other knights, Sir Ector, Arthur's foster-father, who had great possessions near to London; and with him came his son, Sir Key, but recently made knight, to take his part in the **jousting**, and young Arthur also to witness all the sports and fighting.

But as they rode towards the jousts, Sir Key found suddenly he had no sword, for he had left it at his father's house; and turning to young Arthur, he prayed him to ride back and fetch it for him. "I will with a good will," said Arthur; and rode fast back after the sword.

But when he came to the house he found it locked and empty, for all were gone forth to see the tournament. Whereat, being angry and impatient, he said within himself, "I will ride to the churchyard and take with me the sword that sticketh in the stone, for my brother shall not go without a sword this day."

So he rode and came to the churchyard, and **alighting** from his horse he tied him to the gate, and went to the **pavilion**, which was

archbishop of Canterbury: important leader of the Church of England

realm: kingdom

besought: begged

forthwith: immediately

acknowledged: recognized

straightway: right away

ere: before

high renown: great fame

breadth: width

jousting: competition in which knights carrying spears charge at each other on horseback

alighting: getting off

pavilion: large tent

74

pitched near the stone, wherein **abode** the ten knights who watched and kept it; but he found no knights there, for all were gone to see the jousting.

Then he took the sword by its handle, and lightly and fiercely he pulled it out of the stone, and took his horse and rode until he came to Sir Key and delivered him the sword. But as soon as Sir Key saw it he knew well it was the sword of the stone, and riding swiftly to his father, he cried out, "Lo! here, sir, is the sword of the stone, wherefore it is I who must be king of all this land."

When Sir Ector saw the sword, he turned back straight with Arthur and Sir Key and came to the churchyard, and there alighting, they went all three into the church, and Sir Key was sworn to tell truly how he came by the sword. Then he confessed it was his brother Arthur who had brought it to him.

Whereat Sir Ector, turning to young Arthur, asked him—"How gottest thou the sword?"

"Sir," said he, "I will tell you. When I went home to fetch my brother's sword, I found nobody to deliver it to me, for all were **abroad** to the jousts. Yet was I **loth** to leave my brother swordless, and **bethinking me** of this one, I came **hither** eagerly to fetch it for him, and pulled it out of the stone without any pain."

Then said Sir Ector, much amazed and looking **steadfastly** on Arthur, "If this indeed be thus, 'tis thou who shalt be king of all this land—and God will have it so—for none but he who should be rightful Lord of Britain might ever draw this sword forth from that stone. But let me now with mine own eyes see thee put back the sword into its place and draw it forth again."

"That is no mystery," said Arthur; and straightway set it in the stone. And then Sir Ector pulled at it himself, and after him Sir Key, with all his might, but both of them in vain: then Arthur reaching forth his hand and grasping at the **pommel**, pulled it out easily, and at once.

pommel: knob on the handle

Then fell Sir Ector down upon his knees upon the ground before young Arthur, and Sir Key also with him, and straightway did him **homage** as their **sovereign** lord.

homage: honor
sovereign: supreme

But Arthur cried aloud, "Alas! mine own dear father and my brother, why kneel ye thus to me?"

"Nay, my Lord Arthur," answered then Sir Ector, "we are of no blood-kinship with thee, and little though I thought how high thy kin might be, yet wast thou never more than foster-child of mine." And then he told him all he knew about his infancy, and how a stranger had delivered him, with a great sum of gold, into his hands to be brought up and nourished as his own born child, and then had disappeared.

But when young Arthur heard of it, he fell upon Sir Ector's neck, and wept, and made great **lamentation**, "For now," said he, "I have in one day lost my father and my mother and my brother."

lamentation: wailing

"Sir," said Sir Ector presently, "when thou shalt be made king be good and gracious unto me and mine."

"If not," said Arthur, "I were no true man's son at all, for thou art he in all the world to whom I owe the most; and my good lady and mother, thy wife, hath ever kept and fostered me as though I were her own; so if it be God's will that I be king hereafter as thou sayest, [ask] of me whatever thing thou wilt and I will do it; and God forbid that I should fail thee in it."

"I will but pray," replied Sir Ector, "that thou wilt make my son Sir Key, thy foster-brother, **seneschal** of all the lands."

seneschal: agent in charge

"That shall he be," said Arthur, "and never shall another hold that office, save thy son, while he and I do live."

Anon they left the church and went to the archbishop to tell him that the sword had been achieved. And when he saw the sword in Arthur's hand he set a day and **summoned** all the princes, knights, and barons to meet again at St. Paul's Church and see the will of Heaven **signified**. So when they came together, the sword was put back in the stone, and all tried, from the greatest to the least, to move it; but there before them all not one could take it out **save** Arthur only.

summoned: sent for

signified: fulfilled

save: except

Throughout the centuries, the legend of King Arthur has been retold in novels, poetry, plays, operas, and films. Other versions of the tale of King Arthur focus on great battles, epic quests, or searches, and the legendary Knights of the Round Table.

Source: Sir James Knowles, compiler, *King Arthur and His Knights*. New York: Blue Ribbon Books, 1923.

CONTRACT BETWEEN A VASSAL AND LORD **Contract from the 7th century**

During the Middle Ages, many Europeans lived in fear of attack from invaders and from each other. To protect themselves, Europeans developed a system known as feudalism. Under feudalism people provided certain services to each other in exchange for protection. Kings granted large estates to nobles, or lords, who promised to defend the king's territory. In turn the lords made contracts with less powerful nobles called vassals. When a vassal and lord exchanged vows, they often marked the occasion with a grand ceremony. Below is a standard contract between vassal and lord dating from the 7th century. As you read this contract, notice what vassal and lord promise each other. What do you think are some of the benefits and drawbacks of taking such an oath for both lord and vassal?

VASSAL:

I _____ , Since it is known familiarly to all how little I have **whence** to feed and clothe myself, I have therefore **petitioned** your **Piety**, and your good will has permitted me to hand myself over or commend myself to your **guardianship**, which I have thereupon done; that is to say, in this way, that you should aid and **succor** me as well with food as with clothing, according as I shall be able to serve you and deserve it.

whence: with which
petitioned: sought help from
Piety: Lordship
guardianship: care
succor: help

And so long as I shall live I ought to provide service and honor to you, suitably to my free condition; and I . . . must remain during the days of my life under your power or defense.

LORD:

It is right that those who offer to us unbroken **fidelity** should be protected by our aid. And since _____ , a faithful one of ours, by the favor of God, coming here in our palace with his arms, has seen fit to swear trust and fidelity to us in our hand, therefore we herewith **decree** and command that for the future _____ , above mentioned, be **reckoned** among the number of the **antrustions**.

fidelity: loyalty

decree: order
reckoned: counted
antrustions: followers

Life in Europe during the Middle Ages was often harsh and brutal, especially for serfs—the least powerful members of feudal society—who lived and worked on the land belonging to the nobles. Feudal contracts listing the responsibilities of both rulers and subjects had a lasting impact throughout the continent. The great movements for democracy that began in the 17th and 18th centuries built upon the feudal idea of a contract in which government authority is based on the consent of the people.

Source: James Harvey Robinson, *Readings in European History*, Volume 1. Boston: Athenaeum, 1904.

Notebooks from the Renaissance

by Leonardo da Vinci, about 1482–1519

From the 1300s to about 1600 Europe witnessed a rebirth of art, learning, and culture known as the Renaissance. No one embodied the spirit of the Renaissance more than Leonardo da Vinci (1452–1519). An Italian artist, scientist, and inventor, Leonardo studied every part of nature to better understand the world around him. Throughout his life, Da Vinci kept notebooks in which he sketched drawings and jotted down ideas. Da Vinci, who was left-handed, wrote backward from right to left so that his handwriting can only be read by holding it up to a mirror. As you read the selections and look at the drawings from Da Vinci's notebooks, think about how his drawings and ideas capture the spirit of the Renaissance. In what ways is Da Vinci a person far ahead of his time?

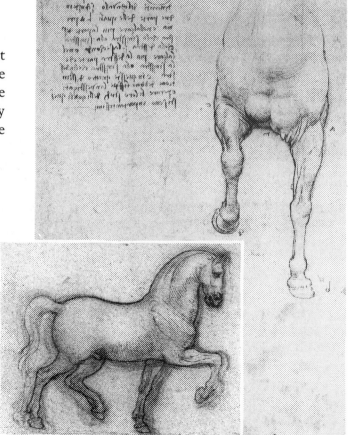

A Man when running throws less weight on his legs than when standing still. And in the same way a horse which is running feels less the weight of the man he carries. Hence many persons think it wonderful that in running, the horse can rest on one single foot.

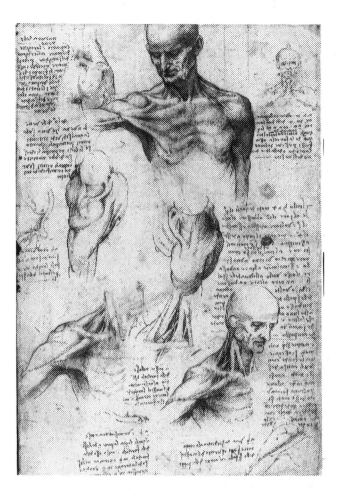

Give the measurement of each muscle, and give the reasons of all their functions, and in which they work and what makes them work. . . . First draw the spine of the back; then clothe it by degrees, one after the other, with each of its muscles and put in the nerves and arteries and veins to each muscle by itself; and besides these note the vertebrae to which they are attached; which of the intestines come in contact with them; and which bones and other organs. . . .

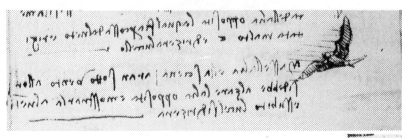

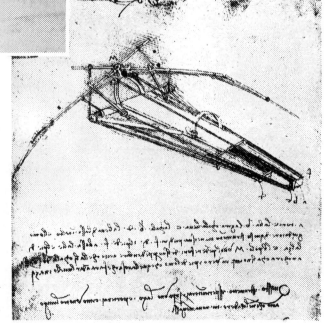

A Bird is an instrument working according to mathematical law, which instrument it is in the capacity of man to reproduce. . . . A man with wings large enough and [properly] attached might learn to overcome the resistance of the air . . . and raise himself upon it. Remember that your bird must imitate no other than the bat, because its membranes serve as . . . the frame of the wings. . . . [Take apart] the bat and on this model arrange the machine. . . .

Nature is [taken in] through the senses, mainly through the sense of sight. The art of painting is [part of] the process of seeing. . . . . The painter must analyze this experience in order to reproduce the visual image appearing in the eye on his picture place. His painting should give the impression of a window through which we look out into a section of the visible world. . . . The mind of a painter should be like a mirror, which always takes the color of the object it reflects and is filled by the images of as many objects as are in front of it. Therefore you must know that you cannot be a good painter unless you . . . represent by your art every kind of form produced by nature.

Leonardo da Vinci is remembered today for some of his great paintings, such as the Mona Lisa and The Last Supper. He is also remembered for his great sketches and ideas for inventions. Many of these inventions—such as the airplane—were so advanced that they could not actually be built for hundreds of years after Da Vinci's death. To learn about another person who also captured the spirit of the Renaissance, *read the next document on page 81.*

Source: Irma A. Richter, ed., *Selections from the Notebooks of Leonardo de Vinci*. London: Oxford University Press, 1952.

This Sceptered Isle

from *Richard II* by William Shakespeare, 1597

The Renaissance that began in Italy in the 1300s gradually spread to the rest of Europe. By the late 1500s the Renaissance was flourishing in England, especially in the theater. Some of the world's greatest plays were written in this period by a London actor named William Shakespeare (1564-1616). Born in the town of Stratford-on-Avon, Shakespeare wrote tragedies, comedies, and histories. The excerpt below is from a speech at the beginning of Richard II, *a historical play that takes place in the late 1300s. In this speech, a duke named John of Gaunt describes England to his nephew, King Richard II. How does Shakespeare's language help express John of Gaunt's feelings about England?*

This royal throne of kings, this **scepter'd** isle,
This earth of majesty, this seat of **Mars**,
This other Eden, **demi**-paradise,
This fortress built by Nature for herself
Against **infection** and the hand of war,
This happy breed of men, this little world,
This precious stone set in the silver sea,
Which serves it in the office of a wall
Or as a moat defensive to a house,
Against the envy of less happier lands,
This blessed plot, this earth, this **realm**,
this England. . . .

scepter'd: royal

Mars: the Roman god of war

demi: half

infection: injury; invasion

realm: kingdom

In this speech John of Gaunt presents a positive view of his nation in the late 1300s. But the play, Richard II, *traces a dark period in England's history when war tore the nation apart.* Richard II *is one of more than 35 plays written by Shakespeare. The beautiful language, complex characters, and great depth of feeling found in all his plays have made Shakespeare one of the finest English-language playwrights who ever lived.*

A Message to the Troops

by Elizabeth I, 1588

In 1558 Elizabeth I (1533-1603) became queen of England. During the middle and late 16th century, Spain was the most powerful country in the world. King Philip of Spain, however, feared the growing strength of England. In 1588 he organized the Spanish Armada, the mightiest fleet of warships that had ever been assembled, and prepared to invade England. At once, Queen Elizabeth rode to a small town called Tilbury to rally her troops. On August 9, 1588, she gave the following speech. To what values does the queen appeal in urging her soldiers to victory?

My loving people, we have been persuaded by some that are careful of our safety to take heed how we commit our self to armed **multitudes** for fear of **treachery**, but I assure you, I do not desire to live to distrust my faithful and loving people. Let Tyrants fear, I have always so behaved myself that under God I have placed my chiefest strength and **safeguard** in the loyal hearts and good will of my subjects. And therefore I [have] come amongst you as you see at this time not for my recreation and **disport**, but being **resolved** in the midst and heat of the battle to live or die amongst you all. To lay down for God and for my kingdom and for my people my honour and my blood even in the dust. I know I have the body of a weak and feeble woman but I have the heart and stomach of a King, and of a King of England too, and think **foul scorn** that **Parma** or Spain or any Prince of Europe should dare invade the borders of my Realm to which rather than any dishonour shall grow by me, I myself will take up arms, I myself will be your General, Judge, and Rewarder of every one of your virtues in the field. I know already for your **forwardness** you have deserved rewards and crowns and we do assure you in the word of a Prince, they shall be duly paid you.

In the meantime my Lieutenant-General shall be in my **stead**, than whom never Prince commanded a more Noble or worthy subject, not doubting but by your obedience to my General, by your **Concord** in the Camp and your **valour** in the field we shall shortly have a famous victory over those enemies of God, of my Kingdom and of my People.

multitudes: crowds
treachery: betrayal

safeguard: defense

disport: amusement
resolved: determined

foul scorn: disapprovingly
Parma: Spanish general

forwardness: boldness

stead: place

concord: togetherness
valour: bravery

Queen Elizabeth's speech inspired her troops. While she waited on land, the English and Spanish fleets fought a fierce battle at sea. The smaller, quicker English ships pounded the Spanish Armada and sent the Spaniards fleeing. A fierce storm at sea also battered many of Spain's ships. England's victory over the Armada helped to make England the world's most powerful nation for hundreds of years. Queen Elizabeth ruled England until her death in 1603 and is considered one of the world's greatest monarchs.

Source: Maria Perry, *The Word of a Prince: A Life of Elizabeth I from Contemporary Documents.* Woodbridge, England: The Boydell Press, 1990.

Clipping the Beards   **Political Cartoon, 1698**

In 1697 Russian Tsar Peter the Great (1672-1725) took a long trip to England and the Netherlands. His travels convinced him that Russia was very backward in its social and technical development compared to other parts of Europe. Upon his return he began efforts to modernize his country. Peter ordered the translation of new science books into the Russian language, planned a large system of canals, promoted the growth of industry, and increased trade. He even declared that nobles could no longer wear beards because he considered them signs of Russian backwardness. In the cartoon below, a woodcut from 1698, a clean-shaven Peter is shown clipping the beard of a noble. A translation of the dialogue appears beside it. How is the noble responding to Peter's action?

The barber is going to cut the dissenter's beard.

Dissenter says: Listen barber, I don't want my beard cut. Agh. I'll soon call the guards to get you.

Under Peter the Great's leadership, Russia modernized and became a powerful country. But Russians paid a steep price for these changes. Peter drained the country's treasury to fight a long war against Sweden. He also arrested many church leaders and brutally put down all opposition to his rule.

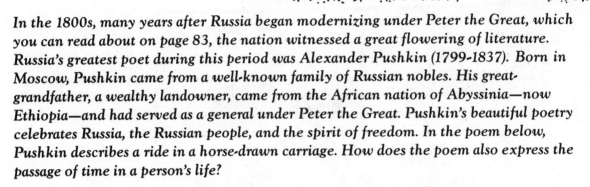

THE COACH OF TIME

by Alexander Pushkin, 1823

In the 1800s, many years after Russia began modernizing under Peter the Great, which you can read about on page 83, the nation witnessed a great flowering of literature. Russia's greatest poet during this period was Alexander Pushkin (1799-1837). Born in Moscow, Pushkin came from a well-known family of Russian nobles. His great-grandfather, a wealthy landowner, came from the African nation of Abyssinia—now Ethiopia—and had served as a general under Peter the Great. Pushkin's beautiful poetry celebrates Russia, the Russian people, and the spirit of freedom. In the poem below, Pushkin describes a ride in a horse-drawn carriage. How does the poem also express the passage of time in a person's life?

Often with heavy burdens **freighted**,
The **coach** rolls on with easy pace.
The driver on the box is seated,
Grey Time, who never leaves his place.

We take our seats at early morning,
And by the **coachman** start the trip;
Our **indolence** and comfort scorning,
We cry: "Now let the horses **rip!**"

When noon comes, we have lost our daring,
We're shaken up; we fear and doubt,
And down steep slopes and **gullies faring**
We cry: "Go slow, you fool! Look out!"

The coach rolls as before unshaken.
We're used to it **ere** day is done.
At last, by **slumber** overtaken,
We reach the inn,—but Time drives on.

freighted: loaded on
coach: horse-drawn carriage

coachman: driver
indolence: laziness
rip: go, move fast

gullies: ditches, ruts
faring: traveling

ere: before
slumber: sleep

In addition to poetry, Pushkin also wrote novels, plays, short stories, and fairy tales. Because many great Russian novelists such as Feodor Dostoyevsky and Leo Tolstoy were influenced by his style of writing, Pushkin is often called the father of Russian literature. He died in a duel at age 37 in 1837.

Source: C.M. Bowra, ed., *A Second Book of Russian Verse*. London: Macmillan and Company, Ltd., 1948.

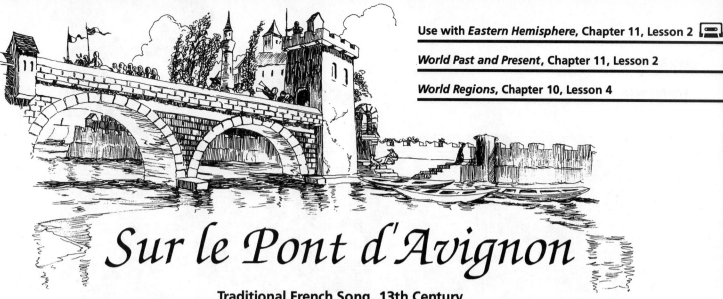

Sur le Pont d'Avignon

Traditional French Song, 13th Century

Festivals in France are always a time for singing and dancing. One of France's best-loved folk songs describes merry-making in an old walled-city in southern France called Avignon. How does this song show many different people from the same community enjoying themselves?

Allegretto

Traditional French Song

On the bridge at   A - vi - gnon, Some are pranc - ing   some are danc - ing.
Sur le pont___   d'A - vi - gnon L'on y pas - se, L'on y dan - se,

On the bridge at   A - vi - gnon They are danc - ing   round and round.
Sur le pont___   d'A - vi - gnon, L'on y dan - se   tout en round.

The beau gal - lants go this   way;   The la - dies fine go this   way.
Les beaux gal - lants font comm' çà;   Les bel - les dames font comm' çà.

Sur le pont d'Avignon
L'on y passe,
L'on y danse,
Sur le pont d'Avignon,
L'on y danse tout en rond.
Les Abbés font comm' çà,
Les soldats font comm' çà.

On the bridge at Avignon,
Some are prancing
Some are dancing.
On the bridge at Avignon
They are dancing round and round.
The Abbés grave go this way,
The soldiers brave go this way.

Source: Dorothy Gordon, *Around the World in Song.* New York: E. P. Dutton & Co., Inc., 1932.

85

WORKING IN THE MINES

by Ann Eggley and Elizabeth Eggley, 1842

One of the main results of the Industrial Revolution, which began in England in the 1700s, was the use of child labor. Children as young as six often worked more than 12 hours a day in crowded mines and factories. In 1842 the British government began an investigation into the effects of child labor. Among the workers interviewed were two teenage sisters, Ann and Elizabeth Eggley. They both worked in the coal mines as "hurriers," people who pushed carts loaded with coal ore that weighed hundreds of pounds. As you read excerpts from their testimony to government officials, notice how the Eggleys feel about their work. Why do you think some people wanted to outlaw child labor?

Ann Eggley, 18 years old

We go [to work] at four in the morning, and sometimes at half-past four. We begin to work as soon as we get down. We get out after four, sometimes at five, in the evening. We work the whole time except an hour for dinner, and sometimes we haven't time to eat. I **hurry** by myself, and have done so for [a long time]. I know the **corves** are very very heavy. They are the biggest corves anywhere about. The work is far too hard for me; the sweat runs off me all over sometimes. I am very tired at night. Sometimes when we get home at night we have not power to wash us, and then we go to bed. Sometimes we fall asleep in the chair. Father said last night it was both a shame and a disgrace for girls to work as we do, but there was **nought** else for us to do. I have

hurry: push carts loaded with coal

corves: carts used in the mines

nought: nothing

tried to get **winding** to do, but could not. I begun to hurry when I was seven and I have been hurrying ever since. I have been 11 years in the pit. The girls are always tired. I was **poorly** twice this winter; it was with headache. I hurry for Robert Wiggins; he is not **akin** to me. I **riddle** for him. We all riddle . . . except the littlest. . . . We don't always get enough to eat and drink, but we get a good supper. I have known my father [to] go at two in the morning to work . . . and he didn't come out till four [in the afternoon]. I am quite sure that we work constantly 12 hours except on Saturdays. We wear trousers and our **shifts** in the pit, and great big shoes. . . . I never went to a dayschool. . . . I walk about and get the fresh air on Sundays. I have not learnt to read.

winding: raising coal to the surface of the mine

poorly: ill

akin: related

riddle: separate materials

shifts: loose shirts or dresses

Elizabeth Eggley, 16 years old

I am sister to the last witness. I hurry in the same pit, and work for my father. I find my work very much too hard for me. I hurry alone. It tires me in my arms and back most. We go to work between four and five in the morning. If we are not there by half past five we are not allowed to go down at all. We come out at four, five, or six at night as it happens. We stop in generally 12 hours, and sometimes longer. . . . I am sure it is very hard work and [it] tires us very much; it is too hard for girls to do. We sometimes go to sleep before we get to bed. We haven't a very good house; we have but two rooms for all the family. I have never been to school except four times. . . . I cannot read. . . .

The testimony of the Eggley sisters and other young workers made people in England more aware of the horrors of child labor. As a result of their testimony, Parliament passed new laws forbidding the employment of children under the age of 10 in the mines. Child labor, however, such as that described by the Eggleys, continued to exist in England for many more years.

Source: Erna Olafson Hellerstein, Leslie Parker Hume, and Karen M. Offen, eds., *Victorian Women*. Stanford, CA: Stanford University Press, 1981.

ALL QUIET ON THE WESTERN FRONT

by Erich Maria Remarque, 1929

World War I was the first major conflict of the 20th century. From 1914 to 1918, millions of soldiers engaged in a new style of fighting called trench warfare. Rather than face each other on large battlefields, soldiers on both sides dug trenches, or deep ditches. From these trenches, soldiers fired guns and threw hand grenades in hopes of driving out the enemy. Trench warfare led to many deaths but few victories. In 1929 a former German soldier named Erich Maria Remarque (1898-1970) wrote a novel describing his experiences in World War I. As you read the following excerpt from All Quiet on the Western Front, notice how Remarque re-creates the experience of trench warfare. How do you think the narrator feels about war?

Quiet, I squat in a **shell-hole** and try to locate myself. More than once it has happened that some fellow has jumped joyfully into a trench, only then to discover that it was the wrong one.

shell-hole: crater formed by an exploded bomb

After a little time I listen again, but still I am not sure. The confusion of shell-holes now seems so **bewildering** that I can no longer tell in my **agitation** which way I should go. Perhaps I am crawling parallel to the lines, and that might go on forever. So I crawl round once again in a wide curve.

bewildering: confusing
agitation: nervousness

These [awful] rockets! They seem to burn for an hour, and a man cannot make the least movement without bringing the bullets whistling round.

But there is nothing for it, I must get out. **Falteringly** I work my way farther, I move off over the ground like a crab and rip my hands sorely on the jagged splinters, as sharp as razor blades. Often I think that the sky is becoming lighter on the horizon, but it may be merely my imagination. Then gradually I realize that to crawl in the right direction is a matter of life or death.

falteringly: unsteadily

A shell crashes. Almost immediately two others. And then it begins in earnest. A bombardment. Machine-guns rattle. Now there is nothing for it but to stay lying low. Apparently an attack is coming. Everywhere the rockets shoot up. **Unceasing.**

unceasing: unending

I lie huddled in a large shell-hole, my legs in the water up to the belly. When the attack starts I will let myself fall into the water, with my face as deep in the mud as I can keep it without suffocating. I must pretend to be dead.

Suddenly I hear the **barrage** lift. At once I slip down into the water, my helmet on the **nape** of my neck and my mouth just clear so that I can get a breath of air.

I lie motionless;—somewhere something clanks, it stamps and stumbles nearer—all my nerves become taut and icy. It clatters over me and away, the first wave has passed. I have but this one shattering thought: What will you do if someone jumps into your shell-hole?—Swiftly I pull out my little dagger, grasp it fast and bury it in my hand once again under the mud. If anyone jumps in here I will go for him. It hammers in my forehead; at once, stab him clean through the throat, so that he cannot call out; that's the only way; he will be just as frightened as I am; when in terror we fall upon one another, then I must be first.

Now our **batteries** are firing. A shell lands near me. That makes me savage with fury, all it needs now is to be killed by our own shells; I curse and grind my teeth in the mud; it is a raving frenzy; in the end all I can do is groan and pray.

The crash of the shells bursts in my ears. If our fellows make a counter-raid I will be saved. I press my head against the earth and listen to the muffled thunder, like the explosions of quarrying—and raise it again to listen for the sounds on top.

The machine-guns rattle. I know our barbed wire entanglements are strong and almost undamaged;—parts of them are charged with a powerful electric current. The rifle fire increases. They have not broken through; they have to retreat.

I sink down again, huddled, strained to the uttermost. The banging, the creeping, the clanging becomes audible. One single cry yelling amongst it all. They are raked with fire, the attack is **repulsed**.

barrage: sound of exploding bombs

nape: back

batteries: guns

repulsed: driven back

More than 8 million soldiers died in World War I. Many people called this conflict "the war to end all wars." But only 20 years after the end of World War I, an even more horrible war would break out in Europe. For a description of one part of this war, read the next document on pages 90-93.

Source: Erich Maria Remarque, *All Quiet on the Western Front*. New York: Fawcett Crest, 1989.

The Diary of Anne Frank

by Anne Frank, 1942–1944

During World War II Nazi Germany attempted to wipe out the entire Jewish population of Europe. In what became known as the Holocaust, the Nazis arrested millions of Jews and sent them to concentration camps where they were starved, tortured, and murdered. To try to save their lives, many Jews fought or fled, while others tried to hide. One of those who hid was a 13-year-old German girl named Anne Frank (1929–1944) living in the Netherlands. With her sister, parents, and four other people, Anne hid in a tiny attic over her father's place of business in Amsterdam. They were helped by Dutch friends who brought them food and other supplies. While in hiding, Anne kept a diary written in Dutch that described her life, her surroundings, and Nazi horrors during World War II. Below is an excerpt from an English translation of Anne Frank's diary. How does her diary express the fears that she and her family had to face every day? How does Anne feel about the war, the world, and the goodness of human beings?

Saturday, 11 July, 1942

Daddy, Mummy, and **Margot** can't get used to the sound of the Westertoren clock yet, which tells us the time every quarter of an hour. I can. I loved it from the start, and especially in the night it's like a faithful friend. I expect you will be interested to hear what it feels like to "disappear"; well, all I can say is that I don't know myself yet. I don't think I shall ever feel really at home in this house, but that does not mean that I **loathe** it here, it is more like being on vacation in a very peculiar boardinghouse. Rather a mad idea [mad way of looking at being in hiding], perhaps, but that is how it strikes me. The "Secret Annexe" is an ideal hiding place. Although it leans to one side and is damp, you'd never find such a comfortable hiding place anywhere in Amsterdam, no, perhaps not even in the whole of **Holland**.

Our little room looked very bare at first with nothing on the walls; but thanks to Daddy who had brought my film-star collection and picture postcards on beforehand, and with the aid of paste pot and

Margot: Anne's sister

loathe: hate

Holland: another name for the Netherlands

90

brush, I have transformed the walls into one gigantic picture. This makes it look much more cheerful, and, when the **Van Daans** come, we'll get some wood from the attic, and make a few little cupboards for the walls and other odds and ends to make it look more lively.

Margot and Mummy are a little bit better now. Mummy felt well enough to cook some soup for the first time yesterday, but then forgot all about it, while she was downstairs talking, so the peas were burned to a cinder and utterly refused to leave the pan. **Mr. Koophuis** has brought me a book called *Young People's Annual*. The four of us went to the private office yesterday evening and turned on the radio. I was so terribly frightened that someone might hear it that I simply begged Daddy to come upstairs with me. Mummy understood how I felt and came too. We are very nervous in other ways, too, that the neighbors might hear us or see something going on. We made curtains straight away on the first day. Really one can hardly call them curtains, they are just light, loose strips of material, all different shapes, quality, and pattern, which Daddy and I sewed together in a most unprofessional way. These works of art are fixed in position with drawing pins, not to come down until we emerge from here.

There are some large business premises on the right of us, and on the left a furniture workshop; there is no one there after working hours but even so, sounds could travel through the walls. We have forbidden Margot to cough at night, although she has a bad cold, and make her swallow large doses of codeine. I am looking for[ward to] Tuesday when the Van Daans arrive; it will be much more fun and not so quiet. It is the silence that frightens me so in the evenings and at night. I wish like anything that one of our protectors could sleep here at night. I can't tell you how oppressive it is *never* to be able to go outdoors, also I'm very afraid that we shall be discovered and be shot. That is not exactly a pleasant prospect. We have to whisper and tread lightly during the day, otherwise the people in the warehouse might hear us.

Someone is calling me.

Friday, 9 October, 1942

I've only got dismal and depressing news for you today. Our many Jewish friends are being taken away by the dozen. These people are treated by the **Gestapo** without a shred of decency, being loaded into cattle trucks and sent to Westerbork, the big Jewish [concentration] camp in **Drente**. Westerbork sounds terrible: only one washing **cubicle** for a hundred people and not nearly enough **lavatories**. There is no separate accommodation. . . .

It is impossible to escape; most of the people in the camp are branded as inmates by their shaven heads and many also by their Jewish appearance.

If it is as bad as this in Holland whatever will it be like in the distant and barbarous regions they are sent to? We assume that most of them are murdered. The English radio speaks of their being gassed.

Van Daans: family in hiding that shared the "secret annexe" with the Franks.

Mr. Koophuis: Dutch man who helped the Franks

Gestapo: secret police force of Nazi Germany
Drente: town in the Netherlands
cubicle: room
lavatories: bathrooms

Perhaps that is the quickest way to die. I feel terribly upset. I couldn't tear myself away while **Miep** told these dreadful stories; and she herself was equally wound up for that matter. Just recently for instance, a poor old crippled **Jewess** was sitting on her doorstep; she had been told to wait there by the Gestapo, who had gone to fetch a car to take her away. The poor old thing was terrified by the guns that were shooting at English planes overhead, and by the glaring beams of the searchlights. But Miep did not dare take her in; no one would undergo such a risk. The Germans strike without the slightest mercy.

Miep: Dutch woman who helped the Franks

Jewess: Jewish woman

Elli too is very quiet: her boy friend has got to go to Germany. She is afraid that the airmen who fly over our homes will drop their bombs, often weighing a million kilos [2.2 million lbs.], on Dirk's head. Jokes such as "he's not likely to get a million" and "it only takes one bomb" are in rather bad taste. Dirk is certainly not the only one who has to go: trainloads of boys leave daily. If they stop at a small station **en route,** sometimes some of them manage to get out unnoticed and escape; perhaps a few manage it. This, however, is not the end of my bad news. Have you ever heard of hostages? That's the latest thing in penalties for **sabotage.** Can you imagine anything so dreadful?

Elli: Dutch woman who helped the Franks

en route: on the way

Prominent citizens—innocent people—are thrown into prison to await their fate. If the **saboteur** can't be traced, the Gestapo simply put about five hostages against the wall. Announcements of their deaths appear in the papers frequently. These outrages are described as "fatal accidents." Nice people, the Germans! To think that I was once one of them too! No, Hitler took away our nationality long ago. In fact, Germans and Jews are the greatest enemies in the world.

sabotage: destruction of enemy property

saboteur: one who commits sabotage

Thursday, 25 May, 1944

There's something fresh every day. This morning our vegetable man was picked up for having two Jews in his house. It's a great blow to us, not only that those poor Jews are balancing on the edge of an abyss, but it's terrible for the man himself.

The world has turned topsy-turvy, respectable people are being sent off to concentration camps, prisons, and lonely cells, and the dregs that remain govern young and old, rich and poor. One person walks into the trap through the black market, a second through helping the Jews or other people who've had to go "underground"; anyone who isn't a member of the **N.S.B.** doesn't know what may happen to him from one day to another.

N.S.B.: initials of the Dutch Nazi party

This man is a great loss to us too. The girls can't and aren't allowed to haul along our share of potatoes, so the only thing to do is to eat less. I will tell you how we shall do that; it's certainly not going to make things any pleasanter. Mummy says we shall cut out breakfast altogether, have porridge and bread for lunch, and for supper fried potatoes and possibly once or twice per week vegetables or lettuce, nothing more. We're going to be hungry, but anything is better than being discovered.

Thursday, 15 June, 1944

I wonder if it's because I haven't been able to poke my nose outdoors for so long that I've grown so crazy about everything to do with nature? I can perfectly well remember that there was a time when a deep blue sky, the song of the birds, moonlight and flowers could never have kept me **spellbound**. That's changed since I've been here.

spellbound: enchanted

At Whitsun, for instance, when it was so warm, I stayed awake on purpose until half past eleven one evening in order to have a good look at the moon for once by myself. Alas, the sacrifice was all in vain, as the moon gave far too much light and I didn't dare risk opening a window. Another time, some months ago now, I happened to be upstairs one evening when the window was open. I didn't go downstairs until the window had to be shut. The dark, rainy evening, the gale, the scudding clouds held me entirely in their power; it was the first time in a year and a half that I'd seen the night face to face. After that evening my longing to see it again was greater than my fear of burglars, rats, and raids on the house. I went downstairs all by myself and looked outside through the windows in the kitchen and the private office. A lot of people are fond of nature, many sleep outdoors occasionally, and people in prisons and hospitals long for the day when they will be free to enjoy the beauties of nature, but few are so shut away and isolated from that which can be shared alike by rich and poor. It's not imagination on my part when I say that to look up at the sky, the clouds, the moon, and the stars makes me calm and patient. It's a better medicine than either valerian or bromine; Mother Nature makes me humble and prepared to face every blow courageously.

Alas, it has had to be that I am only able—except on a few rare occasions—to look at nature through dirty net curtains hanging before very dusty windows. And it's no pleasure looking through these any longer, because nature is just the one thing that really **must be unadulterated**.

must be unadulterated: experienced directly

Seven weeks after Anne wrote this last entry in her diary, the Nazis discovered her family's secret hiding place. They arrested Anne and her family and sent them to a concentration camp. Only Anne's father survived. Anne Frank was one of 6 million Jews murdered by Nazi Germany in concentration camps during the Holocaust. The Nazis also killed 8 million other people in concentration camps, including Poles, Russians, Czechs, and Romanies (sometimes called Gypsies). Anne Frank's courage in the face of one of the greatest horrors in world history remains a testament to the human spirit.

Source: Anne Frank, *The Diary of Anne Frank: The Critical Edition*. New York: Bantam Doubleday Dell Publishing Group, Inc., 1989.

Defeating Nazi Germany

Poster, 1942

When Nazi Germany invaded Poland in 1939, World War II broke out in Europe. By the end of 1941, four of the world's strongest nations—the United States, the Soviet Union, Great Britain, and France—had joined forces to fight Germany and the other Axis nations. In 1942 the United States government printed the following poster to help raise money and build support for the war effort. How does this poster show the joint effort being taken by the Allied nations against Germany?

In 1945 the combined efforts of the Allied nations defeated Germany and the other Axis nations. Altogether, more than 55 million men, women, and children died in World War II, making it the most deadly conflict in history. The cooperation of the United States, the Soviet Union, Great Britain, France, and other countries made victory possible.

Source: Charles Goodrum and Helen Dalrymple, *Advertising in America: The First 200 Years*. New York: Harry N. Abrams, Inc., Publishers, 1990.

New Year's Address

by Václav Havel, 1990

In November 1989 thousands of people jammed the streets in Czechoslovakia's capital city of Prague (präg) to protest communism and Soviet control of their government. Unlike earlier protests in Czechoslovakia that had been crushed, this time the communist government was forced to resign. In December 1989 Czechoslovakia held its first free elections since 1946 and chose Václav Havel (vät′ släf häv′ əl) as president. A leading playwright, Havel had been imprisoned several times for speaking out against the communist government. On January 1, 1990, Havel gave his first major speech as president of Czechoslovakia. As you read an excerpt of his speech, notice how Havel outlines the differences between past governments and the present one. What challenges facing Czechoslovakia does he describe? According to Havel, what are the responsibilities of people in a democracy?

My dear fellow citizens,

For forty years you heard from my **predecessors** on this day different **variations** of the same theme: how our country flourished, how many million tons of steel we produced, how happy we all were, how we trusted our government, and what bright **perspectives** were unfolding in front of us.

I assume you did not propose me for this office so that I, too, would lie to you.

Our country is not flourishing. The enormous creative and spiritual potential of our nations is not being used sensibly. Entire branches of industry are producing goods which are of no interest to anyone, while we are lacking the things we need. A state which calls itself a workers' state **humiliates** and **exploits** workers. Our **obsolete** economy is wasting the little energy we have available. A country that once could be proud of the educational level of its citizens spends so little on education that it ranks today as seventy-second in the world. We have polluted our soil, our rivers and forests, **bequeathed** to

predecessors: past rulers

variations: versions

perspectives: scenes

humiliates: insults

exploits: mistreats

obsolete: outdated

bequeathed: handed down

us by our ancestors, and we have today the most **contaminated** environment in Europe. . . .

But all this is still not the main problem. The worst thing is that we live in a contaminated moral environment. We fell morally ill because we became used to saying something different from what we thought. We learned not to believe in anything, to ignore each other, to care only about ourselves. . . .

We cannot blame the previous rulers for everything, not only because it would be untrue but also because it could **blunt** the duty that each of us faces today, namely, the **obligation** to act independently, freely, reasonably, and quickly. Let us not be mistaken: the best government in the world, the best parliament and the best president, cannot achieve much on their own. And it would also be wrong to expect a general **remedy** from them only. Freedom and democracy include participation and therefore responsibility from us all. . . .

We had to pay, however, for our present freedom. Many citizens perished in jails in the **fifties**, many were executed, thousands of human lives were destroyed, hundreds of thousands of talented people were forced to leave the country. Those who defended the honor of our nations during the Second World War, those who rebelled against **totalitarian** rule, and those who simply managed to remain themselves and think freely, were all **persecuted**. We should not forget any of those who paid for our present freedom in one way or another. . . .

Our country, if that is what we want, can now permanently **radiate** love, understanding, the power of spirit and ideas. . . .

Let us try in a new time and in a new way to restore this concept of politics. Let us teach ourselves and others that politics should be an expression of a desire to contribute to the happiness of the community rather than of a need to cheat. . .the community. . . .

There are free elections and an election campaign ahead of us. Let us not allow this struggle to dirty the so far clean face of our gentle revolution. . . .

You may ask what kind of a republic I dream of. Let me reply: I dream of a republic independent, free, and democratic, of a republic economically prosperous and yet socially just, in short, of a humane republic which serves the individual and which therefore holds the hope that the individual will serve it in turn. Of a republic of well-rounded people, because without such it is impossible to solve any of our problems, human, economic, ecological, social, or political. . . .

People, your government has returned to you!

Czechoslovakia was one of several countries in Eastern Europe to overthrow its communist government and free itself from the control of the Soviet Union in 1989 and 1990. The most remarkable political change of all, however, was the collapse of the Soviet Union in 1991. For a description of this event, read the next document on pages 97-98.

Source: Václav Havel, *Open Letters: Selected Writings 1965–1990*. New York: Alfred A. Knopf, 1991.

contaminated: polluted

blunt: make less clear
obligation: duty

remedy: cure

fifties: 1950s

totalitarian: absolute
persecuted: treated badly

radiate: send out

FAREWELL SPEECH
by Mikhail Gorbachev, 1991

From 1917 to 1991, the Communist Party ruled the Soviet Union. Under communism, the Soviet government denied its citizens many basic freedoms. In 1985 Mikhail Gorbachev came to power and began introducing reforms to promote democracy and improve the economy. In August 1991, however, enemies of Gorbachev in the Soviet government attempted a coup to topple him and undo his reforms. Although the coup failed, it greatly reduced Gorbachev's power. Soon the republics that had made up the Soviet Union began breaking away. In December 1991 some of them agreed to work together by forming a new organization called the Commonwealth of Independent States. As the Soviet Union crumbled, Gorbachev was suddenly left as the leader of a country that no longer existed. Gorbachev resigned from office on December 25, 1991. As you read excerpts from Gorbachev's farewell speech, notice the accomplishments he believes the Soviet Union has made under his leadership. How does Gorbachev feel about these changes? What feelings about the future does he express?

Dear fellow countrymen, compatriots. Due to the situation which has evolved as a result of the formation of the Commonwealth of Independent States, I hereby discontinue my activities at the post of President of the Union of Soviet Socialist Republics. . . .

This being my last opportunity to address you as President of the **U.S.S.R.**, I find it necessary to inform you of what I think of the road that has been **trodden** by us since 1985. . . .

Destiny so ruled that when I found myself at the **helm** of this state it already was clear that something was wrong in this country.

We had a lot of everything—land, oil and gas, other natural resources—and there was intellect and talent in abundance. However, we were living much worse than people in the industrialized countries were living and we were increasingly **lagging** behind them. The reason was obvious even then. This country was suffocating in the **shackles** of the. . .command system. Doomed to **cater to** [communism], and suffer and carry the **onerous** burden of the arms race, it found itself at the breaking point.

All the half-hearted reforms—and there have been a lot of them—fell through, one after another. This country was going nowhere and we couldn't possibly live the way we did. We had to change everything radically. . . .

I am convinced that the democratic reform that we launched in the spring of 1985 was historically correct.

The process of **renovating** this country and bringing about drastic change in the international community has proven to be much more

U.S.S.R.: Union of Soviet Socialist Republics, or Soviet Union

trodden: traveled

helm: head

lagging: falling

shackles: chains

cater to: follow

onerous: heavy

renovating: restoring

complicated than anyone could imagine. However, let us give its due to what has been done so far.

This society has acquired freedom. It has been freed politically and spiritually, and this is the most important achievement that we have yet to fully come to grips with. And we haven't, because we haven't learned to use freedom yet.

However, an effort of historical importance has been carried out. The **totalitarian** system has been eliminated, which prevented this country from becoming a prosperous and well-to-do country a long time ago. A breakthrough has been **effected** on the road of democratic change.

totalitarian: all-powerful government

effected: achieved

Free elections have become a reality. Free press, freedom of worship, representative legislatures and a multi-party system have all become reality. Human rights are being treated as the supreme principle and top priority. Movement has been started toward a [free] economy and the equality of all forms of ownership is being established. . . .

We're now living in a new world. An end has been put to the cold war and to the arms race, as well as to the mad **militarization** of the country, which has crippled our economy, public attitudes and morals. The threat of nuclear war has been removed. . . .

militarization: military buildup

I consider it vitally important to preserve the democratic achievements which have been **attained** in the last few years. We have paid with all our history and tragic experience for these democratic achievements, and they are not to be abandoned, whatever the circumstances, and whatever the **pretexts**. Otherwise, all our hopes for the best will be buried. I am telling you all this honestly and straightforwardly because this is my moral duty. . . .

attained: reached

pretexts: false reasons

I am very much concerned as I am leaving this post. However, I also have feelings of hope and faith in you, your wisdom and force of spirit. We are heirs of a great civilization and it now depends on all and everyone whether or not this civilization will make a comeback to a new and decent living today. I would like, from the bottom of my heart, to thank everyone who has stood by me throughout these years, working for the righteous and good cause.

Of course, there were mistakes made that could have been avoided, and many of the things that we did could have been done better. But I am positive that sooner or later, some day our common efforts will bear fruit and our nations will live in a prosperous, democratic society.

I wish everyone all the best.

After Gorbachev gave his farewell speech on December 25, 1991, the flag of the Soviet Union was lowered for the last time. The Soviet Union, which had been one of the largest and most powerful nations in the world since World War II, ceased to exist. The 15 republics that had made up the Soviet Union are now independent countries.

Source: "Text of Gorbachev's Farewell Address," *The New York Times*, December 26, 1991.

Yellow Submarine

by The Beatles, 1966

Great Britain is known for many things: its literature, its ancient castles, and its long line of kings and queens. But Britain is also famous for something else—its rock-and-roll music. One of the most popular British bands in history was called The Beatles. This band, composed of John Lennon, Paul McCartney, George Harrison, and Ringo Starr, produced one hit song after another from the early 1960s to 1970. The song below was written in 1966 and includes elements of both rock music and folk music. In what ways is this song almost like a fairy tale?

*Words and Music
by John Lennon and Paul McCartney*

In the town_____ where I was born lived a
man_____ who sailed to sea. And he told_____ us of his
life in the land_____ of sub - ma - rines. So we sailed_____ up to the

Source: John Lennon and Paul McCartney, *Yellow Submarine*. Milwaukee, WI: Hal Leonard Publishing Corporation, 1966.

PART

4

AFRICA

Our march to freedom is irreversible.... I have cherished the idea of a democratic and free society in which all persons live together in harmony and with equal opportunities.

Nelson Mandela, 1990

Moon and Sun

Story of the Fon People Retold by Virginia Hamilton, 1988

The people of West Africa have a long tradition of using oral history to pass down their beliefs about the origins of the universe and the world. This oral tradition is made up of songs, poems, and stories, many of which were first told by griots, or storytellers, hundreds of years ago. As you have seen in the documents of the Cree of North America on page 19, the Mayas of Latin America on pages 34-35, and the Vikings of Europe on pages 66-67, people all over the world have stories about their history and how they believe the natural world came to exist. The story below is told by the Fon people of Benin. The Fon were the founders of the powerful kingdom of Dahomey, which flourished in the 18th and 19th centuries in what is today the West African country of Benin. How do the Fon use this story to explain the beginnings of the world?

Nana Buluku, the Great Mother, created the world. She had twins, Mawu and Lisa. She did nothing after that.

Mawu was the moon who had power over the night and lived in the west. Lisa was the sun, who made his home in the east. At first, Mawu and Lisa had no **offspring**. But then, when there was an eclipse—when one of them was in the shadow of the other or another heavenly body—they came together and created children.

offspring: children

Mawu and Lisa were Mother and Father of all the other gods. And there were fourteen of these gods, who were seven pairs of twins. The gods of earth, storm, and iron were born first.

One day, Mawu-Lisa called all of their children to come around them. When they all came, Mawu-Lisa gave each pair of twins a good place to rule. The first twins were told to rule earth.

"Take what you wish from our heaven," Mawu-Lisa told them.

The second pair of twins were told to stay in the sky.

"You will rule over thunder and lightning," said Mawu-Lisa.

The third pair, who were iron, were the strength of their parents.

"You will clear the forests and prepare the land," Mawu-Lisa said. "And you will give humans their tools and weapons."

The next twins were to live in the sea.

"Children, rule all waters and all fishes," Mawu-Lisa commanded.

Other twins would rule over the birds and beasts of the bush country. They would take care of all of the trees everywhere.

More twins were to take care of the space between the earth and sky. "And you will also make the length of time that humans shall live," said Mawu-Lisa.

Then Mawu said, "Come visit me. You will tell me everything that goes on in the world."

Mawu-Lisa took care that none of the lesser gods were ever seen by human beings. That is why people speak so of the sky as a spirit, and speak of storms and lightning as spirits, too.

And all of it is because of the power of the sky gods, Moon and Sun, Mawu-Lisa.

Stories such as this preserve common beliefs among the Fon about the origin of the world. They also suggest the importance of land and nature to the Fon.

Source: Virginia Hamilton, *In the Beginning: Creation Stories from Around the World*. New York: Harcourt Brace Jovanovich, 1988.

THE ROSETTA STONE

Egyptian Decree, 196 B.C.

For hundreds of years one of the world's greatest mysteries could be found on the walls of the pyramids and monuments of ancient Egypt. On these walls Egyptians had carved hieroglyphics, a system of writing that used pictures and signs to stand for objects, sounds, and ideas. At a later time Egyptians had carved another system of writing known as demotic, which used an alphabet to stand for sounds. What did these symbols mean? For years no one knew what they meant because the knowledge of how to read hieroglyphics and demotic writing had been lost.

But in 1799 archaeologists made a remarkable discovery. In the Egyptian town of Rosetta they found a piece of stone marked with carvings in three languages: hieroglyphics, demotic, and Greek. The Rosetta Stone appears in the inset on the facing page. Using their knowledge of Greek, scholars soon learned that the stone recorded the same information in the three different languages. The translation of the Rosetta Stone provided a valuable key for unlocking the secrets of ancient Egypt.

What did the markings on the Rosetta Stone say? It was an order given by a pharaoh named Ptolemy Epiphanes in 196 B.C., demanding that priests in Egypt honor him and accept him as their ruler. To make sure that everyone would obey this order, the pharaoh had it carved in three different languages.

Reading hieroglyphic symbols, or hieroglyphs, is like trying to solve a puzzle. Look at the sentence below taken from the Rosetta Stone. The meaning of each hieroglyph is given below it in English. Try to put the hieroglyphs together to make a sentence.

GOOD   EVERYTHING   HEALTH   STRENGTH   LIFE   MIGHT   VICTORY   THE GODS AND GODDESSES   GAVE HIM

This sentence appears on the facing page in the enlargement of the top right section of the Rosetta Stone. It is in the line beside the arrow. Can you find it? In English, this sentence reads: "The gods and goddesses have given him [Pharaoh] victory, might, strength, health, and every other good thing." You can use some of these symbols to decode other hieroglyphs as well. For example, you already know the symbol for life, which appears above. The symbol for eternal, shown below, is a snake. When these two symbols appear together, they mean eternal life. See if you can find this phrase on the next page. Notice that by combining symbols you can make longer phrases. Look at the symbols for day, seven, and ten. Now see if you can find the phrase 17 days on the Rosetta Stone. Try to locate the other symbols and phrases explained below. What do you suppose that the other hieroglyphs on the Rosetta Stone might mean?

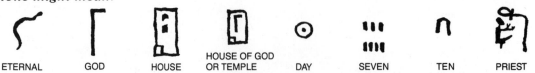

ETERNAL   GOD   HOUSE   HOUSE OF GOD OR TEMPLE   DAY   SEVEN   TEN   PRIEST

Thanks to the Rosetta Stone, people can now read hieroglyphic writing to learn about life in ancient Egypt. To find out about one of the most important Egyptian leaders in history, read the next document on page 106.

A Queen's Promise

by Hatshepsut, 1500 B.C.

One of ancient Egypt's best-known rulers was Queen Hatshepsut (hat shep' süt) (1520-1482 B.C.), the first woman ruler known to history. During her reign, from about 1503 to 1482 B.C., Egypt enjoyed peace and prosperity and expanded its trade with East Africa and Asia. Like other Egyptian rulers, Hatshepsut ordered the building of gigantic monuments and temples. One of them was a huge stone obelisk, a tall four-sided pillar. Hatshepsut's obelisk is made of a single piece of red granite and still stands today. Like most Egyptian monuments, it is carved with hieroglyphics. Thanks in part to the Rosetta Stone, which you can read about on pages 104-105, historians have been able to translate Hatshepsut's obelisk. As you read part of the obelisk below, notice that Hatshepsut connects herself to the gods. In what ways does she claim to be a powerful ruler?

Now my heart turns **to and fro**,
In thinking what will the people say,
They who shall see my monument in after years,
And shall speak of what I have done. . . .
In order that my name may endure in this temple,
For eternity and everlastingness,
They are each of one block of hard granite,
Without seam, without joining together! . . .
Lo, the god knows me well,
Amun, Lord of **Thrones-of-the-Two-Lands**;
He made me rule **Black Land** and **Red Land** as reward,
No one rebels against me in all lands.
All foreign lands are my subjects,
He placed my border at the limits of heaven,
What **Aten** encircles labors for me.
He gave it to him who came from him,
Knowing I would rule it for him.
I am his daughter in very truth,
Who serves him, who knows what he **ordains**.
My reward from my father is **life-stability-rule** . . .
    eternally like **Re**.

to and fro: back and forth

Thrones-of-the-Two-Lands: Upper and Lower Egypt

Black Land: the Nile Valley

Red Land: the desert

Aten: the sun

ordains: orders

life-stability-rule: rule for life

Re: the sun god

After Queen Hatshepsut's death her stepson, Thutmose III, became ruler of Egypt. Because he had long been her rival for power, he tried to destroy everything Hatshepsut had built. However, because she had built so many temples and monuments, many survived untouched.

Source: Joanna Bankier and Deirdre Lashgari, eds., *Women Poets of the World*. New York: Macmillan Publishing Co., Inc., 1983.

THE KINGDOM OF
KUSH

Ancient Artifacts and Accounts, 450 B.C.–A.D. 77

After soldiers of Kush conquered Egypt in 751 B.C., the Kushites established an empire that dominated part of the Nile River Valley in what is today Sudan for the next 1,000 years. The Kushites built pyramids and a great capital city named Meroë (mer ə wē'). They also developed their own written language. Unlike Egyptian hieroglyphics, whose symbols have been decoded, no one has been able to decode the language of Kush. As a result, we know far less about ancient Kush than we do about ancient Egypt. Our knowledge of Kush comes from ancient artifacts and written accounts by people who visited Kush long ago.

The pictures of engravings and artifacts on pages 108-109 were all found at the site of ancient Kush. You can also read several descriptions of Kush adapted from Greek and Roman writers. Notice that these writers often called the Kushites "Ethiopians." Although Greeks and Romans used Ethiopians as a general term for black Africans, in the following passages they are mostly referring to the Kushites. What do the artifacts and travelers' accounts tell you about ancient Kush? Think of each of the following items as a clue in a puzzle. What do these clues reveal about the Kushites?

Herodotus, about 450 B.C.

After the forty days' journey on land from Egypt one takes another boat and in twelve days reaches a big city named Meroë. This city is said to be the capital of the Ethiopians. The inhabitants worship only the Gods of Zeus and Dionysus, and hold them in great honor. There is an **oracle** of Zeus in the city which directs the Ethiopians when it commands them to go to war. The Ethiopians are said to be the tallest and handsomest men in the whole world. In their customs they differ greatly from the rest of mankind, and particularly in the way they choose their kings. They find out the man who is the tallest of all the citizens, and of strength equal to his height. They appoint this man to be their ruler.

oracle: temple

Diodorus Siculus, about 50 B.C.

Historians tell us that the Ethiopians were the first of all men. The proofs of this statement, they say, are obvious. Historians say that the black peoples of Kush were the first to be taught to honor the gods and to hold sacrifices and processions and festivals by which men honor the gods. It is generally held that the sacrifices practiced among the Ethiopians are those which are the most pleasing to heaven. As witness to this these historians call upon the poet who is perhaps the oldest and certainly the most respected among the Greeks. For in the *Iliad*, Homer describes both Zeus and the rest of the gods with him on a visit to Ethiopia. The gods share in the sacrifices and the banquet which were given annually by the Ethiopians for all the gods together.

Strabo, 25-24 B.C.

When Gallus was leader of Egypt, I accompanied him in 25 and 24 B.C. We traveled up the Nile as far as Syene and the frontiers of Kush. I learned that as many as 120 vessels were sailing from Myos Hormos, a port on the Red Sea, all the way to India. In older times under the Egyptians, only a very few ventured to undertake the voyage and to carry on trade in Indian merchandise.

**Gold mask of
Queen Malaqaye**

Example of the Kush alphabetic script

:ƧȜƧȜ:VꝽ//:Ꞩ<V4ẟ/Ƙ: ꝽꞨȜꝵƘ:4Ȝꝵ<
44ꞨV///ꞨȜȜ:VꝽ//:ꞨƖȜƖꝵꞨ:Ꞩ<ꝵꞨꞨVȜꞨȜ
                    VꝽ//Ƙ/ȜȜ:
ƖꞨˑ:44ȜꞨƖȜ:ƘꞨѠVꝵ:<ꝵꞨꞨVꝵȜȜ:44ꝵ
Vꝵẟ:Ɩꝵ4ẟ/ƦꞨ:Ꞩ<ꝵVV//:VꝽ//:ꞨȜꝵ44
                    Ѡ<:ƘѠ
ƖȜꞨ:4ẟVV//:4<<Ѡ4:/Ȝ4ẟȜ:ꞨȜꝵ<Ȝ
:ẟꝵѠ//ѠVꞨȜ:ẟꝵ///4ȜȜ:ƘȝꞨ:ꝵ4ẟV//Ꞩ

Pliny the Elder, about A.D. 77

Meroe had once enjoyed great fame and had maintained four thousand artisans.... The queens of the country bore the name Candace, a title that had passed from queen to queen for many years.

Kush god carved on the stone wall of a temple at Meroë

These accounts and artifacts provide evidence of a rich civilization widely admired by other peoples. They reveal that the Kushites traded far beyond their borders, created beautiful art, developed an original system of writing, were deeply religious, and chose both men and women as their rulers. In the second century A.D. the Kush empire began to decline. The nearby kingdom of Axum conquered the capital city of Meroë in 325 and the Kush empire gradually disappeared.

Source: Basil Davidson, *African Civilization Revisited*. Trenton, NJ: Africa World Press, 1991.
Basil Davidson, *Africa in History*. New York: Macmillan Publishing Company, 1974.

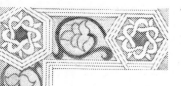

Mali Under Mansa Musa

by Daniel Chu and Elliott Skinner, 1990

In the 1300s, 1,000 years after the fall of the Kush Empire in eastern Africa, which was described on pages 107-109, another great African empire arose thousands of miles to the west. Known as the empire of Mali, its major trading center was Timbuktu, and its greatest leader was a king named Mansa Musa (1297-1322) who ruled from 1307 to 1332. Mansa Musa encouraged the spread of arts and culture and extended the Mali Empire westward to the Atlantic Ocean and eastward across the Sahara. During his reign, Mansa Musa took a fabulous journey across Africa. To learn about this journey and why he took it, read the selection below from a recent book called A Glorious Age in Africa. According to the authors, what were some of Mansa Musa's personal qualities? How did he shape his empire?

Mansa Musa ruled the empire of Mali for twenty-five years. In that quarter of a century the fame of Mali spread across the Sahara to the Middle East, and across the Mediterranean Sea to Europe. Mansa Musa's name was known throughout the world.

Mansa Musa's achievements were many. He extended the boundaries of Mali by **diplomacy** and war. He promoted trade and commerce. He encouraged the spread of learning. He was a lover of the arts (designs, architecture, literature). Above all Mansa Musa was devoutly religious.

diplomacy: negotiations

Several of the Moslem rulers of Mali, starting with **Mansa Wali**, had made pilgrimages to Mecca, the holy city of Islam. The hajj, as these pilgrimages are called, is one of the five basic observances of the Islamic faith. . . .

Mansa Wali: ruler of Mali from 1255 to 1270

Mansa Musa made his hajj in 1324, in the seventeenth year of his reign. The fact that he made the pilgrimage was not unusual. But the way he made it was.

For Mansa Musa's hajj was one of the grandest grand tours ever recorded. The spectacular wealth displayed by his **entourage** so dazzled the people on his line of march that their descendants still talked about it one hundred years after it occurred.

entourage: traveling party

As the ruler of the richest empire in West Africa, possibly in the world, at that time, Mansa Musa could easily afford the expenses involved. Even so, it was a hard journey. Arabia, where Mecca is located, was thousands of miles from Musa's capital city, Niani. His caravan would be traveling across some of the most barren wastelands on earth.

Months before the journey, the Mansa's officials and servants went through the empire to collect the necessary food and supplies for the trip. To make sure that the Mansa would have plenty of money, they assembled some 80 to 100 camel-loads of gold dust, each load weighing about 300 pounds [135 kg].

By the time the caravan was finally assembled, it had become possibly the biggest moving crowd that Africa had ever seen. . . . Some sources say that the caravan consisted of 60,000 people! . . .

Mansa Musa's glittering caravan entered Cairo, Egypt, in July 1324, and he was an immediate sensation. The Sultan of Cairo honored the distinguished visitor from the western **Sudan** with elaborate ceremonies. . . .

Sudan: name for savanna area south of the Sahara

Mansa Musa's generosity was probably as impressive as his religious faith. He freely gave gifts in the holy cities of Mecca and Medina, and he also gave generously to all those who performed some service for him. On his return trip from Arabia to Mali, Mansa Musa passed through Egypt once more and reportedly "spread the waves of his generosity all over Cairo. There was no one, officer of the court or holder of any official job, who did not receive a sum of gold from him.". . .

The enormous prestige that came to Mansa Musa as a result of his fabulous hajj has been well documented. In time the fame of the Emperor of Mali spread to Europe. In the fourteenth century European mapmakers produced a series of [maps] which marked the position of Mali and **depicted** the wealth of its emperor. . . .

depicted: showed

At the height of its powers under Mansa Musa, the empire of Mali covered an area about equal to that of Western Europe.

The political **subdivisions** within Mali were well organized. . . . [The provinces] were so well policed that merchants and their caravans could travel through them without any fear of robbers. . . .

subdivisions: districts

The industrious people of Mali skillfully put their country's resources to use. Every large city or middle-sized village had its own craftsmen, woodcarvers, silversmiths, goldsmiths, coppersmiths, blacksmiths, weavers, tanners, and dyers.

But the greatest source of income for the government of Mali was neither agriculture nor manufacturing. It was trade. Having replaced Ghana as the greatest power of the western Sudan, Mali also took over the trans-Saharan gold-salt trade. . . .

The cross-desert journey was long, always hard, and often dangerous. Yet the caravans kept coming in greater numbers because the profits from trade in Mali apparently made it worth the effort and risk. Arab travelers reported that even the common people of Mali seemed to be well-off. They marveled that some of the Malian households were lighted at night by candles, which were not common items in those days.

Under Mansa Musa's rule Mali became the greatest empire in Africa. What would it have been like to visit this empire in the 1300s and get to know the people of Mali? To find out, read the next document on pages 112-113.

Source: Daniel Chu and Elliott Skinner, *A Glorious Age in Africa*. Trenton, NJ: Africa World Press, Inc., 1990.

Observations
of a 14th-Century Traveler

by Ibn Battutah, 1352–1353

In 1352, 20 years after Mansa Musa died, a Moroccan writer named Muhammed Ibn Abdullah Ibn Battutah (1304-1369) visited the empire of Mali. A world traveler, Ibn Battutah had journeyed to India, China, and many parts of Africa, Europe, and southwest Asia. He found Mali one of the most interesting places he had ever visited. In a book he wrote in Arabic about his travels, Ibn Battutah described life in the royal palace and the customs of the people of Mali. As you read the excerpt below from Ibn Battutah's book, notice how King Mansa Sulayman of Mali, Mansa Musa's grandson, greets visitors. How does the king make himself appear great? How does this firsthand description by Ibn Battutah compare to the more recent account of the Mali Empire described in the document on pages 110-111?

On certain days the **sultan** [Mansa Sulayman] holds audiences in the palace yard, where there is a platform under a tree, with three steps; this they call the *pempi*. It is carpeted with silk and has cushions placed on it. [Over it] is raised the umbrella...made of silk, **surmounted** by a bird in gold, about the size of a falcon. The sultan comes out of a door in a corner of the palace....The sultan is preceded by his musicians, who carry gold and silver two-stringed guitars, and behind him come three hundred armed slaves. He walks in a leisurely fashion, affecting a very slow movement, and even stops from time to time. On reaching the *pempi* he stops and looks round the assembly, then ascends it in the **sedate** manner of a preacher ascending a **mosque**-pulpit. As he takes his seat the drums, trumpets, and bugles are sounded....

Among the admirable qualities of these people, the following are to be noted:

1. The small number of acts of injustice that one finds there; for the Negroes are of all peoples those who most **abhor** injustice. The sultan pardons no one who is guilty of it.

2. The complete and general safety one enjoys throughout the land. The traveler has no more reason than the man who stays at home to fear...thieves....

sultan: king

surmounted: topped

sedate: calm
mosque: Muslim house of worship

abhor: hate

3. The blacks do not **confiscate** the goods of [North Africans] who die in their country, not even when these consist of big treasures. They deposit them, on the contrary, with a man of confidence among the [North Africans] until those who have a right to the goods present themselves and take possession.

confiscate: seize

4. They make their prayers punctually; they **assiduously** attend their meetings of the faithful, and punish their children if these should fail in this. On Fridays, anyone who is late at the mosque will find nowhere to pray, the crowd is so great. Their custom is to send their servants to the mosque to spread their prayer-mats in the due and proper place, and to remain there until they, the masters, should arrive. These mats are made of the leaves of a tree resembling a palm, but one without fruit.

assiduously: devotedly

5. The Negroes wear fine white garments on Fridays. If by chance a man has no more than one shirt or a soiled **tunic**, at least he washes it before putting it on to go to public prayer.

tunic: short jacket

6. They **zealously** learn the Koran by heart.

zealously: enthusiastically

Ibn Battutah was one of the great travel writers of his time. His descriptions of life in the three different continents he visited in the 1300s are among the liveliest and most interesting travel books ever written. His descriptions of Mali are especially important because less than 100 years after his visit the empire began to decline. In the late 1400s the Songhai Empire conquered Mali, and the once-great Mali empire collapsed.

Source: Basil Davidson, *African Civilization Revisited*. Trenton, NJ: Africa World Press, 1991.

CAPTURED!

by Olaudah Equiano, 1789

When Europeans arrived in Africa in the late 1400s, they greatly expanded the slave trade that Arab merchants had been carrying on for hundreds of years. They also began to forcibly transport Africans overseas to the Americas. In 1756 Olaudah Equiano (1745-1797) was an 11-year-old boy living in the village of Benin in what is today Nigeria. One day slave traders came to his village and changed his life forever. In his autobiography, written in 1789, Equiano described this fateful day and what happened afterward. As you read the following excerpt from his autobiography, think of the horrors he describes. How does he manage to endure this experience?

One day, when all our people were gone out to their works as usual, and only I and my dear sister were left to mind the house, two men and a woman got over our walls, and in a moment seized us both; and, without giving us time to cry out, or make resistance, they **stopped** our mouths, and ran off with us into the nearest wood. Here they tied our hands, and continued to carry us as far as they could, till night came on, when we reached a small house, where the robbers halted for refreshment, and spent the night. We were then unbound; but were unable to take any food; and, being quite overpowered by fatigue and grief, our only relief was some sleep, which **allayed** our misfortune for a short time.

    The next morning we left the house, and continued travelling all the day. For a long time we had kept [to] the woods, but at last we came into a road which I believed I knew. I had now some hopes of being **delivered**; for we had advanced but a little way before I discovered some people at a distance, [and] I began to cry out for their assistance; but my cries had no other effect than to make them tie me [tighter] and stop my mouth, and then they put me into a large sack. They also stopped my sister's mouth, and tied her hands; and in this manner we proceeded till we were out of the sight of these people.

stopped: stuffed something into

allayed: eased

delivered: rescued

When we went to rest the following night they offered us some **victuals**; but we refused them; and the only comfort we had was in being in one another's arms all that night, and bathing each other with our tears. But alas! We were soon deprived of even the smallest comfort of weeping together. The next day proved a day of greater sorrow than I had yet experienced; for my sister and I were then separated, while we lay clasped in each other's arms: it was in vain that we **besought** them not to part us: she was torn from me, and immediately carried away, while I was left in a state of **distraction** not to be described. I cried and grieved continually; and for several days did not eat any thing but what they forced into my mouth. . . .

victuals: food

besought: begged

distraction: worry

From the time I left my own nation I always found somebody that understood me till I came to the sea coast. The languages of different nations did not totally differ, nor were they so **copious** as those of the Europeans, particularly the English. They were therefore easily learned; and, while I was journeying thus through Africa, I **acquired** two or three different **tongues**.

copious: full of words

acquired: learned
tongues: languages

In this manner I had been travelling for a considerable time, when one evening, to my great surprise, whom should I see brought to the house where I was but my dear sister? As soon as she saw me she gave a loud shriek, and ran into my arms—I was quite overpowered: neither of us could speak, but, for a considerable time, clung to each other in mutual embraces, unable to do any thing but weep. Our meeting affected all who saw us; and indeed I must acknowledge, in honour of those **sable** destroyers of human rights, that I never met with any ill treatment, or saw any offered to their slaves, except tying them, when necessary, to keep them from running away. When these people knew we were brother and sister, they **indulged** us to be together; . . . and thus for a while we forgot our misfortunes in the joy of being together; but even this small comfort was soon to have an end; for scarcely had the **fatal** morning appeared, when she was again torn from me forever! I was now more miserable, if possible, than before. . . .

sable: dark

indulged: allowed

fatal: dreaded

I continued to travel, sometimes by land, sometimes by water, through different countries, and various nations, till, at the end of six or seven months after I had been kidnapped I arrived at the sea coast.

After arriving on the west coast of Africa, Olaudah Equiano was sold to European slave traders. They transported him overseas to Barbados. Equiano was one of more than 14 million Africans kidnapped and carried by force to the Americas from the late 1400s to the 1800s. Equiano, however, was more fortunate than most. A British sea captain later bought him and made him a sailor. Although enslaved, Equiano managed to earn money and bought his freedom in 1766. As a free man, he traveled the world and explored the northern Arctic. Years later he settled in England and wrote his autobiography. The book was widely read in the 1790s and helped the growth of the anti-slavery movement.

Source: Olaudah Equiano, *The Interesting Narrative of the Life of Olaudah Equiano, or Gustavus Vassa, the African. Written by Himself*. London: W. Durell, 1791.

Attack on the Congo River: One View

by Henry M. Stanley, 1885

During the Age of Imperialism, which began in the mid-1800s, European powers conquered much of Africa and divided the continent into colonies. During these years Europeans and Africans often failed to understand each other's cultures. The document below and the next document on pages 118-119 give an example of one of these misunderstandings. In 1877 a reporter named Henry Stanley explored the Congo River, known today as the Zaire River, in central Africa. Stanley was an American citizen, but his trip was being paid for by the government of Belgium. At a spot near where the Congo River joins the Lualaba River, Stanley and his traveling party encountered a group of the Basoko. Eight years later Stanley wrote a book describing this encounter. As you read the excerpt below from Stanley's book, notice some of the harsh terms he uses to describe the Basoko. What does Stanley believe the Basoko are trying to do to him? After you read this excerpt, compare Stanley's view of the encounter to the description by Chief Mojimba, a Basoko leader, on pages 118-119.

At 2 P.M., we emerge out of the shelter of the deeply wooded banks [at the place where the Congo River joins the Lualaba River.] As soon as we have fairly entered its waters, we see a great **concourse** of canoes hovering about some islets, which stud the middle of the stream. The canoe-men, standing up, give a loud shout as they **discern** us, and blow their horns louder than ever. We pull briskly on to gain the right bank...when, looking up stream, we see a sight that sends the blood tingling through every nerve and fibre of the body...a **flotilla** of gigantic canoes bearing down upon us, which both in size and numbers utterly **eclipse** anything encountered **hitherto**! Instead of aiming for the right bank, we form in line, and keep straight down

concourse: crowd

discern: notice

flotilla: fleet
eclipse: surpass
hitherto: before

river, the boat taking position behind. Yet after a moment's reflection, as I note the numbers of the savages, and the daring manner of the pursuit, and the apparent desire of our canoes to abandon the steady **compact** line, I give the order to drop anchor. . . .

We have sufficient time to take a view of the mighty force bearing down on us, and to count the number of war-vessels, which have been collected from the [Congo-Lualaba River]. There are fifty-four of them! A monster canoe leads the way, with two rows of upstanding paddles, forty men on a side. . . . All the paddles are headed with ivory balls, every head bears a feather crown, every arm shows gleaming white ivory **armlets**. . . .

The crashing sound of large drums, a hundred blasts from ivory horns, and a thrilling chant from two thousand human throats, do not tend to soothe our nerves or to increase our confidence. . . . We have no time to pray, or to take [a] sentimental look at the savage world, or even to breathe a sad farewell to it. So many other things have to be done speedily and well.

As the **foremost** canoe comes rushing down, and its **consorts** on either side beating the water into foam . . . I turn to take a last look at our people, and say to them:

"Boys, be firm as iron; wait until you see the first spear, and then take good aim. Don't fire all at once. Keep aiming until you are sure of your man. Don't think of running away, for only your guns can save you.". . .

The monster canoe aims straight for my boat, as though it would run us down; but, when within fifty yards [45 m] off, swerves aside and, when nearly opposite, the warriors above the manned **prow** let fly their spears, and on either side there is a noise of rushing bodies. But every sound is soon lost in the ripping, crackling **musketry**. For five minutes we are so absorbed in firing that we take no note of anything else; but at the end of that time we are made aware that the enemy is **reforming** about 200 yards [180 m] above us.

Our blood is up now. It is a murderous world, and we feel for the first time that we hate the filthy, **vulturous ghouls** who inhabit it. We therefore lift our anchors, and pursue them upstream along the right bank, until rounding a point we see their villages. We make straight for the banks, and continue the fight in the village streets and those who have landed, hunt them out into the woods, and there only sound the retreat, having returned the daring cannibals the compliment of a visit.

compact: closely united

armlets: bracelets worn high up on the arm

foremost: front
consorts: accompanying boats

prow: front of a boat

musketry: gunfire

reforming: organizing again

vulturous: like vultures
ghouls: evil beings

Like many other Europeans during the Age of Imperialism, Henry Stanley looked down on Africans. In his encounters with the Basoko people, Stanley believed he understood the situation correctly and was right in attacking. Stanley, however, was not the only one to give a description of this encounter. For a different view, read the next document on pages 118-119.

Source: Henry M. Stanley, *Through the Dark Continent.* New York: Harper and Brothers, 1885.

Attack on the Congo River: Another View

by Mojimba, 1907

In 1907, 30 years after Henry Stanley and the Basoko people encountered each other in what is today the nation of Zaire, Chief Mojimba, a Basoko leader, described the same encounter to a Belgian missionary. As you read Mojimba's account, compare it to Stanley's account that you read on pages 116–117. On what parts do they agree? On what parts do they differ? What do these differences tell you about relationships between Europeans and Africans during the Age of Imperialism?

When we heard that the man with the white flesh was journeying down the Lualaba [River] we were open-mouthed with astonishment. We stood still. All night long the drums announced the strange news—a man with white flesh. That man, we said to ourselves, has a white skin. He must have got that from the river-kingdom. He will be one of our brothers who were drowned in the river. All life comes from the water and in the water, he has found life. Now he is coming back to us, he is coming home. . . .

We will prepare a feast, I ordered, we will go to meet our brother and escort him into the village with rejoicing! We **donned** our ceremonial **garb**. We assembled the great canoes. We listened for the gong which would announce our brother's presence on the Lualaba. Presently the cry was heard: He is approaching. . . . Now he enters the river! Halloh! We swept forward, my canoe leading, the others following with songs of joy and with dancing to meet the first white man our eyes had beheld, and to him honor.

donned: put on
garb: clothing

But as we drew near his canoes there were loud **reports**, *bang! bang!* and **fire-staves** spat bits of iron at us. We were paralyzed with fright; our mouths hung wide open and we could not shut them. Things such as we had never seen, never heard of, never dreamed of—they were the work of evil spirits! Several of my men plunged into the water. . . . What for? Did they fly to safety? No—for others fell down also, in the canoes. Some screamed dreadfully—others were silent—they were dead, and blood flowed from little holes in their bodies. "War! that is war!" I yelled. "Go back!" The canoes sped back to our village with all the strength our spirits could **impart** to our arms.

reports: sounds
fire-staves: guns

impart: give to

That was no brother! That was the worst enemy our country had ever seen.

And still those bangs went on; the long staves spat fire, flying pieces of iron whistled around us, fell into the water with a hissing sound, and our brothers continued to fall. We fled into our village—they came after us. We fled into the forest and flung ourselves on the ground. When we returned that evening, our eyes **beheld** fearful things; our brothers, dead, dying, bleeding, our village **plundered** and burned, and the water full of dead bodies.

beheld: saw

plundered: robbed

The robbers and murderers had disappeared.

Now tell me: has the white man dealt fairly by us? O, do not speak to me of him! You call us wicked men, but you white men are much more wicked! You think, because you have guns you can take away our land and our possessions. You have sickness in your heads, for that is not justice.

The Basokos' ceremonial throwing of spears to greet Henry Stanley in 1877 was actually very similar to the European custom of firing cannons to salute an honored visitor. But as was often the case during the late 1800s, Europeans and Africans failed to understand each other. In the 1900s, many Africans began fighting to regain their independence and freedom, and to bring an end to colonial rule. To learn more about this movement, read the next two documents on pages 120-125.

Source: Heinrich Schiffers, *The Quest for Africa*. New York: G. P. Putnam's Sons, 1958.

THE MAN WHO SHARED HIS HUT

by Jomo Kenyatta, 1938

In the middle 1800s European powers began dividing up the continent of Africa into colonies by adopting a policy called imperialism. Under imperialism Africans had little control over their land. Europeans set up their own laws and ruled most of the continent. In the 1900s many Africans began fighting to regain their independence. One of the leaders of this fight was Jomo Kenyatta (1897-1978), a Kikuyu who was born near Nairobi, Kenya. In 1938 Kenyatta wrote Facing Mount Kenya, *a study of the Kikuyu people and culture. In this book, Kenyatta wrote the following tale, a story about the history of imperialism and how European nations had treated Africa. But in this story, called* The Man Who Shared His Hut, *no European nations are named. Instead, all the characters except one are animals. As you read this story, try to figure out who and what the different characters represent. How does Kenyatta describe the relationship between Africans and Europeans?*

Once upon a time an elephant made a friendship with a man. One day a heavy thunderstorm broke out, the elephant went to his friend, who had a little hut at the edge of the forest, and said to him: "My dear good man, will you please let me put my trunk inside your hut to keep it out of this **torrential** rain?"

torrential: pouring

The man, seeing what situation his friend was in, replied: "My dear good elephant, my hut is very small, but there is room for your trunk and myself. Please put your trunk in gently."

The elephant thanked his friend, saying: "You have done me a good deed and one day I shall return your kindness."

But what followed? As soon as the elephant put his trunk inside the hut, slowly he pushed his head inside, and finally flung the man out in the rain, and then lay down comfortably inside his friend's hut, saying: "My dear good friend, your skin is harder than mine, and as there is not enough room for both of us, you can afford to remain in the rain while I am protecting my delicate skin from the hailstorm."

The man, seeing what his friend had done to him, started to grumble, the animals in the nearby forest heard the noise and came to see what was the matter. All stood around listening to the heated argument between the man and his friend the elephant.

In this **turmoil** the lion came along roaring, and said in a loud voice: "Don't you all know that I am the King of the Jungle! How dare anyone disturb the peace of my kingdom?"

turmoil: confusion

On hearing this the elephant, who was one of the high ministers in the jungle kingdom, replied in a soothing voice, and said: "My Lord, there is no disturbance of the peace in your kingdom. I have only been having a little discussion with my friend here as to the possession of this little hut which your **lordship** sees me occupying."

lordship: title of respect

The lion, who wanted to have "peace and tranquility" in his kingdom, replied in a noble voice, saying: "I command my ministers to appoint a **Commission of Inquiry** to go thoroughly into this matter and report accordingly." He then turned to the man and said: "You have done well by establishing friendship with my people, especially with the elephant who is one of my honorable ministers of state. Do not grumble any more, your hut is not lost to you. Wait until the sitting of my **Imperial Commission**, and then you will be given plenty of opportunity to state your case. I am sure that you will be pleased with the findings of the Commission."

Commission of Inquiry: panel of investigation

Imperial Commission: government panel

The man was very pleased by these sweet words from the King of the Jungle, and innocently waited for his opportunity, in the belief that, naturally, the hut would be returned to him.

The elephant, obeying the command of his master, got busy with other ministers to appoint the Commission of Inquiry. The following elders of the jungle were appointed to sit on the Commission: (1) Mr. Rhinoceros; (2) Mr. Buffalo; (3) Mr. Alligator; (4) The **Rt. Hon.** Mr. Fox to act as chairman; and (5) Mr. Leopard to act as Secretary to the Commission.

Rt. Hon.: Right Honorable, title of respect

On seeing the **personnel**, the man protested and asked if it was not necessary to include in this Commission a member from his side. But he was told that it was impossible, since no one from his side was well enough educated to understand the **intricacy** of jungle law. Further, that there was nothing to fear, for the members of the Commission were all men of **repute** for their **impartiality** in justice, and as they were gentlemen chosen by God to look after the interests of races less adequately **endowed** with teeth and claws, he might rest assured that

personnel: people appointed

intricacy: complicated matters

repute: honor
impartiality: fairness
endowed: furnished

they would investigate the matter with the greatest care and report impartially.

The Commission sat to take the evidence. The Rt. Hon. Mr. Elephant was first called. He came along with a superior air, brushing his tusks with a **sapling** which Mrs. Elephant had provided, and in an **authoritative** voice said: "Gentlemen of the Jungle, there is no need for me to waste your valuable time in relating a story which I am sure you all know. I have always regarded it as my duty to protect the interests of my friends, and this appears to have caused the misunderstanding between myself and my friend here. He invited me to save his hut from being blown away by a hurricane. As the hurricane had gained access owing to the unoccupied space in the hut, I considered it necessary, in my friend's own interests, to turn the undeveloped space to a more economic use by sitting in it myself; a duty which any of you would undoubtedly have performed with equal readiness in similar circumstances."

After hearing the Rt. Hon. Mr. Elephant's **conclusive** evidence, the Commission called Mr. Hyena and other elders of the jungle, who all supported what Mr. Elephant had said. They then called the man, who began to give his own account of the dispute. But the Commission cut him short, saying: "My good man, please confine yourself to **relevant** issues. We have already heard the circumstances from various **unbiased** sources; all we wish you to tell us is whether the undeveloped space in your hut was occupied by anyone else before Mr. Elephant **assumed** his position?"

The man began to say: "No, but—" But at this point the Commission declared that they had heard sufficient evidence from both sides and retired to consider their decision.

After enjoying a delicious meal at the expense of the Rt. Hon. Mr. Elephant, they reached their verdict, called the man, and declared as follows: "In our opinion this dispute has arisen through a **regrettable** misunderstanding due to the backwardness of your ideas. We consider that Mr. Elephant has fulfilled his sacred duty of protecting your interests. As it is clearly for your good that the space should be put to its most economic use, and as you yourself have not yet reached the stage of **expansion** which would enable you to fill it, we consider it necessary to arrange a compromise to suit both parties. Mr. Elephant shall continue his occupation of your hut, but we give you permission to look for a site where you can build another hut more suited to your needs, and we will see that you are well protected.

The man, having no **alternative**, and fearing that his refusal might expose him to the teeth and claws of members of the Commission, did as they suggested. But no sooner had he built another hut than Mr. Rhinoceros charged in with his horn lowered and ordered the man to quit. A Royal Commission was again appointed to look into the matter, and the same finding was given. This procedure was repeated until Mr. Buffalo, Mr. Leopard, Mr. Hyena and the rest were all accommodated with new huts.

sapling: young tree
authoritative: official

conclusive: convincing

relevant: timely, important
unbiased: fair, open-minded
assumed: took

regrettable: unfortunate

expansion: growth

alternative: other choice

Then the man decided that he must adopt an effective method of protection, since Commissions of Inquiry did not seem to be of any use to him. He sat down and said: "*Ng'enda thi ndeagaga motegi*," which literally means "there is nothing that treads on the earth that cannot be trapped," or in other words, you can fool people for a time, but not for ever.

Early one morning, when the huts already occupied by the jungle lords were all beginning to decay and fall to pieces, he went out and built a bigger and better hut a little distance away. No sooner had Mr. Rhinoceros seen it than he came rushing in, only to find that Mr. Elephant was already inside, sound asleep. Mr. Leopard next came in at the window, Mr. Lion, Mr. Fox, and Mr. Buffalo entered the doors, while Mr. Hyena howled for a place in the shade and Mr. Alligator basked on the roof.

Presently they all began disputing about their rights of penetration, and from disputing they came to fighting, and while they were all embroiled together the man set the hut on fire and burnt it to the ground, jungle lords and all.

Then he went home, saying: "Peace is costly, but it's worth the expense," and lived happily ever after.

Just like the man in the story, some people in Africa turned to violence to rid their land of European imperialists. Kenya regained its independence from Britain in 1963, and Jomo Kenyatta later served as its president.

Source: Jomo Kenyatta, *Facing Mount Kenya*. London: Martin Secker & Warburg Ltd., 1953.

THE VISION THAT I SEE

by Kwame Nkrumah, 1953

During the 1800s European nations divided Africa into colonies and ruled almost the entire continent. In the middle 1900s, however, many Africans began fighting to regain their independence and freedom, and to bring an end to colonialism. One leader of this fight was Jomo Kenyatta, who wrote the story that appears on pages 120-123. Another major leader in the struggle against imperialism and colonial rule was Kwame Nkrumah (kwäm′ ē en krü′ mə, 1909-1972), a member of the Nzima people. Nkrumah was born in Nkroful, a village in the British colony called the Gold Coast. Although imprisoned for his beliefs, Nkrumah continued to fight for an end to colonialism. In 1953 he delivered a speech expressing his hopes for the Gold Coast and the rest of Africa. As you read an excerpt from this speech, notice Nkrumah's goals and beliefs. In what ways does Nkrumah use history to support his ideas?

The subject I have chosen to address you on this evening is "The Vision that I See.". . . It is better to be free to manage, or mismanage, your own affairs, than not to be free to mismanage or manage your own affairs. . . .

You know, **Providence** must be at work. I don't want to go back into history because I might be repeating sad memories but imagine the whole question of the slave trade, how Negroes from the West Coast of Africa were all carried over to the United States. And look into Negro history. You see the suffering and **tribulation** these people went through, and yet they survived in the United States of America and the **West Indies**. That's Providence. God Himself came, and, as in the days of Moses and the Israelites, who spent so many hard years in Egypt under all kinds of suffering, what was the result? The day came, yes, when God Himself brought up the man, and that man led them out of Egypt. A greater **exodus** is coming in Africa today, and that exodus will be established when there is a united, free and independent West Africa.

Again I don't want to bore you with history. It is a sad story. Look at the whole country of Africa today. With the possible exception of Liberia, Egypt and Ethiopia, the entire country is divided and sub-divided. . . .

Africa for the Africans! Is this some new concept that has come into being?. . .no! We are bringing into being another Africa for Africans, with a different concept, and that concept is what? A free and independent state in Africa. We want to be able to govern ourselves

providence: God's guidance of human destiny

tribulation: pain

West Indies: Caribbean islands

exodus: mass departure

in this country of ours without outside interference. And we are going to see that it is done.

Ladies and gentlemen, a people without a Government of their own is silly and absurd. Let us therefore **forge ahead** and develop our own countries, politically and economically. We must work for a greater glory and majesty, greater than the civilizations of our **grandsires**, the civilization of Ghana, the civilization of the [Mali] Empire and the civilization of the [Songhai] Empire. Long before the slave trade, long before Imperialistic rivalries in Africa began, civilizations of the Ghana Empire were in existence. And here, you even discover that at one time, at the great University of Timbuktu, Africans **versed** in the science of art and learning were studying their works translated in Greek and Hebrew, and at the same time exchanging professors with the University of Cordova in Spain. These were the brains, and today they come and tell us that we cannot do it. No, give the African a chance and he will show you that he can do it. . . .

And not only that, there have been great Africans, . . . who have distinguished themselves in the **cabinet** and in the field of battle. I need mention only a few: Anthony Amu, a man from the **Gold Coast**, was the first African to graduate with the degree of doctor of philosophy from the University of Wittenberg. Amu became professor of philosophy at the University of Berlin, 1954. He was an African. He came and died in the Gold Coast. That was a brain. . . . And not only that. In the field of battle there is **Toussaint**. Yes, these are the men who have put up the torch of light that we men of today, the youth of Africa, want to learn and **emulate** them, forge ahead, until Africa is **redeemed**, until we are free to manage or mismanage our own affairs in this country.

We believe in the equality of races. We believe in the freedom of the people of all races. We believe in cooperation. In fact it has been one of my **theses** that in this struggle of ours, in this struggle to redeem Africa, we are fighting not against race and colour and creed. We are fighting against a system—a system which degrades and exploits, and wherever we find that system, that system must be **liquidated**. Yes, we believe in peace and cooperation among all countries, but we also **abhor** Colonialism and Imperialism. We abhor man's inhumanity against man. . . .

We must learn to live together. The age of **aristocracy** is gone. God made all of us equal. In the sight of God we are one. We must combine. . . .

forge ahead: move forward

grandsires: male ancestors

versed: educated

cabinet: government

Gold Coast: present-day country of Ghana

Toussaint: Toussaint L'Ouverture, the liberator of Haiti

emulate: equal or surpass

redeemed: freed

theses: beliefs

liquidated: destroyed

abhor: hate

aristocracy: government by a privileged upper class

Four years after delivering this speech, Kwame Nkrumah helped to lead his country to independence. On March 6, 1957, the colony of the Gold Coast became the free nation of Ghana. Nkrumah served as president of Ghana from 1960 to 1966 and inspired many other Africans to fight to regain their independence. One by one during the 1950s and 1960s, Africans liberated their nations from European rule.

Source: Bankole Timothy, *Kwame Nkrumah—From Cradle to Grave.* Dorchester, Dorset, Great Britain: The Gavin Press Limited, 1981.

In the Streets of Accra

by Andrew Amankwa Opoku, 1958

What is it like to be in the bustling city of Accra, the capital of Ghana? Take a tour of this large West African city with poet Andrew Amankwa Opoku. Born in 1912, Opoku has been a sculptor, farmer, and teacher, as well as a poet. In what ways does he describe Accra as a lively place?

This is the road!
This is the main highway!
Shouters, we are in the street!
Shooters, restrain your guns!
This is Accra.

This is the town,
The street of the **municipality**.   **municipality:** city
Strangers, we are in the streets.
Townsmen, stretch out your sleeping mats
This is Accra.

This is the beach,
This is the pilgrim's **haven**—   **haven:** shelter
A vast town, but where is the sleeping place?
A great crowd but where is an acquaintance?
This is Accra. . . .

What is this buzzing noise?
What means this paa! paa!
Is this where you walk daily?
And you have lived so long!
This is Accra.

Stay let me have a look.
If such a collection of merchandise
Crowd even the streets so,
What of the market?
This is Accra.

126

What does this ringing of the bell signify?
This shouting and tinkling noise
This running in the blazing sun
This sweat that is skimmed off with the hands?
This is Accra.

Could women monopolize a street so?
In vain you try to elbow your way through
If you stop they will roll over you
If you turn away a vehicle is knocking you down.
This is Accra.

If it is like this on the edge, how will it be in the depth?
So grand as it is at the backyard
How will it be inside at the dance?
How the electric lights **scintillate**!   scintillate: sparkle
This is Accra. . . .

Andrew Amankwa Opoku is one of Ghana's leading poets of the 20th century. If you were to write a poem about the place where you live, what sights and sounds would you describe?

Source: Barbara Nolen, ed., *Africa Is Thunder and Wonder.* New York: Charles Scribner's Sons, 1972.

Fall Rain Fall Rain by Ladysmith Black Mambazo, 1987

What is the most important thing that falls from the sky? To most people throughout the world the most important thing is rain. Without rain most crops can't grow and animals can't live. In the following song, the South African band Ladysmith Black Mambazo combine rock and Zulu rhythms to create a chant that celebrates rain. What other parts of nature does this song describe?

Oh rain, oh rain
Oh rain, oh rain, beautiful rain
Don't disturb me, beautiful rain
Oh come, never come, oh come, never come
Oh come to me beautiful rain
Rain
Rain, rain, rain, rain
Beautiful rain
Rain, rain, rain, rain
Beautiful rain
Oh come, never come, oh come, never come
Oh come to me beautiful rain
When the sun says good night to the mountain
I am dreaming of the sun
Say good night
When the sun says good night to the mountain
I am dreaming of the sun
Say good night
When the sun goes down, the birds on the trees
Are singing sweet for the night
When the sun says good night to the mountain
I am dreaming of the sun
Say good night
When the sun goes down, the birds on the trees
Are singing sweet for the night
When the sun says good night to the mountain
I am dreaming of the sun
Say good night
Rain
Rain, rain, rain, rain
Beautiful rain
Rain, rain, rain, rain
Beautiful rain
Oh come, never come, oh come, never come
Oh come to me beautiful rain

Source: Ladysmith Black Mambazo, *Intokozo.* Gallo Music Productions.

Test of a Friendship

Yoruba Tale Retold by Barbara Walker, 1968

As the story on pages 102-103 showed, griots, or storytellers, play an important role in many parts of West Africa. Griots tell stories and help to pass on their people's culture, values, and history. Often these stories and tales have an important message or lesson to teach. The tale below is from the Yoruba people of Nigeria. What is the griot's message in this tale?

Long ago and far away there were two good friends named Olaleye [ō lä le ye] and Omoteji [ō mō te jē]. Each had a farm directly across the footpath from the other, and day after day they would greet each other as they went about their work. Finally their great friendship raised a question in the heart of their wise neighbor, and he determined to test their friendship for one another.

Secretly, he made a hat for himself which was red on one side and green on the other. Then one day after putting on his new hat, he strolled along the footpath.

"Good morning!" he greeted Omoteji as the good fellow bent over the **yams** in his field.

yams: sweet potatoes

"Good morning," answered Omoteji, standing up to stretch himself a little from his bending. "I see you have a fine new red hat."

"Oh, yes," answered the other. "I am happy that you noticed it." And he set his new hat more firmly upon his head. He walked on along the footpath, and Omoteji returned to his work.

A few moments later, he saw Olaleye pulling weeds in his yam patch. "Good morning, Olaleye!" he called.

Olaleye looked up and returned the man's greeting. Then, "Oho," said he. "I see you have a fine new green hat."

129

"Yes, indeed," answered the neighbor. "I looked a long time before I found the one I wanted." After a moment's chatting with Olaleye, he went on his way down the footpath, well satisfied with himself.

When the sun stood at the **zenith**, Olaleye stopped his work and went to eat his lunch with his good friend Omoteji. As they ate, Omoteji said, "Did you notice the fine new red hat our neighbor had?"

zenith: highest point

"*Red* hat!" exclaimed Olaleye. "My friend, you must have been a little dazzled by the sun."

"What do you mean?" asked Omoteji.

"It wasn't a red hat our neighbor was wearing. It was a *green* hat," explained Olaleye. And he smiled at his friend's mistake.

"A green hat!" exclaimed Omoteji. "Oh, no, my friend. It was *not* green. It was red. I know, for I remarked on it to our neighbor."

"And so did I," returned Olaleye, becoming a little impatient.

Omoteji, irritated by his friend's impatience, continued to argue that the hat was red, while Olaleye for his part maintained that the hat was green. From words, the quarrel grew to blows, and Omoteji was still **reeling** from Olaleye's stout blow when their neighbor hurried toward them.

reeling: staggering

"What's this!" he exclaimed. "You two fighting! I thought you were the best of friends. How can friends come to blows this way?"

Olaleye and Omoteji, their excitement somewhat cooled by this interruption, stared at their neighbor. This time, Omoteji saw the green side of the hat, and Olaleye saw the red side.

"Oh, my friend Omoteji," said Olaleye quickly. "You were right, after all. Our neighbor's hat *is* red."

"Oh, no," returned Omoteji earnestly. "I was wrong and you were right. I must have been dazzled by the sun, after all. Our neighbor's new hat *is* green."

Their difference of opinion would shortly have led to blows again if their neighbor had not laughed. Taking off his hat, he showed them the red side and then the green one. "Look here, my friends," he said. "You were both right about the hat. But you were both wrong about your friendship. You are not the best of friends if you cannot examine both sides of a question without anger, whether it be a hat or whether it be something more important."

"You are right," declared Olaleye. "One never knows about a friendship until it has been put to a test. As for me, a hat can be either green or red. It doesn't matter, as long as I have my good friend, Omoteji."

"Nor does it matter to me," agreed Omoteji.

And **thenceforth** the two were stronger friends than ever.

thenceforth: from then on

In gathering together to hear and respond to griots' stories like the one above, many people in West Africa share their beliefs and pass down their traditions. West Africans also pass down their traditions by writing literature. For an example of West African literature, read the document on pages 131-133.

Source: Barbara Walker, *The Dancing Palm Tree and Other Nigerian Folktales.* 1968.

THE PRAISE-SINGER

by Camara Laye, 1954

For thousands of years, gold has been an important metal to people all over the world. In West Africa the tradition of crafting gold has been passed down from generation to generation for as long as people can remember. The excerpt below is from **The Dark Child**, *an autobiography written in 1954 by a famous novelist from Guinea named Camara Laye (1924-1980). As you read this excerpt about Laye's memories of his childhood in a West African village, notice the different roles played by people in the community who take part in the gold-crafting process. What are some of the traditions that Laye describes?*

Of all the different kinds of work my father engaged in, none fascinated me so much as his skill with gold. No other occupation was so noble, no other needed such a delicate touch. And then, every time he worked in gold it was like a festival—indeed it *was* a festival—that broke the **monotony** of ordinary working days.

So, if a woman, accompanied by a go-between, crossed the **threshold** of the workshop, I followed her in at once. I knew what she wanted: she had brought some gold, and had come to ask my father to transform it into a **trinket**. . . .

monotony: dull routine

threshold: entryway

trinket: small ornament

These women never came alone. They knew my father had other things to do than make trinkets. And even when he had the time, they knew they were not the first to ask a favor of him, and that, consequently, they would not be served before others. . . .

Therefore, to **enhance** their chances of being served quickly and to more easily persuade my father to interrupt the work before him, they used to request the services of an official praise-singer, a go-between, arranging in advance the fee they were to pay him for his good offices.

The go-between installed himself in the workshop, turned up his cora, which is our harp, and began to sing my father's praises. This was always a great event for me: I heard recalled the **lofty** deeds of my father's ancestors and their names from the earliest times. . . .

[My father] would take the clay pot that was kept specially for **smelting** gold, and would pour the grains into it. . . .

When finally the gold began to melt I could have shouted aloud—and perhaps we all would have if we had not been forbidden to make a sound. . . .

The woman for whom the trinket was being made, and who had come often to see how the work was progressing, would arrive for the final time, not wanting to miss a moment of this spectacle—as marvelous to her as to us—when the gold wire, which my father had succeeded in drawing out from the mass of **molten** gold and charcoal, was transformed into a trinket. . . .

No one—no one at all—would be more enchanted than she as my father slowly turned the trinket back and forth between his fingers to display its perfection. Not even the praise-singer whose business it was to register excitement would be more excited than she. Throughout this **metamorphosis** he did not stop speaking faster and ever faster, increasing his **tempo, accelerating** his praises and **flatteries** as the trinket took shape, shouting to the skies my father's skill.

For the praise-singer took a curious part—I should say rather that it was direct and effective—in the work. . . . He shouted aloud in joy. He plucked his *cora* like a man inspired. He sweated as if he were the trinket-maker, as if he were my father, as if the trinket were his creation. . . . He was a man who created his song out of some deep inner necessity. And when my father, after having **soldered** the large grain of gold that crowned the summit, held out his work to be admired, the praise-singer would no longer be able to contain himself. He would begin to **intone** the *douga*, the great chant which is sung only for celebrated men and which is danced for them alone. . . .

At the first notes of the *douga* my father would arise and . . . dance the glorious dance.

No sooner had he finished, than workmen and apprentices, friends and customers in their turn, not forgetting the woman for whom the trinket had been created, would flock around him, congratulating him, showering praises on him and complimenting the praise-singer at the

enhance: improve

lofty: proud and noble

smelting: melting

molten: melted

metamorphosis: change
tempo: speed
accelerating: speeding up
flatteries: compliments

soldered: welded together under high heat

intone: recite in a singing voice

same time. The [praise-singer] found himself **laden** with gifts—almost
his only means of support, for the praise-singer leads a wandering life
after the fashion of the **troubadours** of old. Aglow with dancing and
the praises he had received, my father would offer everyone cola nuts,
that small change of Guinean courtesy.

    Now all that remained to be done was to redden the trinket in a
little water to which chlorine and sea salt had been added. I was at
liberty to leave. The festival was over!

laden: loaded

troubadours: poet-musicians

*Camara Laye's novels provide a colorful portrait of village life in West Africa. His
numerous books have made him one of Guinea's leading writers.*

Source: Camara Laye, *The Dark Child*. New York: The Noonday Press, 1954.

Song for the Dance of Young Girls

Poem of the Didinga People, 1971

The Didinga people live in the East African nation of Sudan. Like the people of Guinea, whom Camara Laye described in the story on pages 131-133, the Didinga have many traditions based on different crafts. The poem below is a song often chanted by Didinga women and girls as they mold clay into pottery. How does this poem describe the process of making pottery?

We mold a pot as our mothers did.
The pot, where is the pot?
The pot, it is here.
We mold the pot as our mothers did.

First, the base of the pot.
Strip by strip, and layer by layer.
Supple fingers **kneading** the clay,
Long fingers molding the clay,
Stiff thumbs shaping the clay,
Layer by layer and strip by strip,
We build up the pot of our mother.

supple: agile, flexible
kneading: shaping

We build up the pot of our mother,
Strip by strip and layer by layer.
Its belly swells like the **paunch** of a hyena,
Of a hyena which has eaten a whole sheep.
Its belly swells like a mother of twins.
It is a beautiful pot, the pot of our mother.
It swells like a mother of twins.

paunch: stomach

Didinga women and children chant this poem as they work to express the beauty of their craft. Which poems might you chant as you work to describe the different tasks you do?

Source: Jay David and Helise Harrington, eds., *Growing Up African*. New York: William Morrow and Company, Inc., 1971.

Famine in Ethiopia

by Roberta Oster, 1992

In the East African nation of Ethiopia, civil war, drought, and famine have made thousands of people homeless. Roberta Oster is a television news producer from the United States who visited Ethiopia in 1991 with UNICEF, the United Nations children's relief organization. In 1992 Oster wrote a newspaper article about her visit. As you read an excerpt from this article, notice the dangers and hardships of life today in Ethiopia and in Somalia, the nation directly to the east. According to Oster, what are some of the needs and hopes of the Ethiopian people?

If there were a place called the "end of the earth," it would probably be the Ogaden region in southeastern Ethiopia: an expansive stretch of desert-like **terrain** dotted with small tufts of gray-green scrub bordering Somalia. Life has never been easy for the nomads and **pastoral farmers** who live here, but once again, drought and civil war have turned their simple existence into a desperate fight for survival. Today, more than 1 million are at risk of starvation in the Ogaden. . . .

terrain: land

pastoral farmers: farmers who raise herds of animals

Over the past year, more than 500,000 Somalis fleeing civil war in their country have crossed over the Ethiopian border into the Ogaden. Around the same time, more than 200,000 Ethiopians who had been refugees in Somalia for 14 years headed in the same direction. Known as "returnees," the Ethiopians are now **subsisting** in thousands of little huts made from thorn bush branches scattered along the sides of an endless, dusty road. They could not have picked a worse time to come home. The Ogaden has **endured** its second straight year of severe drought and more than half a million residents were already in need of food aid. . . .

subsisting: surviving

endured: suffered through

Shurki Abdi-Adam endured a five-day walk in 120 degree heat across the Somali desert. She and her husband and their three-year-old son reached the **Kelafo** refugee camp several months ago.

Kelafo: town in eastern Ethiopia

"While we are living in our home," she recalls, "we didn't have any problems, then the civil war was starting, and the shooting was starting and everybody was running away from the house. . . . Many people died."

Shurki has spent almost all of her life . . . struggling as an Ethiopian refugee in Somalia. She never went to school, and she's still uncertain about her own future, but she dreams that one day her son will be able to get an education. For now, here in Kelafo, her only concern is feeding her child.

Every morning, Shurki brings her baby to the intensive feeding center, a cluster of tents and temporary thatched structures, where only the most severely **malnourished** children are fed and given medical treatment. Five times a day, they eat porridge made with faffa (a mix of cereal, milk powder and vitamins) and high protein biscuits. Some are too sick to eat. Shurki tries to **entice** her child to taste the porridge but each time the spoon nears his mouth, he quickly turns his head. . . .

malnourished: underfed, starving

entice: encourage

Gode and Kelafo have recently benefited from a successful UNICEF-led emergency relief effort. Since July 25, [1991], about eight C-110 cargo planes carrying 20 metric tons of grain have been landing on a small airstrip in Gode every day. As soon as they hear the **drone** of engines in the distance, about 25 Ethiopian men run out to the airstrip to unload. Chanting to make the work go faster, they carry hundreds of sacks of grain off the plane and load them onto trucks. . . .

Gode: town in eastern Ethiopia

drone: sound

The side effects of civil war, drought and famine extend beyond the images of malnourished children—families are slowly losing their ability to provide for themselves and seem to be caught in a vicious cycle. Forced to sell off their livestock, they wind up in refugee centers and become accustomed to eating faffa and grain. . . .

For Berhane Berhe, a UNICEF agricultural engineer who has been working in the Ogaden for more than 10 years, emergency food relief is only the first step. "We are feeding these people to save their lives, but to save their lives for how long?" he asks. "Unless they can go back to their original areas in Ethiopia and live the same way they've been living for ages, then really, we will not have been successful at all."

If the funding lasts and the intensive feeding center at Kelafo can stay open, women such as Shurki Abdi-Adam will continue to spend their days trying to bring their children back to life, spoonful by spoonful.

As the African sun sinks beyond the horizon, Shurki walks slowly back to her tent, carrying her unhealthy child in a cloth wrapped around her shoulders. When asked, she talks about the future and her hopes for her family, but each sentence has a bitter **refrain:** "All I want is food." As she speaks of her child's future, dreams of school, dreams of a home, she repeats **ceaselessly:** "I want food. I just want food for my family, then I can think about what else I will do."

refrain: repeated saying

ceaselessly: nonstop

For many years people all over the world have been trying to provide relief for the people of Ethiopia. However, many Ethiopians like Shurki Abdi-Adam continue to suffer. Famine in Ethiopia is not the only serious problem facing Africa. To learn about another dangerous situation in the southern part of the continent, read the next two documents on page 137-140.

Source: Roberta Oster, "Visiting the place where a million people may die." *In These Times,* Jan. 29-Feb. 4, 1992.

AMANDLA! AMANDLA!

by Nelson Mandela, 1990

In 1948, the nation of South Africa set up a system of apartheid to separate black South Africans from white South Africans. Apartheid denied blacks the right to vote or to live in most parts of South Africa. Apartheid also limited the public places, such as parks or beaches, that black South Africans could visit. During the 1950s a black lawyer named Nelson Mandela became a leader of the African National Congress, an organization fighting to end apartheid. The South African government arrested Mandela in 1962 and put him in jail. Mandela's courage and dedication to his cause— even when imprisoned—inspired millions to speak out against apartheid. In order to protest apartheid, many nations, including the United States, adopted sanctions that limited trade with South Africa. Finally, on February 11, 1990, after 27 years in jail, Nelson Mandela was freed by South Africa's president F. W. de Klerk. On the first day of his freedom, Mandela delivered a speech to his supporters and to the world. As you read excerpts from this speech, notice what type of government Mandela wants for South Africa. In what ways does he hope South Africa will achieve this goal?

Amandla! Amandla! i-Afrika, mayibuye! My friends, comrades and fellow South Africans, I greet you all in the name of peace, democracy and freedom for all. I stand here before you not as a **prophet** but as a humble servant of you, the people.

amandla: power
i-Afrika: Africa
mayibuye: let it come back
prophet: one who predicts the future

Your tireless and heroic sacrifices have made it possible for me to be here today. I therefore place the remaining years of my life in your hands.

On this day of my release, I extend my sincere and warmest gratitude to the millions of my **compatriots** and those in every corner of the globe who have campaigned tirelessly for my release. . . .

compatriots: fellow citizens

Today the majority of South Africans, black and white, recognize that apartheid has no future. It has to be ended by our own decisive mass actions in order to build peace and security. The mass campaigns of **defiance** and other actions of our organizations and people can only **culminate** in the establishment of democracy.

The [harm caused by] apartheid. . .on our **subcontinent** is **incalculable**. The fabric of family life of millions of my people has been shattered. Millions are homeless and unemployed. . . .

defiance: opposition
culminate: end
subcontinent: region of Africa
incalculable: very great

137

The need to unite the people of our country is as important a task now as it always has been. No individual leader is able to take all these enormous tasks on his own. It is our task as leaders to place our views before our organization [the African National Congress] and to allow the democratic structures to decide on the way forward. . . .

Today, I wish to report to you that my talks with the Government have been aimed at **normalizing** the political situation in the country. We have not as yet begun discussing the basic demands of the struggle. . . .

Negotiations cannot take place—negotiations cannot take up a place above the heads or behind the backs of our people. It is our belief that the future of our country can only be determined by a body which is democratically elected on a **nonracial** basis. . . .

Our struggle has reached a decisive moment. We call on our people to seize this moment so that the process toward democracy is rapid and uninterrupted. We have waited too long for our freedom. We can no longer wait. Now is the time to **intensify** the struggle on all fronts. . . .

We call on our white compatriots to join us in the shaping of a new South Africa. The freedom movement is the political home for you, too. We call on the international community to continue the campaign to isolate the apartheid **regime**.

To lift sanctions now would be to run the risk of **aborting** the process toward the complete **eradication** of apartheid. Our march to freedom is **irreversible**. We must not allow fear to stand in our way.

Universal **suffrage** on a common voters roll in a united democratic and nonracial South Africa is the only way to peace and racial harmony.

In conclusion, I wish to go to my own words during my trial in 1964. They are as true today as they were then. I wrote: I have fought against white **domination**, and I have fought against black domination. I have cherished the idea of a democratic and free society in which all persons live together in harmony and with equal opportunities.

It is an ideal which I hope to live for and to achieve. But if needs be, it is an ideal for which I am prepared to die.

My friends, I have no **words of eloquence** to offer today except to say that the remaining days of my life are in your hands. . . .

normalizing: making normal

negotiations: talks

nonracial: without regard to race

intensify: strengthen

regime: government

aborting: stopping

eradication: doing away

irreversible: unstoppable

suffrage: voting rights

domination: control

words of eloquence: beautiful phrases

After his release from prison in 1990, Nelson Mandela continued to fight the system of apartheid. In 1991 and 1992, the South African government ended most of the laws of apartheid. In 1992 white South Africans voted to support negotiations between blacks and whites for the creation of a new constitution that would grant all South Africans the right to vote. This nation of 35 million people—less than 25 percent of whom are white—faces an uncertain future. For a description of how South Africa has both changed and remained the same since the 1960s, read the next document on pages 139-140.

Source: Nelson Mandela, "Apartheid Has No Future," *Vital Speeches of the Day* (Volume LVI, Number 10, March 1, 1990).

My Return to South Africa

by Dennis Brutus, 1991

Nelson Mandela, whose speech you read on pages 137-138, was not the only fighter against apartheid to be jailed by the government of South Africa. During the past 40 years, thousands of blacks have been imprisoned, killed, and tortured for their beliefs. Dennis Brutus, a black teacher and poet who has long been opposed to apartheid, was shot and wounded by South Africa's secret police in 1963. He was sent to prison and then forced to leave South Africa in 1966. Brutus later moved to the United States, where he continued working to end apartheid. In July 1991, 17 months after Mandela's release from prison, Brutus returned to his homeland. In a newspaper article based on a journal he kept during his visit to South Africa, Brutus described how the country had changed in the 25 years since he had been exiled. As you read an excerpt from this article, notice the effects of apartheid on the people and the landscape of South Africa. According to Brutus, what steps must be taken for South Africa to be free?

The British Airways 747 begins a bumpy descent through broken clouds to **Johannesburg's** Jan Smuts Airport....

Suddenly, in the bright morning sunlight, the wide landscape appears below and I realize that this airport is truly unique. Nowhere else would you see those great flat-topped mounds of dirt dominating the landscape.... The great mounds of dirt are **slag heaps** excavated from the gold mines that run for miles and miles under the very foundations of Johannesburg's skyscrapers.

When the light is at the right angle, the mounds have a golden **hue** that says to me: wealth and **oppression**, the essential twin features of South African society. Gold, diamonds and coal are the source of the country's **prosperity**. Black labor in the mines was the energy that created vast wealth at an untold cost of human suffering. There is no way to think of South Africa without thinking **simultaneously** of those two elements: great wealth—great **deprivation**. To make the mining enterprise ever more profitable, people were deprived of their basic rights and humanity. Made to labor in the dark, to produce wealth....

During my return, I went to visit my boyhood home in **Port Elizabeth**. It has been converted into a body repair shop. The neighborhood that I grew up in is now all-white. Though the **"Group Areas Act"** has been **repealed**, the community of my childhood is now closed to me. It is a well-documented fact that empty schools in white neighborhoods have been destroyed, rather than being opened to non-white (usually black) children who so desperately need them.

Johannesburg: one of South Africa's largest cities

slag heaps: piles of waste matter

hue: color
oppression: cruel power

prosperity: wealth

simultaneously: at the same time
deprivation: poverty

Port Elizabeth: city on the south coast of South Africa
Group Areas Act: an apartheid law
repealed: ended

As I traveled on the bus between Port Elizabeth and **Cape Town,** I was impressed with all of the construction that has gone on since I left. **High rises** dominate the horizons of the major cities. The National Road is fully **comparable** to the best of the interstate highways in the U.S.

Yet, on this National Road, I viewed things that troubled me terribly. Shantytowns and squatter camps have grown up along this modern thruway. These camps are characterized by tin-roofed shacks cobbled together with whatever materials are available. Even as you whisk along the highway, you can see how cramped and filthy the places are.

One afternoon, for the first time, I visited the grave of my mother who died and was buried while I was in prison on Robben Island. Nearby was the grey bulk of the prison called "Rooi Hel" (Red Hell). In 1965, I was released from there to go under house arrest, so that my home could be my prison.

Nearby Rooi Hel are segregated townships for white workers. In the distance are shanties of those who came from the [black] townships of New Brighton and Kwazakele. The area has been subdivided. There is now a new city called Ibhayi which has its own city council. The town clerk is white though the city's inhabitants are black. All the foul legacy of apartheid still presses with full weight on both black and white.

So while my old neighborhood, taken over by whites, has thrived, the situation for the black majority has seriously **deteriorated** in the past quarter century. Even if blacks and other non-whites were allowed to settle freely, without **intimidation** and interference, only about 1 percent could financially afford to do so. . . .

Also, there is a tremendous exhaustion fueled by the weight of having to struggle every day for basic necessities such as food, housing, sanitation, health care, transportation, and education. . . .

There have been some good changes, of course. The economy is picking up though unemployment is still high—about 35 percent among blacks. More expressways, highways and high rises have been built. And some blacks are beginning to move out of **menial** jobs into white-collar professions. So there's no doubt that there have been changes. The trouble is that the fundamental changes haven't come yet.

For instance, [Nelson] Mandela still can't vote. Neither can **Bishop [Desmond] Tutu.** Seventy percent of the population can't vote. . . .

You either have a democracy or you don't, and a democracy is a society in which everybody has the vote. . . .

South African society is getting better for some. But it was always better for some. Our goal, as I understand it, is that it should be better for all.

Dennis Brutus had hoped to regain his South African citizenship during his visit, but his application was denied by the South African government. Brutus returned to the United States, where he remained a poet and college professor and continued to speak out against apartheid.

Source: Dennis Brutus, "Reflections on a Return to the Land of Sirens, Knuckles, Boots." *In These Times,* Nov. 6–12, 1991.

Cape Town: one of the capitals of South Africa

high rises: tall buildings

comparable: equal

deteriorated: worsened

intimidation: threats

menial: low-paying

Bishop Desmond Tutu: a leading black opponent of apartheid

JI-NONGO-NONGO

African Riddles Collected by Verna Aardema, 1978

The oral tradition in Africa of storytelling by griots, which you read about in the documents on pages 102–103 and 129–130, also includes riddles. Griots often entertain a crowd by telling riddles before beginning a tale. Besides providing fun, the riddles also describe acceptable ways of behaving or make wise observations about life. Verna Aardema, an author who specializes in African folklore, collected the following riddles from various groups of people throughout the continent. See if you can guess the answers to the riddles. The answers are printed upside down. What are some of the ideas and values expressed in the riddles?

Accra
When is it safe to play with the leopard cubs?
Answer: When their mother is far away.

Congo
Why shouldn't you grow pumpkins on the side of a hill?
Answer: Because when they are ripe, they would roll down.

Ga
What is soft and flat, but cannot be slept upon?
Answer: The surface of the lake.

What leaps down the mountain, but cannot climb back up?
Answer: The mountain stream.

What is it that you look at with one eye, but never with two?
Answer: The inside of a bottle.

Hausa

Why is a man like a pepper?
Answer: Until you have tested him, you can't tell how strong he is.

What lies down when it's hungry and stands up when its full?
Answer: A rice sack.

What looks at the valley, but never goes into it?
Answer: The hill.

Bantu

Who is it that always stands, and never sits down?
Answer: A tree.

Masai

What doesn't run from the prairie fire?
Answer: The bare spot.

I have two skins—one to lie upon and the other to cover me. What are they?
Answer: The ground and the sky.

Wolof

What is long but has no shadow?
Answer: The road.

Yoruba

What thing in the forest frightens even the lion?
Answer: The forest fire.

They cut off its head. They cut off its feet. And its middle calls the town together. What is it?
Answer: A drum.

What is long and can be shortened by the feet, but not with a hatchet?
Answer: The path.

What can the buffalo do that two strong men can not?
Answer: Grow horns.

Today, Africans are recording their rich oral tradition by collecting stories, poems, legends, and riddles and publishing them in books. At the same time others are keeping the oral tradition alive in storytelling sessions, often combined with music and dance.

Source: Verna Aardema, *Ji-Nongo-Nongo Means Riddles*. New York: Four Winds Press, 1978.

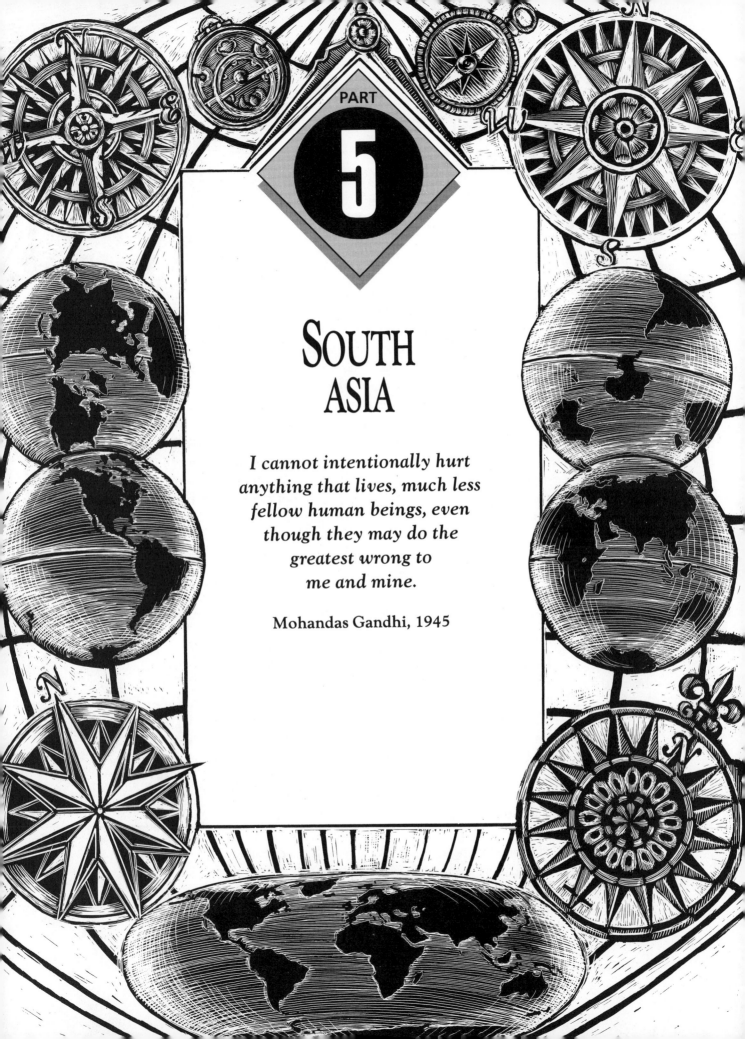

PART

5

SOUTH ASIA

I cannot intentionally hurt anything that lives, much less fellow human beings, even though they may do the greatest wrong to me and mine.

Mohandas Gandhi, 1945

Praying at the Western Wall

by Brent Ashabranner, 1984

Judaism is one of the world's oldest religions, its traditions dating back thousands of years. Around 960 B.C., Solomon became king of the Jewish people, and built a magnificent building—known as the First Temple—in Jerusalem. The First Temple became the center of the Jewish religion. Four hundred years later the First Temple was destroyed and a new temple was built. This new temple, called the Second Temple, was remodeled by King Herod around 30 B.C. But 100 years later, in A.D. 70, Roman soldiers attacked Jerusalem and destroyed the Second Temple. All that remained of it was one giant wall. Today this wall is known as the Western Wall, or Kotel, and is the most sacred monument of Judaism. Many Jews travel to the Western Wall to pray. Among them is a 12-year-old boy named Gavriel, who lives in Jerusalem. In the following excerpt from a book describing his life, Gavriel attends morning prayer at the Western Wall with his father and four brothers. What are some of the rituals that Gavriel performs with his father? How do these rituals relate to Gavriel's religious beliefs?

When Abe and his sons go to morning prayer, the sun is just turning the eastern sky a rosy pink. Gavriel has learned from his father that morning prayer cannot be said until the light is just right. "Just enough to tell a light blue thread from a white one," Abe says. Gavriel rubs the sleep from his eyes as they walk to the Kotel, the Western Wall, but he does not wish that he were back in bed.

He has a special feeling for the Jewish quarter at this time of day, before the noise and bustle have really begun, before the narrow streets are crowded. He likes going to prayer with his father. He carries a blue velvet pouch which holds his father's prayer shawl and *tefillin*, which are small leather boxes containing Biblical verses.

They pass the rebuilt ruins of a **Crusader** lodging place and then walk down several flights of stone stairs—140 steps in all—to reach the Kotel. Morning is Gavriel's favorite time to come to the Western Wall. Some people are always there when they arrive but not so many as there will be later in the day. The sounds of prayer rise clearly in the cool, clean air. Swallows swoop overhead making little cries. It is a peaceful place to be.

Abe puts on his prayer shawl and the *tefillin*, which are provided with long leather straps. He places one of the *tefillin* on his left arm facing his heart and winds the leather strap around his left forearm seven times. The other *tefillin* he places in the center of his forehead, looping the leather strap around his head to keep the *tefillin* in place.

Crusader: name for Christian soldiers who fought from the 11th to 13th centuries to recapture Jerusalem from the Muslims

Gavriel knows the *tefillin* signify that the **covenant** with God is a matter of serious concern every day of the week. He remembers the passage from **Deuteronomy**: "And these words which I command thee this day shall be upon thine heart...And thou shalt bind them for thine hand, and they shall be for **frontlets** between thine eyes."

When the *tefillin* are properly attached, Abe begins to pray, and his sons join him. He has taught them the proper way of prayer just as he learned it from his father. They pray aloud, and Gavriel concentrates intently, not just saying words but thinking very hard about what they mean. This concentration, this thinking about what the prayer means, is called *kavvanah*, and it is of great importance. As with his father and other men in prayer at the Wall, the intensity of his concentration causes Gavriel's eyes to close and his body to sway.

"... O purify our hearts to serve Thee in truth, for Thou art God in truth, and Thy word is truth, and endureth forever...."

On many nights Abe helps Gavriel in his study of the **Talmud**. In just a few months Gavriel will become *bar mitzvah*, a son of the commandment. This will happen on the day he is thirteen years old. Then, in a religious sense, he will be a man and able to understand the commandments of the Torah and observe them on his own responsibility. Now it is Abe's responsibility to see that Gavriel really has that understanding.

Gavriel takes his religion seriously. Whenever he leaves the apartment or returns to it, he touches a piece of the **Torah**, called *mezuzah*, which has been nailed to the doorframe. He does the same with a piece of the Sacred Book that has been fastened to his classroom door at school.

And at family gatherings around the dinner table on the holy day of **Shabbat** or at **Passover**, when songs of praise and thanksgiving are sung, Gavriel's clear voice is loudest, after that of his father.

covenant: agreement

Deuteronomy: holy book of Jewish scripture

frontlets: decorated headbands

Talmud: Jewish law based on interpretations of sacred texts

Torah: Jewish scripture

Shabbat: Jewish sabbath from sundown Friday to sundown Saturday

Passover: Jewish holiday celebrating Exodus from Egypt

Today about 18 million people—or 1 in 300 people in the world—are Jews. Judaism emerged in the Middle East almost 4,000 years ago in what is today the nation of Israel. About 2,000 years ago, another major religion—called Christianity—developed in the same region. To learn more about Christianity, read the next document on pages 146-147.

Source: Brent Ashabranner, *Gavriel and Jemal: Two Boys of Jerusalem*. New York: Dodd, Mead & Company, 1984.

A Craftsman in Bethlehem

by Avram Hissan, 1981

Almost 2,000 years ago, a Jewish woman named Mary gave birth to a son in Bethlehem, a town that still exists in Israel today. Mary's son was named Jesus. According to the New Testament of the Bible, Jesus grew up in the town of Nazareth and practiced the religion of Judaism. When he was about 30 years old, Jesus started preaching. As he traveled from village to village, he stressed that love for God required showing love for other people. Jesus won many followers, who called him the Savior, a term for a person who has come to save humanity from evil. These followers of Jesus began a new religion called Christianity. Avram Hissan is a Christian who lives in Bethlehem. In the excerpt below, Hissan expresses his love for his town and his job. How does Christianity shape his life?

This is a magic city. It's a quiet and friendly town — not so quiet at Christmas, Easter and festivals, when thousands of pilgrims from all over the world pour into our city. Its link with the Jewish people began nearly 4,000 years ago when Jacob, passing through the town, lost his young wife Rachel in childbirth. Bethlehem today has a population of 32,000 — mainly Christian Arabs with professions. Many of them are gold smiths, skilled in carving. Every visitor is attracted to the Church of the Nativity, traditionally the birthplace of Jesus, where Mary gave birth and laid the child in the manger because there was no room for him in the inn. The Church of the Nativity is one of the holiest shrines **in Christendom.**

For many generations now we've sold articles carved in olive wood and also goods made of mother-of-pearl. They are the most sought-after goods in Bethlehem, extremely popular with the tourists. The olive-wood industry is famous here. We have our own factory beneath our store where we make all kinds of figures and nativity sets. The majority of the olive-wood goods sold in the store are made on the premises.

in Christendom: among Christian worshipers

We call olive wood the holy wood. We carve very large pieces too—large manager sets are bought and taken all over the world, especially at Christmas time.

Thank God, without religion we cannot live. I pray in St. Mary's Church in Bethlehem. Our services are held in the **Aramaic** language in our churches all over the world. This was the language of the Lord Our Saviour, and of our **Prophets**, Abraham, Isaac and Jacob.

I work in the store every day from 8 o'clock [in the morning] until 7 or 8 o'clock in the evening. On Sundays I go to church in the morning and then go to work. I like to take vacations, but only a day at a time. I usually go with my brother George. I like to go in and around Bethlehem, sometimes to King Solomon's Pools. This is one of our main beauty spots; it's fertile and the pool is spring-fed. . . . It was erected some 500 years ago, and is now ringed by a well-grown pine forest. These great open reservoirs form a green and beautiful park, an ideal picnic spot.

I also like to go to Jericho and to the Dead Sea where the climate is much warmer and drier than here. I'm very much a family man and I enjoy staying at home in the evenings with my family; so many friends come in to visit us and, of course, business people, mainly from the United States.

Christians and Moslems live together in Bethlehem. We have very good relations with the Jews; we have lived together now for fourteen years. We are happy and we hope for peace in the future.

Aramaic: ancient language used widely in the Middle East from 600 B.C. to A.D. 800

prophets: persons who deliver messages believed to be from God

Christianity spread rapidly throughout the Roman Empire and much of Europe. It also spread into Africa and Asia. Europeans later introduced Christianity to other parts of the world. Today more than 1.6 billion people—or almost one in three people in the world—are Christians. To learn about another important religion that emerged in the Middle East, read the next document on pages 148-149.

Source: Gemma Levine, *We Live in Israel*. New York: The Bookwright Press, 1983.

Pilgrimage to Mecca

by Samaan bin Jabir Al Nasaib, 1987

During the seventh century, a major religion called Islam emerged in the Middle East. According to Islamic faith, around A.D. 610 an Arab merchant named Muhammad heard a voice tell him that there is only one God—for which the Arabic word is Allah—and that he, Muhammad, was Allah's messenger. Followers of Muhammad's teachings became known as Muslims, or "followers of Islam." After Muhammad's death, these teachings were gathered into a book called the Koran. The Koran is believed by Muslims to be the very word of God. The Koran teaches that Muhammad is the last in the line of prophets, or people who deliver a message believed to be from God. Muslims believe that earlier prophets were Abraham, Moses, and Jesus. One of the duties that all Muslims try to fulfill at least once in their lives is to make a journey to the city of Mecca, the birthplace of Muhammad. What is this journey like? In the following selection from an oral history, a Muslim from Saudi Arabia named Samaan bin Jabir Al Nasaib describes his recent pilgrimage to Mecca. What are some of the rituals that Jabir Al Nasaib performs during his pilgrimage? How do these rituals relate to his religious beliefs?

*M*y family traces its **descent** from the oldest of the tribes of this part of the world. Some say that we can trace our heritage back to Adam. Whether or not this is so, we have been landowners and **sheikhs** in the **Wadi Najran** for as long as anybody can remember. We grow corn, wheat and citrus fruit here.

descent: origins

sheikhs: Arab leaders
Wadi Najran: region in southwest Saudi Arabia

I suppose the high spot of my life was performing the Hajj [häj] in the company of my son Maana. The Hajj is the name we give to the pilgrimage that Muslims make to Mecca, to the Holy Kaaba [kä′ bə], Abraham's "House of God." This pilgrimage is one of the "five pillars of Islam," the other four being the belief in one God, prayer five times a day, the giving of **alms** and fasting during the holy month of Ramadan. What a proud and spiritually rewarding moment it was for me to make my seven rounds of the Kaaba with my son beside me!

alms: aid to the poor

The Hajj requires great physical stamina as well as religious **zeal**. The Hajjis, as pilgrims are called, must all wear a special garment consisting of two white lengths of cotton, without seams, emphasizing the equality of all men in the sight of God. We put the garment on at the start of our journey, after ritual washing and prayer.

zeal: enthusiasm

On arrival in Mecca, after further washing and prayer, the pilgrims go directly to the Kaaba and circle it seven times in an anti-clockwise

direction. On passing the Black Stone, they should try either to kiss it or at least touch it. This stone is a meteorite and is traditionally held to be a link between the Prophet **Mohammed**, Abraham and Adam.

Mohammed: Muhammad

After the duties of the Kaaba, pilgrims are required to run between two hills, Al Safa and Al Marwah, which both have links with Abraham's wife, Hagar. While doing this they are praying all the while. Pilgrims may then drink from the spring of Zam Zam, which is referred to in the Old Testament [of the Bible]. Male pilgrims then have their heads shaved, or more commonly today, their hair cut.

Now follows a visit to Mount Arafat, where Mohammed gave his farewell sermon. A whole afternoon is spent in the open air, on the Plain of Arafat, standing bareheaded, glorifying God and reading the Koran.

Crowds of pilgrims spend the night under the stars at Musdalifah, and each collects seventy small pebbles. Then they make their way to Mina, the end of the journey, where there are three stone pillars. Seven of the pebbles are then cast at the pillars, an act symbolic of mankind casting out the evil from within. Then animals are sacrificed and the meat given to the poor. Before returning home, the pilgrims throw the remaining pebbles at the pillars.

The pilgrimage ends after a final symbolic cutting of hair. Some pilgrims take this opportunity of going on to Medina, where they can visit the Tomb of Mohammed, and the Prophet's **Mosque**.

mosque: Islamic house of worship

Back on my farm in the Wadi Najran, I often remember those privileged days I spent in Mecca.

Today about 900 million people—or one in six people in the world—are Muslims. Judaism, Christianity, and Islam all emerged in the Middle East. Thousands of miles to the east, two other major religions also developed long ago. To learn more about these other two religions, read the next two documents on pages 150-153.

Source: Abdul Latif Al Hoad, *We Live in Saudi Arabia*. New York: The Bookwright Press, 1987.

Use with *Eastern Hemisphere*, Chapter 18, Lesson 2

World Past and Present, Chapter 18, Lesson 2

World Regions, Chapter 25, Lesson 1

Life of a Hindu Priest

NATARAJ

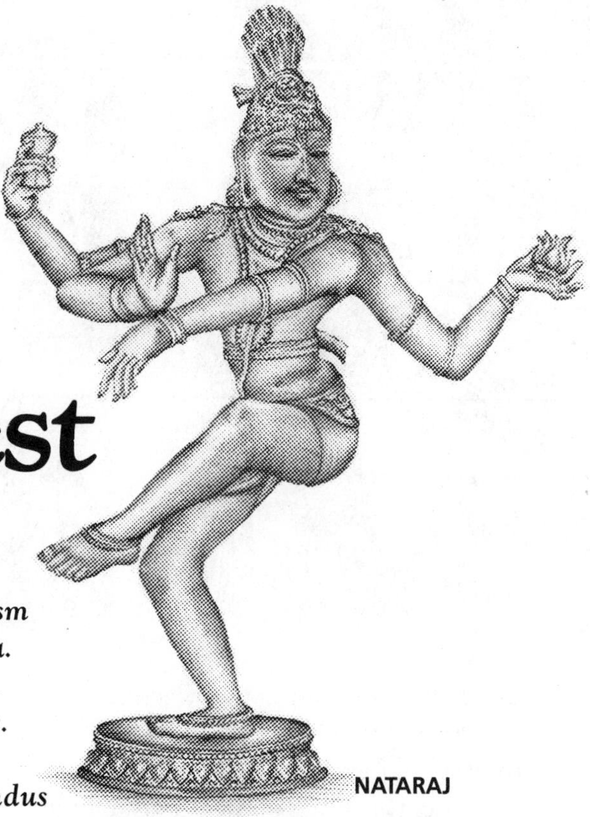

by Hardwari Lal, 1984

About 4,000 years ago, the religion of Hinduism began to develop on the subcontinent of India. Hinduism developed from ancient beliefs and stories. Hindus believe in many different gods. Some of these gods are pictured in the illustrations accompanying this selection. Hindus also believe that all parts of nature are holy. Hardwari Lal is a 55-year-old Hindu **pandit,** *or priest, who works at a temple in Bhatinda, a town in northern India near the Pakistani border. As you read Hardwari Lal's description of his duties in a selection from an oral history, think about how the rituals he and other Hindus perform relate to their religious beliefs.*

My day at the temple begins at half-past four in the morning and ends at eight o'clock every night. It's a long day, but I don't mind one bit, as I devote all the time to the service of God.

Which God, you ask? Well, we Hindus have 330 million **deities.** We believe that the God Brahma is the Creator of the World. Vishnu is the God who preserves the world and the God Shiva is the destroyer of the world.

deities: gods

Among the more popular gods and goddesses are Radha and Krishna, Ram and Sita, Hanuman the monkey god, Ganesha the elephant-headed god, and the Goddess Durga, who rides a tiger. We have lots of **idols** of these gods and goddesses in our temple. You'll find lots of temples in India, at least one every mile or so, for religion is very important here.

idols: statues

It's part of my duty as a priest to offer prayer to the idols, to bathe them with milk and honey, and to dress them. Then, every day, other temple priests and I have to organize the distribution of free food. Our temple feeds about thirty or forty poor people every day. The temple gets its money from donations.

Only a **Brahman** can become a priest in a temple. He must be learned in the ancient Sanskrit texts known as *Vedas*. He must also know how to conduct weddings, birth and death ceremonies, and so on.

Brahman: member of the Hindu priest class

Most marriages are finally arranged after comparing the horoscopes of the boy and girl. If the astrologer feels that they will get along, he fixes an **auspicious** day and hour for the wedding. Last year, for almost eight months, practically no weddings took place, as the stars weren't in the right position.

Anyhow, on the chosen day, the bridegroom dresses in style with a shining crown on his head and **garlands** of flowers and **rupees** round his neck. He then sits on a white horse—though some people prefer automobiles nowadays. Escorted by a band of drummers and trumpeters and a whole lot of relatives and friends, the groom goes through the streets to the bride's home. The bride has to wear lots of jewelry and dress in red or pink.

The priests light the sacred fire of sandalwood and incense and begin reciting **mantras** from the *Vedas*. Then we take a pink cloth and tie one end to the bridegroom and the other end to the bride. The bride and bridegroom have to walk around the sacred fire seven times to become husband and wife. For tens of centuries, Hindu weddings have been performed in the same way.

As for funerals, we Hindus usually burn our dead, though we bury infants.

There are so many holy cities and places. They're usually on the banks of rivers or up on the snowy mountains. Cities like Hardwar, Rishikesh and Varanasi are on the riverside. Pilgrimage centers like Badrinath, Kedarnath and Amarnath are high up in the mountains. Half the year the pilgrims can't get to them because of the snow.

But I must tell you about the Kumbh *Mela*, which is held every twelve years and is the world's greatest religious fair. At Kumbh, millions and millions of Hindus gather from all over India to take a bath in the holy Ganges [River].

With so much going on, life remains busy and full for me. I can't tell you how happy and fortunate I feel serving God and the people.

auspicious: lucky

garlands: wreaths
rupees: Indian coins

mantras: prayers

SHIVA   **PARVATI**   **KRISHNA**   **RAMA**   **SITA**

Today about 700 million people—or one in eight people in the world—are Hindus. Most Hindus live in India and Southeast Asia. Around 2,500 years ago, a Hindu prince founded another major religion of the world. To learn about this religion, read the next document on pages 152-153.

Source: Veenu Sandal, *We Live in India*. New York: The Bookwright Press, 1984.

Becoming a Buddhist Master

by Sek Bao Shi, 1985

Around 563 B.C., a Hindu prince named Siddhartha Gautama was born in the foothills of the Himalaya Mountains in what is today Nepal. After trying for years to understand suffering and find wisdom, Siddhartha decided that suffering was caused by desire and attachment. By freeing himself of these qualities, Siddhartha said he found nirvana, a peaceful state that is free of pain and suffering. When he told friends what he had learned they began to call him the Buddha, a title meaning "the Awakened One." From Siddhartha's teachings a new religion called Buddhism developed and spread throughout Southeast Asia. Sek Bao Shi is a 41-year-old resident of Singapore who is working toward becoming a Buddhist Master. As you read this account of her life from an oral history, notice the different rituals and practices that she follows. How do her Buddhist beliefs shape her life?

*I*t's 4:30 A.M. The sky is dark and it's rather cold, but I'm up and so are the other five members of our Buddhist Order. Only women live in our temple. By 5:00 A.M. we're chanting Buddhist **sutras** at our first service of the day.

sutras: teachings, scriptures

At 7:00 A.M. we make our first offering of biscuits or bread and a cup of tea to Lord Buddha. A short service accompanies the offering.

152

Then we have our breakfast of bread or oatmeal and a hot drink. We are **vegetarians**, because we don't believe in harming any living creature.

After breakfast, there are chores to do. These include cleaning, washing and preparing lunch. At 11:00 A.M., after the rice is cooked, we make a second offering to Lord Buddha. We have our lunch soon after and this is the final meal of the day.

To become a member of the Buddhist Order, it's customary to follow a Master or *Shi Fu* of one's choice for five years. When I decided to leave home, give up my job, rid myself of my worldly possessions, shave my head and devote myself to practicing Lord Buddha's teachings, I asked to be her **disciple**. I was very happy to be accepted. I have been my *Shi Fu's* disciple for three years now.

disciple: follower

My decision to join the Buddhist Order was not made overnight. I had been thinking about it since I was 9. As a child, I often accompanied my mother, a devout Buddhist, to the Kuan Yin Temple to make offerings to Kuan Yin, the Goddess of Mercy.

After completing my secondary schooling, I entered the civil service. Still deeply interested in the teachings of Lord Buddha, I became a vegetarian. As a lay devotee I went to the Buddhist Union Shrine to help out in religious and administrative activities. I also resolved to abstain from harming others, from stealing, from telling lies, from being unchaste and from all forms of intoxicating drinks and drugs. I spent seventeen years in this way until finally deciding to join the Buddhist Order at the age of 38.

Since then, I have been staying at the Leng Jin Temple to study the Buddhist scriptures with my *Shi Fu*. In addition, she teaches me how to **meditate**, conduct Buddhist services and beat the drum and cymbals during special ceremonies. I also have more than 500 rules to observe now.

meditate: focus one's thoughts

I've found peace and happiness in the teachings of our Lord Buddha who said, "The gift of Truth excels all other gifts." I want to seek this Truth through the study of the Buddhist scriptures. I know it can be found within ourselves.

I am glad for the opportunity to practice what I believe in. There's complete freedom of worship in Singapore and wherever you go you will see temples, mosques, churches and other places of worship near to each other.

As a Buddhist, I'm very happy to see our people understanding and accepting one another's customs and religion. It makes for a much happier world.

Today more than 300 million people—or 1 in 18 people in the world—are Buddhists. Buddhism, along with Judaism, Christianity, Islam, and Hinduism, which you read about on pages 144-151, all began in South Asia. Over the course of hundreds of years, these five religions have spread to every part of the world. They have had an enormous impact on both world civilization and history.

Source: Jessie Wee, *We Live in Malaysia & Singapore.* New York: The Bookwright Press, 1985.

The Epic of Gilgamesh

Sumerian Epic, 3000–2000 B.C.

One of the oldest stories in the world is The Epic of Gilgamesh, *an ancient Sumerian tale that was written between 4,000 and 5,000 years ago. The story comes from Mesopotamia—in what is today the Middle East—and is so old that instead of being written on paper, it was originally carved on clay tablets. Gilgamesh was the king of Uruk, an ancient city in Mesopotamia, around 2700 B.C. In the epic Gilgamesh goes on a long journey in search of eternal youth and encounters monsters, gods, and the mighty forces of nature. In the excerpt below, a god tells Gilgamesh about a great flood that once swept the land. How does the god manage to survive the flood?*

For six days and six nights the winds blew, torrent and **tempest** and flood overwhelmed the world, tempest and flood raged together like warring hosts. When the seventh day dawned the storm from the south **subsided**, the sea grew calm, the flood was stilled; I looked at the face of the world and there was silence, all mankind was turned to clay. The surface of the sea stretched as flat as a roof-top; I opened a hatch and the light fell on my face. Then I bowed low, I sat down and I wept, the tears streamed down my face, for on every side was the waste of water. I looked for land in vain, but fourteen leagues distant there appeared a mountain, and there the boat grounded; on the mountain of Nisir the boat held fast, she held fast and did not budge. One day she held, and a second day on the mountain of Nisir she held fast and did not budge. A third day, and a fourth day she held fast on the mountain and did not budge; a fifth day and a sixth day she held fast on the mountain. When the seventh day dawned I loosed a dove and let her go. She flew away, but finding no resting-place she returned. Then I loosed a swallow, and she flew away but finding no resting-place she returned. I loosed a raven, she saw that the waters had retreated, she ate, she flew around, she **cawed**, and she did not come back. Then I threw everything open to the four winds, I made a sacrifice and poured out a **libation** on the mountain top.

tempest: storm

subsided: died down

cawed: squawked

libation: liquid offering

After telling this story, the god presents Gilgamesh with a plant that will give him eternal life. A serpent tricks him, however, causing Gilgamesh to lose the plant and the promise of eternal life. The Epic of Gilgamesh *is the oldest epic known to human history. Like* The Iliad *and the* Aeneid, *which you can read excerpts from on pages 68–72, it is considered one of the world's greatest works of literature.*

Source: N. K. Sandars, ed., *The Epic of Gilgamesh*. London: Penguin Group, 1960.

The Ringdove

by Bidpai, about A.D. 300
Translated by Abdallah Ibn al-Muqaffa,
about A.D. 750

The Ringdove is a fable from an ancient book that has been one of the most popular tales in the Middle East for centuries. According to legend, around the year A.D. 300, an Indian king asked a teacher and philosopher named Bidpai to write a book that would guide him toward being a better ruler. Bidpai hid himself away for a year and wrote the Kalila wa Dimna, a collection of fables in which animals are the main characters. Bidpai based the Kalila wa Dimna on stories that had been told in India for hundreds of years. About 450 years later, a writer named Abdallah Ibn al-Muqaffa translated the Kalila wa Dimna into Arabic. Ibn al-Muqaffa's version is the oldest translation that still exists. In 1354, an Arab artist created a set of beautiful drawings to accompany Ibn al-Muqaffa's version of the Kalila wa Dimna. The pictures on these pages, which combine drawings and Arabic writing, are from this version. As you read The Ringdove, notice how the animals— both in pictures and in words—demonstrate human qualities. What does this fable say about friendship and cooperation? What might a king who lived hundreds of years ago have learned about ruling by reading this fable?

The king said to the philosopher that now that he had heard the story of the envious and **deceitful** man who brought **corruption** among friends, he would like to know how a man is received into brotherhood among his fellows and how strangers of **alien** races can come to love and trust one another.

deceitful: dishonest
corruption: bad habits
alien: different

The philosopher answered that nothing is equal in value to brotherhood because brothers can help in times of trouble, rescue one another from hidden **snares**, and protect their **kin** from enemies, like the crow, the mouse, the tortoise, and the gazelle.

snares: traps
kin: relatives

There was a fertile region with abundant grass and trees frequented by **fowlers** and hunters. An old and wise crow lived in a tree that was particularly large and rich in **foliage**. One day the crow saw a hunter

fowlers: people who catch birds
foliage: leaves

155

spreading a net below the tree and covering it with safflower seeds. Soon a flock of doves flew in. Their leader, a ringdove, spotted the seeds but did not notice the net. When the doves landed on the ground to feast on the seeds, the snare was drawn and they were caught in the net.

The ringdove suggested that the group unite and fly away together before they were caught by the hunter. The birds followed his advice, flapped their wings **in unison**, and took off with the net just as the hunter was approaching.

The crow decided to follow them. The doves flew over hills and houses with the hunter in hot pursuit. They eventually lost the man and landed near a burrow where a mouse lived. The ringdove called her friend, Zirak, the mouse, who came out of his burrow and saw the birds entangled in the net. He began to gnaw the ropes and finally cut through the snare. The doves rejoiced at being freed; they congratulated each other and thanked the mouse before flying off. Zirak returned to his home.

The crow, impressed by the friendship between the ringdove and the mouse, decided to stay on. He called out to Zirak and told the mouse that he would like them to be friends. Zirak, knowing well that crows are the natural enemies of mice, was slightly **apprehensive** at first but became convinced of the crow's sincerity and accepted his offer of brotherhood. A strong bond soon developed between the two, and they came to rely on one another.

The crow, noticing that their homes were too close to men, suggested that they move to another area. He knew of a **secluded** region full of vegetation and water where his friend, the tortoise, lived.

The mouse agreed and the crow took him by the tail and flew to the pond of the tortoise. The three friends enjoyed each other's company and passed their days in peace and happiness.

One day a gazelle came running into their neighborhood and frightened them. The tortoise dove into the water, the mouse scurried into his burrow, and the crow took flight and hid in a tree. When they saw that no one was pursuing the gazelle and that the animal was merely thirsty, they came out of hiding. The gazelle told them that he was running away from hunters. The friends asked him to join them and live in their peaceful place. The gazelle moved in, enjoyed good company and **ample** food and drink.

It became the custom of the four friends to meet every day, talk about their lives and experiences, and share their meal together. One day the gazelle failed to show up and the crow, the mouse, and the tortoise were worried that some misfortune had **befallen** him. The crow took to the air, searched for the gazelle, and saw that he was caught in a hunter's net. He reported what he had seen to the mouse and the tortoise, who then set out to rescue their friend. When they reached the gazelle, the mouse began to gnaw the net and eventually freed him. The gazelle turned to the tortoise and said that if the hunter came back, he could run away, the crow could fly, and the mouse could hide; but, the slow and defenseless tortoise would probably be caught. As they were talking, the hunter arrived; the gazelle, the crow, and the mouse ran away and hid, but the tortoise, who could not move fast enough, was captured by the man. The hunter bound him and took him away, slung over his shoulders.

The friends, distressed by the loss of their brother, devised a plan to free him. They decided that if the gazelle pretended to be wounded and lay down with the crow who would appear to lick his wound, they might deceive the hunter. The gazelle followed their plan and lay down in the path of the hunter with the crow over him; the mouse hid nearby and they waited for the man. When the hunter arrived and saw them, he let go of the tortoise and went after the gazelle. The crow took flight and the gazelle jumped up and ran, luring the hunter away from the tortoise. The mouse quickly went to the tortoise and severed the ropes binding him.

By the time the hunter returned, the friends were safely far away. The man was disappointed and ashamed of himself for having lost his catch. He had become quite **leery** of this region and moved onto another area.

leery: suspicious

The crow, the mouse, the tortoise, and the gazelle rejoiced; they embraced and kissed each other, greatly relieved that now they could live in complete peace and happiness.

The tales of the Kalila wa Dimna *have been translated into dozens of languages. Why do you think such stories survive for centuries and remain popular worldwide? If you wrote a fable, what would your story be about, and what qualities would you give to different animals? What would your fable teach?*

Source: Esin Atil, *Kalila wa Dimna: Fables from a Fourteenth-Century Arabic Manuscript*. Washington, DC: Smithsonian Institution Press, 1981.

Mountains of Israel

Song about Israel, 1950

Bordered by the Mediterranean Sea on its western coast, the nation of Israel is a land of great beauty. Mountains, valleys, and deserts cover much of the country. How does the Israeli song below describe the geography of this part of the Middle East?

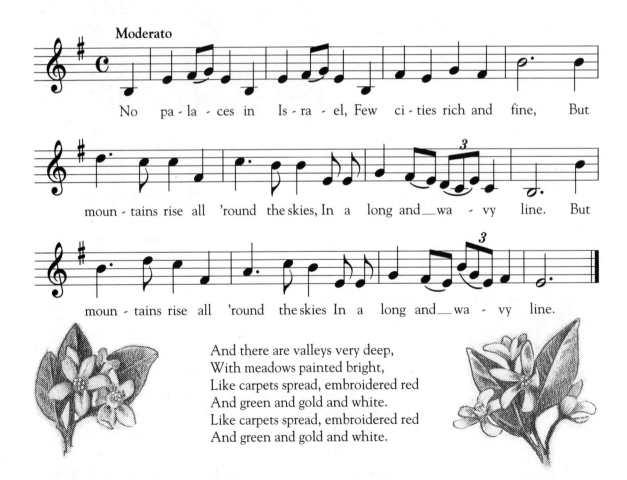

Moderato

No pal - a - ces in Is - ra - el, Few ci - ties rich and fine, But

moun - tains rise all 'round the skies, In a long and wa - vy line. But

moun - tains rise all 'round the skies In a long and wa - vy line.

And there are valleys very deep,
With meadows painted bright,
Like carpets spread, embroidered red
And green and gold and white.
Like carpets spread, embroidered red
And green and gold and white.

Source: Harry Coopersmith, *The Songs We Sing.* New York: The United Synagogue of America, 1950.

Road to Peace

by Yitzhak Shamir and Haidar Abdel-Shafi, 1991

For thousands of years people living in the Middle East have fought over this land, the birthplace of three of the world's major religions—Judaism, Christianity, and Islam. The conflict heated up in 1948 when the nation of Israel was created as a homeland for the Jewish people. The creation of the country of Israel upset many Arabs, some of whom had been living in this territory—which they called Palestine—for many hundreds of years. These Arabs, known as Palestinians, wanted this territory set aside for a Palestinian homeland. As a result of this situation, Israel and its Arab neighbors have fought several wars against each other since 1948, and violence has broken out many times. In 1987 Palestinians began an uprising known as the intifada to regain certain lands claimed or occupied by Israel. In trying to put down the intifada, Israel has killed, arrested, and exiled many Palestinians. Finally, in late 1991, Israel, the Palestinians, and the Arab nations met in Madrid, Spain, for their first peace conference. Below are excerpts from the opening speeches, given on October 31, 1991, by Yitzhak Shamir, the prime minister of Israel, and Haidar Abdel-Shafi, the leader of the Palestinian delegation. As you read these speeches, notice how each side uses distant and recent history to defend its position. What are some of the demands that need to be addressed to achieve peace?

Speech by Yitzhak Shamir

To appreciate the meaning of peace for the people of Israel, one has to view today's Jewish **sovereignty** in the Land of Israel against the background of our history. Jews have been **persecuted** throughout the ages in almost every continent. Some countries barely tolerated us, others **oppressed**, tortured, slaughtered and exiled us. This century saw the Nazi regime set out to **exterminate** us. The . . . Holocaust, the catastrophic **genocide** of unprecedented proportions which destroyed a third of our people, became possible because no one defended us. Being homeless, we were also defenseless. . . .

No nation has expressed its bond with its land with as much intensity and consistency as we have. . . . For **millennia** our prayers, literature and folklore have expressed powerful longing to return to our land. Only . . . the Land of Israel is our true homeland. Any other country, no matter how **hospitable**, is still a . . . temporary station on the way home. . . .

sovereignty: political control

persecuted: mistreated

oppressed: treated cruelly

exterminate: destroy

genocide: large-scale killing

millennia: thousands of years

hospitable: friendly

159

Regrettably the Arab leaders, whose friendship we wanted most, opposed a Jewish state in the region. With a few distinguished exceptions, they claimed that the Land of Israel is part of the Arab **domain** that stretches from the Atlantic [Ocean] to the Persian Gulf. . . .

domain: territory

In its declaration of independence on May 15, 1948, Israel stretched out its hand in peace to its Arab neighbors, calling for an end to war and bloodshed. In response, seven Arab states invaded Israel. . . .

We **repulsed** the Arab onslaught, prevented Israel's **annihilation**, declared its independence and established a **viable** state and government institutions within a very short time. After their attack on Israel failed, the Arab regimes continued their fight against Israel with boycott, blockade, terrorism and outright war. . . .

repulsed: drove back
annihilation: destruction
viable: working

Arab hostility to Israel has also brought tragic human suffering to the Arab people. Tens of thousands have been killed and wounded. Hundreds of thousands of Arabs who lived in . . . Palestine were encouraged by their own leaders to flee from their homes. Their suffering is a blot on humanity. . . .

We, who over the centuries were denied access to our holy places, respect the religion of all faiths in our country. Our law guarantees freedom of worship and protects the holy places of every religion. . . .

I stand before you today in yet another quest for peace, not only on behalf of the State of Israel, but in the name of the entire Jewish people, that has maintained an unbreakable bond with the Land of Israel for almost 4,000 years. . . .

We are a nation of four million. The Arab nations from the Atlantic to the gulf number 170 million. We control only 28,000 square kilometers [11,200 sq. mi.]. The Arabs possess a land mass of 14 million square kilometers [5,600,000 sq. mi.]. The issue is not territory but our existence. . . .

Today it is a dream, but we have seen, in our own lifetime, some of the most fantastic dreams become reality. Today, the gulf separating the two sides is still too wide, the Arab hostility to Israel too deep, the lack of trust too immense, to permit a dramatic, quick solution. But, we must start on the long road to **reconciliation** with this first step in the peace process. . . .

reconciliation: peaceful settlement

Speech by Haidar Abdel-Shafi

We, the people of Palestine, stand before you in the fullness of our pain, our pride, and our anticipation for we have long harbored a yearning for peace and a dream of justice and freedom. . . .

As we speak, thousands of our brothers and sisters are **languishing** in Israeli prisons and detention camps, most detained without evidence, charge or trial, many cruelly mistreated and tortured in **interrogation**, guilty only of seeking freedom or daring to defy the occupation. We speak in their name, and we say, "Set them free." . . .

languishing: wasting away

interrogation: questioning

As we speak, the eyes of thousands of Palestinian refugees [and] **deportees** . . . are haunting us for exile [as] a cruel fate. Bring them

deportees: people forced to leave a country

160

home. They have the right to return. As we speak, the silence of demolished homes echoes through the halls and in our minds.

We must rebuild our homes and our free state. And what do we tell the loved ones of those killed by army bullets? How do we answer the questions and the fear in our children's eyes, for one out of three Palestinian children under occupation has been killed, injured, or detained in the past four years?

How can we explain to our children that they are denied education or schools so often closed by the army . . . or why their life is in danger for raising a flag in the land where even children are killed or jailed? What **requiem** can be sung for trees uprooted by army bulldozers? And, most of all, who can explain to those whose lands are **confiscated** and free waters stolen? . . .

requiem: service to honor the dead
confiscated: taken away

Remove the barbed wire, restore the land and its life-giving water. The settlements must stop now. Peace cannot be waged while Palestinian land is confiscated. . . .

In the name of the Palestinian people, we wish to directly address the Israeli people, with whom we have had a prolonged exchange of pain. Let us share hope, instead. We are willing to live side by side on the land and the promise of the future.

Sharing, however, requires two partners willing to share as equals. . . .

Our homeland has never ceased to exist in our minds and hearts. . . .

Self-determination . . . can neither be granted nor withheld at the will of the political self-interests of others. For it is **enshrined** in all international charters and humanitarian law. We claim this right. We firmly assert it here before you and in the eyes of the rest of the world.

self-determination: right of a people to decide the form of government they shall have
enshrined: contained
inviolable: unquestionable

For it is a sacred and **inviolable** right which we shall relentlessly pursue and exercise with dedication and self-confidence and pride. Let's end . . . this unnatural condition of occupation, which has already claimed too many lives.

No dream of expansion or glory can justify the taking of a single life. Set us free to **reengage** as neighbors and as equals on our holy land. To our people in exile and under occupation who have sent us to this appointment, laden with their trust, love and **aspirations**, we say that the load is heavy and the task is great, but we shall be true.

reengage: come together again
aspirations: hopes

In the words of our great national poet, Mahmoud Darwish, "My homeland is not a suitcase and I am no traveler."

To the exiled and the occupied, we say you shall return and you shall remain and we will prevail, for our cause is just.

The peace talks that began in 1991 marked the first time that Israel, the Palestinians, and any Arab nations met face to face to work out their problems. The first round of negotiations, however, failed to produce any major solutions. Many people hope the talks will continue and that a peaceful settlement in the Middle East will one day be achieved. To learn how young people hope to bring peace to this region, read the next document on page 162.

Source: *"3 Speeches: The Area is 'a Dangerous Battleground.' "* The New York Times. November 1, 1991.

Poems for Peace

by Tali Shurek and Mahmud Abu Radj, 1974

Peace negotiators, such as the ones you read about on pages 159-161, are not the only people in the Middle East who want peace. Young people living in this region of the world also want to make the Middle East a safer place in which to live. Below are two poems that were written in Israel. The one on the left is by Mahmud Abu Radj, a 12-year-old Arab, and the one on the right is by Tali Shurek, a 13-year-old Jew. How do these two poems use different images to present similar ideas?

When Will It Come, The Day

When will peace take over?
When will it come, the day?
When with armies and bombs will they do away
When all this hostility cease,
A day on which battleships
Will become palaces of leisure and fun
Floating on the seas.

A day on which the steel of guns
Will be melted into pleasure cars;
A day on which generals will begin to raise flowers.

When peace
Will include all the peoples of these neighboring
   lands,
When Ishmael and Israel
Will go hand in hand,
And when every Jew—
The Arab's brother will be.
When will it come, the day?

Mahmud Abu Radj

The Paint-Box

I had a paint-box—
Each color glowing with delight;
I had a paint-box with colors
Warm and cool and bright.
I had no red for wounds and
   blood,
I had no black for an orphaned
   child,
I had no white for the face of
   the dead,
I had no yellow for burning
   sands.
I had orange for joy and life.
I had green for buds and
   blooms,
I had blue for clear bright skies.
I had pink for dreams and rest.
I sat down
and painted
Peace.

Tali Shurek

Young people such as Tali Shurek and Mahmud Abu Radj hope that their poetry can help make the world a more peaceful place. If you were to write a poem about peace, what images would you use?

Source: Jacob Zim, *My Shalom My Peace*. Tel Aviv, Israel: American Israel Publishing Co. Ltd., 1974.

Separation

by Sherko Bekas, 1988

One of the many groups of people living in the Middle East is the Kurds. The Kurdish people, who number more than 20 million, have lived in parts of Iraq, Iran, Turkey, and Syria for more than 4,000 years. Although the Kurds have been ruled by different groups for the past 2,500 years, they have never stopped fighting for their freedom and the right to form their own nation. Most recently they have been fighting to free themselves from the rule of Iraqi leader Saddam Hussein. One of these Kurdish freedom fighters is a poet named Sherko Bekas, who was born in Iraq in 1940. From reading the poem below, recently translated by Hussain Sinjari, what do you think Bekas believes are the essential parts of life? Why do you think he named his poem "Separation"?

If within my poems

You take out the flower

From the four seasons

One of my seasons will die

If you exclude love

Two of my seasons will die

If you exclude bread

Three of my seasons will die

And if you take away freedom

All four seasons and I will die.

Since 1965 Sherko Bekas has been working with the Kurdish National Liberation Movement. He has endured both oppression and exile in his efforts to bring attention to the cause of the Kurds. He now lives in Sweden, where he continues to write poetry and to work for the freedom of the Kurdish people.

Source: Sherko Bekas, *Index on Censorship*. London, 1988.

The Mahabharata

Ancient Indian Epic, about 400 B.C.

About 2,500 years ago—no one knows exactly when—a great Hindu poem was written in India. This ancient epic, called the Mahabharata *(məha′ ba′ rətə), consists of 100,000 stanzas and tells the heroic story of two families who fought to control a kingdom in northern India. Combined with the story are legends, tales, and religious discussions. These religious discussions deal with many basic Hindu ideas. Below are two precepts, or principles, from the* Mahabharata. *What are some of the lessons that these precepts teach Hindus about life?*

Enjoy the pleasure
bestowed on you,

and bear the pain
bestowed on you,

wait patiently for
what time brings,

as does the farmer
with the fruit.

Let us overcome
the angry man
  with gentleness,

the evil man
  with goodness,

the miser
  with generosity,

the liar
  with truth.

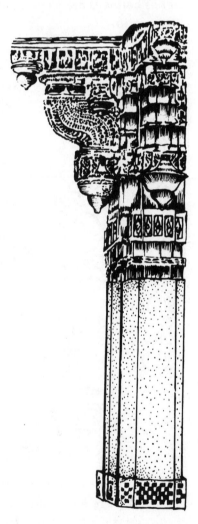

The Mahabharata *is one of two great Hindu epics. Its deeply religious poems continue to be read by people all over the world.*

Source: Daisy Aldan, *Poems from India*. New York: Thomas Y. Crowell Company, 1969.

Why India Must Be Free

by Mohandas Gandhi, 1930 and 1945

Great Britain ruled India as a colony for many years. In the early 1900s many Indians began fighting for the independence of their nation. The leader of this movement was a lawyer named Mohandas Gandhi (1869-1948). He urged Indians to seek independence without violence by practicing civil disobedience—the refusal to obey unjust laws. Gandhi wrote the letter on this page to Lord Irwin, the British governor of India, in 1930. He wrote the letter on page 166 to Jawaharlal Nehru, another Indian independence leader, in 1945, just after World War II. How does Gandhi separate his feelings about British rule from his feelings about the British people? What does he believe individuals must do to change the world?

Letter to Lord Irwin

March 2, 1930
Dear Friend,

Before **embarking** on civil disobedience and taking the risk I have dreaded to take all these years, I would **fain** approach you and find a way out.

My personal faith is absolutely clear. I cannot intentionally hurt anything that lives, much less fellow human beings, even though they may do the greatest wrong to me and mine. Whilst, therefore, I hold the British rule to be a curse, I do not intend harm to a single Englishman or to any **legitimate** interest he may have in India.

I must not be misunderstood. Though I hold the British rule in India to be a curse, I do not, therefore, consider Englishmen in general to be worse than any other people on earth. I have the privilege of claiming many Englishmen as dearest friends. Indeed much that I have learnt of the evil of British rule is due to the writings of frank and courageous Englishmen who have not hesitated to tell the **unpalatable** truth about that rule.

And why do I regard the British rule as a curse?

It has **impoverished** . . . millions by a system of progressive **exploitation** and by a ruinously expensive military and civil administration which the country can never afford.

embarking: setting out
fain: rather

legitimate: rightful

unpalatable: unpleasant

impoverished: made poor
exploitation: misuse

Letter to Jawaharlal Nehru

October 5, 1945
Jawaharlal . . .

I believe that if India, and through India the world, is to achieve real freedom, then sooner or later we shall have to go and live in the villages—in huts, not in palaces. Millions of people can never live in cities and palaces in comfort and peace. Nor can they do so by killing one another, that is, by resorting to violence and untruth. I have not the slightest doubt that, **but for** the pair, truth and nonviolence, mankind will be doomed. We can have the **vision** of that truth and nonviolence only in the simplicity of the villages. That simplicity **resides** in the spinning-wheel and what is implied by the spinning-wheel. It does not frighten me at all that the world seems to be going in the opposite direction. For the matter of that, when the moth approaches its doom it whirls round faster and faster till it is burnt up. It is possible that India will not be able to escape this moth-like circling. It is my duty to try, till my last breath, to save India and through it the world from such a fate. The sum and substance of what I want to say is that the individual person should have control over the things that are necessary for the **sustenance** of life. If he cannot have such control the individual cannot survive. Ultimately, the world is made up only of individuals. If there were no drops there would be no ocean.

but for: without
vision: dream

resides: is found

sustenance: support

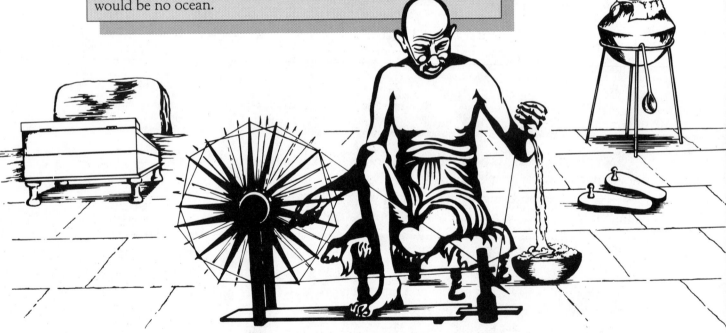

Gandhi's nonviolent campaign succeeded. In 1947 India won its independence from Great Britain, and Gandhi's friend, Jawaharlal Nehru became the country's first prime minister. Gandhi's methods of peaceful protest later inspired a young American minister, Martin Luther King, Jr. In the 1950s and 1960s King was a leader of the civil rights movement, which used nonviolent protest in the fight for equal rights for all Americans.

Source: Martin Green, ed., *Gandhi in India: In His Own Words.* Hanover, NH: University Press of New England, 1987.

The Sayings of Confucius

by Confucius, about 500 B.C.

For thousands of years, China has been shaped by the values of family loyalty and hard work. A major influence on Chinese civilization has been Confucius (kən fū′ shəs), a philosopher and teacher born in 551 B.C. In the hope of preventing wars, Confucius taught that kindness and respect in the family form the foundation of a peaceful society. Confucius stressed that rulers are also obligated to be honest and just. The passages below are some of Confucius's teachings that his students later wrote down. How do the teachings of Confucius still relate to life today?

Having only **coarse** food to eat, plain water to drink, and a bent arm for a pillow, one can still find happiness therein. Riches and honor acquired by **unrighteous** means are to me as drifting clouds.

coarse: simple

unrighteous: unjust

Those who know the truth are not up to those who love it; those who love the truth are not up to those who delight in it.

By nature men are pretty much alike; it is learning and practice that set them apart.

Shall I teach you what knowledge is? When you know a thing, say that you know it; when you do not know a thing, admit that you do not know it. That is knowledge.

Tzu Kung asked: "Is there any one word that can serve as a principle for the conduct of life?" Confucius said: "Perhaps the word '**reciprocity**': Do not do to others what you would not want others to do to you."

The gentleman first practices what he preaches and then preaches what he practices.

The gentleman understands what is right; the inferior man understands what is **profitable**.

The gentleman makes demands on himself; the inferior man makes demands on others.

A government is good when those near are happy and those far off are attracted.

reciprocity: mutual sharing

profitable: money-making

After Confucius died in 479 B.C., his teachings were handed down by others. His ideas about respect and honesty became part of the fabric of Chinese society and spread across Southeast Asia. His teachings remain a major influence throughout much of Asia and the world.

Source: Wm. Theodore de Bary, ed., *Sources of Chinese Tradition*, New York and London: Columbia University Press, 1960.

The Splendors of Hangzhou

by an Unknown Chinese Traveler, 1235

For thousand of years, bustling, exciting cities have been an important part of Chinese life. One of the most ancient cities in China is Hangzhou (hang′ jō). This city along the east coast of China served as the nation's capital in the 12th and 13th centuries. During this period, Hangzhou overflowed with markets, goods, and endless types of entertainment. The drawing on the next page, which was created by a Chinese artist living in Hangzhou during the 1200s, shows one of the city's many silk shops. In 1235 a Chinese traveler visited this fascinating city and described its attractions. As you read this traveler's account, think of what you might do if you had one day to spend in ancient Hangzhou. How do the attractions of 13th-century Hangzhou compare with attractions of cities today?

Markets

In the evening, with the exception of the square in front of the palace, the markets are as busy as during the day. The most attractive one is at Central Square, where all sorts of **exquisite artifacts**, instruments, containers, and hundreds of varieties of goods are for sale. In other marketplaces, sales, auctions, and exchanges go on constantly. In the wine shops and inns business also thrives. Only after the fourth drum does the city gradually quiet down, but by the fifth drum, court officials already start preparing for audiences and merchants are getting ready for the morning market again. This cycle goes on all year round without **respite**. . . .

exquisite artifacts: beautiful hand-crafted goods

respite: rest

Commercial Establishments

Various businesses are designated by the word "company" (*hang*), which is a taxation category **imposed** by the government and is used for all businesses dealing in **commodities**, regardless of their size. Even physicians and fortunetellers are included. Other trades sometimes also borrow the word "company" for their own use, such as liquor company and food company. Some businesses are called "gatherings" (*ho*), such as a flower gathering, fruit gathering, dried-fish gathering. . . . **Artisans** sometimes call their businesses "workshops" (*tso*), such as comb workshop, belt workshop, gold-and-silver plating workshop. There are some businesses that use unusual names; for example, shops dealing in the "seven treasures" (gold, silver, pearl, amber, etc.) may call themselves **curio** companies, whereas a bathhouse may be designated a fragrant-water company.

imposed: set up
commodities: goods

artisans: skilled workers

curio: rare goods

In general, the capital attracts the greatest variety of goods and has the best craftsmen. For instance, the flower company at Superior Lane does a truly excellent job of flower arrangement, and its caps, hairpins, and collars are **unsurpassed** in craftsmanship. Some of the most famous specialties of the capital are the sweet-bean soup at the **Miscellaneous** Market, the pickled dates of the Ko family, the thick soup of the Kuang family at Superior Lane, the fruit at the Great Commons marketplace, the cooked meats in front of Eternal Mercy Temple, Sister Sung's fish broth at Penny Pond Gate, the juicy lungs at Flowing Gold Gate, the "lamb rice" of the Chih family at Central Square, the boots of the P'eng family, the fine clothing of the Hsüan family at Southern Commons, the sticky rice pastry of the Chang family, the flutes made by Ku the Fourth, and the Ch'iu family's Tatar whistles at the Great Commons. . . .

unsurpassed: not topped

miscellaneous: varied

Entertainment Centers

The hundred games used to be the official entertainment of the old capital. The experts . . . can climb high poles, do somersaults, walk on stilts, juggle spears . . . play with swords, display horsemanship, and so on.

The various skills of the entertainers have their respective high-sounding names. Their acts include: kicking bottles, juggling plates, kicking musical stones, twirling drumsticks, kicking writing brushes, playing ball. There are also performances with trained insects, fish or bears, fireworks, fire shows, water shows, puppet shows, and marksmanship of all kinds.

Puppet shows include string-puppets, cane-top puppets, water-puppets, and flesh-puppets. The stories are usually fictitious and fantastic. Shadow plays originated in the old capital. At first the figures were made with white paper; later they were made of leather and painted various colors. The stories of the shadow plays are pretty much the same as those used by the storytellers; generally speaking, they are a mixture of truth and fiction. The loyal and righteous are given a handsome appearance, whereas the wicked and **treacherous** are depicted as monstrously ugly—a kind of **implicit** criticism that is easily understood by the people in the streets. The storytellers can be divided into four groups: those who specialize in social tales, mysteries, and miracle tales; those who deal with military adventures; those who **explicate sutras** by telling religious tales; and those who relate historical events. . . .

treacherous: untrustworthy

implicit: understood

explicate: explain

sutras: sacred Buddhist teachings

Boats

The capital is encircled by a river on the left side and by West Lake on the right; thus the most convenient way to travel is by boat. The boats for hire on West Lake vary greatly in size. Some are 50 feet [15 m] long and have a capacity of more than 100 passengers; others are 20 to 30 feet [6 to 9 m] long and can take 30 to 50 passengers. All of them are exquisitely constructed, with carvings on the railings and paintings on the beams. They sail so smoothly that the passengers may forget that they are on water. These boats are for hire in all seasons and never lack patrons. They are also well equipped with everything; a tourist can get on board in the morning, drink wine, and enjoy himself; at dusk he may walk home by following a trail. It is not tiring but is rather expensive. Some wealthy families have their own pleasure boats, and these are even more exquisitely built and more luxuriously fitted out.

Dragon boat competitions are held in spring at the West Lake and in autumn at the Che River. The dragon boats are light and swift and make a grand **spectacle**. . . .In early and mid-autumn there are swimmers in the Che River, who, **brandishing** pennants and poles, display the most breathtaking skills. I believe this is a unique attraction of the capital. . . .

spectacle: show

brandishing: waving

Specialty Stores

Some famous fabric stores sell exquisite brocade and fine silk which are unsurpassed elsewhere in the country. Along the river, close to the Peaceful Ford Bridge, there are numerous fabric stores, fan shops, and **lacquerware** and porcelain shops. Most other cities can only boast of one special product; what makes the capital unique is that it gathers goods from all places. Furthermore, because of the large population and busy commercial traffic, there is a demand for everything. There are even shops that deal exclusively in used paper or in feathers, for instance.

lacquerware: varnished wood products

The treasures of Hangzhou and other parts of China were among the greatest in the world. After Marco Polo visited China in the late 1200s, tales of China's wealth began to spread to Europe. Europeans wanted these fabulous goods and luxuries, and a busy trade soon flourished. During the 1400s Europeans, who were eager for such treasures, began racing to find the shortest route to China and Asia.

Source: Patricia Buckley Ebrey, ed., *Chinese Civilization and Society.* New York: The Free Press, 1981.

Massacre at Tian An Men Square

Signs of Protest, 1989

In May 1989 thousands of students began gathering at Tian An Men Square, one of the largest open spaces in Beijing, the capital of China. These students were protesting against the oppressive communist government. Each day more and more students gathered in the square and were soon joined by workers, journalists, and others. Within two weeks the number of people demonstrating in Tian An Men Square reached 1 million. Demonstrations were held in more than 80 cities across China in support of the students. What did these protesters want? On this page are pictures showing signs carried during the demonstration in Tian An Men Square. Look at these signs and then read their English translations. How do the signs express the demands of the protesters?

1. This is a completely peaceful demonstration. This is not an act of violence. We object to the way the government ignores our needs. Until the government negotiates new terms with us as we requested, we shall fast.

2. Liberty or Death.

3. In One Voice the Citizens of Beijing Support University Students.

4. We Want to Speak but Can't.

5. Down with the Corrupt Officials.

The Chinese government opposed the demands of the protesters and ordered the demonstration to end. The protesters refused. On June 4, 1989, the government sent in tanks and troops to break up the demonstration. In the massacre that followed, hundreds of people were killed and more than 100,000 were arrested. Many of those who were arrested remain in jail to this day. The courage of the protesters who challenged their oppressive government remains an inspiration to millions of Chinese people today.

The Tale of Genji

by Murasaki Shikibu, early 1000s

In the late 10th century, Japanese literature began to flower with stories and poems about the rituals and ceremonies of the island nation's palace life. Around the year 1000, Murasaki Shikibu (mùr ä sak' ē   shē' kē bù, 978-1031), a woman who worked for the empress, wrote Genji monogatari, *which translates as* The Tale of Genji (gen' je). *This book, often considered the world's first novel, is about the adventures of a prince named Genji and numbers more than 4,000 pages. In the following excerpt, the prince gets caught in a dangerous storm while he is away from the emperor's palace. What does this story tell you about the customs and beliefs of Japanese society in the 11th century?*

𝓘t was the day of the serpent, the first such day in the Third Month. "The day when a man who has worries goes down and washes them away," said one of his men, admirably informed, it would seem, in all the **annual observances.**

Wishing to have a look at the seashore, Genji set forth. Plain, rough curtains were strung up among the trees, and a **soothsayer** who was doing the circuit of the province was **summoned** to perform the **lustration.**

Genji thought he could see something of himself in the rather large doll being cast off to sea, bearing away sins and **tribulations**. . . .

The bright open seashore showed him to wonderful advantage. The sea stretched placid into **measureless** distances. He thought of all that had happened to him, and all that was still to come. . . .

Suddenly a wind came up and even before the services were finished the sky was black. Genji's men rushed about in confusion. Rain came pouring down, completely without warning. Though the obvious course would have been to return **straightway** to the house, there had been no time to send for umbrellas. The wind was now a howling **tempest**, everything that had not been tied down was **scuttling** off across the beach. The surf was biting at their feet. The sea was white, as if spread over with white linen. Lightning flashed and thunder roared. Fearful every moment of being struck down, they finally made their way back to the house.

"I've never seen anything like it," said one of the men. "Winds do come up from time to time, but not without warning. It is all very strange and very terrible."

annual observances: yearly ceremonies

soothsayer: fortune teller

summoned: called

lustration: purifying ceremony

tribulations: sufferings

measureless: great

straightway: at once

tempest: storm

scuttling: scurrying

The lightning and thunder seemed to announce the end of the world, and the rain to beat its way into the ground; and Genji sat calmly reading a **sutra**. The thunder **subsided** in the evening, but the wind went on through the night.

sutra: sacred Buddhist teaching
subsided: lessened

"Our prayers seem to have been answered. A little more and we would have been carried off. I've heard that tidal waves do carry people off before they know what is happening to them, but I've not seen anything like this.". . .

Genji offered prayers to the king of the sea and countless other gods as well. The thunder was increasingly more terrible, and finally the gallery adjoining his rooms was struck by lightning. Flames sprang up and the gallery was destroyed. The confusion was immense; the whole world seemed to have gone mad. Genji was moved to a building out in back, a kitchen or something of the sort it seemed to be. It was crowded with people of every station and rank. The **clamor** was almost enough to drown out the lightning and thunder. Night descended over a sky already as black as ink.

clamor: noise

Presently the wind and rain subsided and stars began to come out. The kitchen being altogether too mean a place, a move back to the main hall was suggested. The **charred** remains of the gallery were an ugly sight, however, and the hall had been badly muddied and all the blinds and curtains blown away. . . . .

charred: burned

[Genji] opened a **wattled** door and looked out. The moon had come up. The line left by the waves was white and dangerously near, and the surf was still high. There was no one here whom he could turn to, no student of the deeper truths who could **discourse** upon past and present and perhaps explain these wild events. All the fisherfolk had gathered at what they had heard was the house of a great gentleman from the city. They were as noisy and impossible to communicate with as a flock of birds, but no one thought of telling them to leave.

wattled: woven with poles and reeds

discourse: talk

"If the wind had kept up just a little longer," someone said, "absolutely everything would have been swept under. The gods did well by us."

Genji goes through many adventures before this 11th-century novel comes to a close. In addition to writing this novel, Murasaki Shikibu also kept a diary that reveals much about life in ancient Japan.

Source: Murasaki Shikibu, *The Tale of Genji.* New York: Vintage Books, 1990.

ATTACK ON PEARL HARBOR

from *The New York Times*, 1941

After World War II broke out in 1939, the United States tried to remain at peace. But on December 7, 1941, without any warning, Japan made a surprise attack on a United States naval base in Pearl Harbor, Hawaii. Below is the front page of The New York Times reporting this event the next day. As you read this front page, try to imagine that it is December 8, 1941, and you have just bought this newspaper. How might you have reacted to the news?

United States President Franklin D. Roosevelt called December 7, 1941, "a day that will live in infamy." The day after the attack, the United States declared war on Japan. Soon after, Germany declared war on the United States. World War II now became truly a world conflict—a war that affected people all over the world.

When the A-Bomb Fell

by Yoshihiro Kimura, 1951

By the summer of 1945, the United States had been fighting Japan in World War II for more than three and a half years. In an effort to force the Japanese to surrender, the United States dropped an atomic bomb on the Japanese city of Hiroshima (hîr ō shē′ mə) on August 6, 1945. This bomb, the first nuclear weapon ever used in a war, shattered people's lives along with buildings. In a matter of seconds, more than 75,000 people died. Many more thousands were injured or made homeless. One of those injured was a third-grade student named Yoshihiro Kimura. In 1951, six years after the bombing a Hiroshima professor named Dr. Arata Osada collected the stories of children who were in Hiroshima when the bomb exploded. In the following account, Yoshihiro describes that tragic day when the bomb fell. How does he cope with the disaster?

On the morning of August 6th, my father was running a temperature and he didn't get up. My brother . . . was toasting some dried **squid**. After everyone had gone off, I and my father and my mother and my other sister were left. The two of us got ready to go to school.

squid: sea animal

My sister went to the real school and I went to the branch school. . . . My friends and I were talking about the war.

We heard a voice saying, "Air raid alarm."

I hurried home and was playing. This is because I was already used to this sort of thing. Then the alert ended and I went back to school. . . .

Pretty soon we heard a hum and saw a little aeroplane in the sky to the southeast. And this gradually grew larger and came over our heads. I was watching the aeroplane the whole time. I [couldn't] tell whether it [was] a foreign plane or a Japanese plane. Then suddenly a thing like a white parachute came falling. Five or six seconds later everything turned yellow in one instant. It felt the way it does when you get the sunlight straight in your eye. A second or two later, CRASH! There was a tremendous noise. Everything became dark and stones and roof tiles came pouring down on our heads. For a while I was **unconscious**. A whole lot of lumber came piling around my hips and I wanted to protest, "Stop, that hurts!" I **came to** again with the pain. I quickly crawled outside. There were lots of people lying around there; the faces of most of them were **charred**. I got out to the street and just as I heaved a sigh of relief my right hand suddenly began to hurt. When I looked closely at it I found that the skin of my right arm was peeled off from my elbow to my fingers and it was all red. I wanted

unconscious: knocked out

came to: woke up

charred: burned

175

to go home right away and I figured out the direction and started to walk toward the house when I heard a voice call . . . and I turned and looked and it was my sister. Her clothes were torn to rags and her face was so changed that I was amazed.

The two of us started off toward the house together, but the house was flattened and there was no one there. We searched around the neighborhood and then came back and looked and there was Father. Father was pulling off the roof and trying to get something out. But then he seemed to give that up and he came toward us.

When I asked, "Mother?" he said tiredly, "She's dead." . . .

Pretty soon a muddy rain began to fall so we went under the railroad bridge. The railroad bridge was making a **sputtering** noise as it **smoldered**. When the rain stopped it suddenly got cold. . . .

sputtering: hissing
smoldered: burned slowly

I got terribly thirsty so I went to the river to drink. From upstream a great many black and burned **corpses** came floating down the river. I pushed them away and drank the water. At the **margin** of the river there were corpses lying all over the place. Among them were some who weren't dead yet and there were some children who were screaming, "Mother! Mother!" When I saw the corpses I was already so used to it I didn't think anything of it. There were also some people who came **tottering** to the edge of the river and fell in and died just like that. Pretty soon my sister too—was it because of her burns?—fell down on the road. My father carried her and laid her down where our house had been. In the evening my brother came back. . . .

corpses: dead bodies
margin: edge

tottering: wobbling

There are only four left: I and Father and my big brother and the other sister. I didn't have the strength to say another thing. Everybody was in a sort of **daze**. That night I couldn't sleep either. When I got up to go to the bathroom I tried calling, "Mother."

daze: confusion

But Mother wasn't there anymore. When I finally realized she was dead, I can't describe to you the loneliness and sorrow that attacked me. I cried with my whole soul. But no matter how hard I cry, Mother won't come back. . . .

After a while another misfortune came to us. On the 15th of August at about three o'clock my sister finally died. . . . That day the war ended. . . .

The deaths of my kind mother and sisters are all because of that war. I wouldn't hate any special person, blaming him for my mother's death. However, only war alone I *will* hate. I hope that this hateful war will never be repeated.

War is the enemy of everyone. If we can do away with war and if peace comes, I am certain that my mother in heaven will be happy.

Three days after dropping the atomic bomb on Hiroshima, the United States dropped a second atomic bomb on Nagasaki. Six days later Japan surrendered, ending World War II. The people of Hiroshima and Nagasaki have since rebuilt their cities. Each year in August, the Japanese hold ceremonies to honor the atomic bomb victims and urge an end to warfare.

Source: Dr. Arata Osada, ed., *Children of the A-Bomb: The Testament of the Boys and Girls of Hiroshima.* London: Peter Owen Limited, 1963.

Governing Japan Today

by Michitada Takasugi, 1984

Since the destruction caused by World War II, which was described on pages 175-176, Japan has made great progress in rebuilding its society and its economy. It has also rebuilt its government. Like the United States, Japan has a democratic form of government and two major political parties. Japan's major parties are the Liberal Democrats and the Socialists. Michitada Takasugi is a member of the Diet, the national legislature of Japan. In the excerpt below, he describes some of his duties on a typical workday. What does Takasugi feel are his responsibilities as a politician? What is his attitude toward world peace?

*T*he National Diet consists of two houses, the House of Representatives (the Lower House) and the House of Councillors (the Upper House). The Lower House has 511 members and the Upper House has 252 members—all elected by popular vote. I am a member of the House of Councillors and I belong to the Japan Socialist Party, which is the present **opposition**.

opposition: political
party not in power

177

I was just 20 when Japan was defeated in World War II. I saw my country in ruins and in a state of confusion. Being a sensitive and **idealistic** youth, my sense of responsibility was strongly awakened. I thought that the work of rebuilding this defeated country was up to the young to carry out. Japan started the war and was defeated. We saw the pictures of the hell at Nagasaki and Hiroshima after the atom bombs were dropped. We shall never repeat this mistake again. We must build a peaceful society so that we will never see nuclear weapons used. This is why I decided to go into politics as a socialist.

idealistic: hopeful, believing that the world can be a better place

When I graduated from college I took a job as a secretary to a member of the House of Councillors. This was my first step forward in the world of politics. I was elected a member of the House in 1974, and have been a member ever since.

A politician's life is a very busy one. I get up at 7:30 A.M. and immediately go through the newspapers and the news on TV. Every other day I have a breakfast meeting with other members and we exchange our ideas. There follow official meetings and committee work until the House convenes at 10:30 A.M. When the work of the House is finished I go back to the official residence for members of the House and have dinner. But even after dinner there are policy research meetings and so on waiting for me, and it is not unusual for work to continue until midnight.

As a member of the House my present job is chairman of the special Price Countermeasure Committee. The job of this committee is to examine ways of **stabilizing** prices and combating inflation. So we tackle all sorts of price problems from food to gasoline. Fortunately, in the last two or three years, Japanese prices have been very stable compared with those of the U.S.A. and Europe. I feel happy and proud that this is partly as a result of our hard work. I am also involved in encouraging social welfare works for the aged, the disabled and children.

stabilizing: maintaining

On Saturdays and Sundays the Diet is closed so I return to my home in the **Ibaraki district**. But I do not go back home to take a rest. I go back in order to listen to the opinions of the people who elected me and I talk to them. I cover every corner of my area on my own feet. I believe it is a basic political duty to talk to people and to reflect their views in national policy.

Ibaraki district: legislative district north of Tokyo

At first glance, all this work may seem like a drop in the ocean when compared with the huge problems facing the world today. But it is only by long and consistent effort that good results are reached in politics.

Thanks to political leaders like Michitada Takasugi, Japan has had a stable democratic government since World War II ended in 1945. During this period Japan has become one of the leading industrial nations of the world.

Source: Kazuhide Kawamata, *We Live in Japan*. New York: The Bookwright Press, 1984.

The Tiger and the Three Wise Rabbits

Ancient Korean Tale Retold by Carol J. Farley, 1991

The Korean peninsula is home to one of the world's oldest cultures. For thousands of years, Koreans have maintained a distinctive culture on this peninsula, despite having been ruled by other nations—including China and Japan—at different periods during their history. Like many people around the world, Koreans have a strong tradition of storytelling. Many Korean tales are about tigers, who once roamed the peninsula. According to ancient Korean beliefs, tigers were considered one of four gods that ruled the land. While many American tales begin with the words, "Once upon a time," most Korean stories begin with the words, "When tigers smoked long pipes." In the tale below, what does the tiger learn?

When tigers smoked long pipes, there were three rabbits in a large forest. They lived in constant fear of a huge tiger who often hunted nearby. One day, they decided to have a talk with the tiger.

"Uncle Tiger," the bravest one said, "what makes you think you have the right to chase us? All day, every day, we must worry. We could not enjoy our dinner in the bamboo garden in the spring because we feared you might pounce on us. We could not sit beside the forest pond in the summer and admire the lotus blossoms because you might have been lurking behind a tree. We can scarcely sleep these cool autumn nights because of trembling with fear of you. Why can't you live in peace and harmony with us?"

The tiger waved his paws. "What a foolish question!" he roared. "I must chase you because I must eat!"

"But couldn't you eat the fish?" the smallest rabbit asked. "They don't enjoy the bamboo grove or the lotus blossoms or the beautiful mountain scenery. Perhaps they wouldn't mind having you chase them."

The tiger swished his long tail. He ran his paw under the chin string of his fine horsehair hat. "But how would I chase them? I run on land. They live in the water."

"We have a plan," the wisest rabbit said. "We can help you catch a whole bundle of those tasty fish. All you have to do is to sit right by the creek with your beautiful tail dangling in the water. We will lead the fish upstream to you while you relax and smoke your favorite pipe. When they reach you, you will feel them. Pull your tail up quickly, and you will have your dinner attached to it."

The tiger, who was a vain, lazy fellow, **switched** his long tail back and forth again. Yes, indeed, it was a beautiful tail. No fish would be

switched: moved

179

able to resist its beauty. And sitting beside the creek would certainly be easier than having to run all over the forest for his dinner. "I'll do it," he agreed.

Happily, he waved to the three rabbits as they began chasing the fish. "Be certain you sit quietly, Uncle Tiger," they called back, "or you will frighten those tasty fish away. Be patient and allow us time to fetch you a mighty bundle." As they disappeared around a bend and into the forest, the tiger dropped his tail into the cold water and took out his long pipe.

Soon his beautiful tail felt cold and heavy, but he continued to sit quietly. It would never do to have those unworthy rabbits see that he was unable to be patient. Still, though, he felt as cold as the stones on the mountains. As a fierce wind began to blow, he felt hungry, too. He grew hungrier as light snowflakes began to fall. Soon, the flakes grew large enough to drown the ashes in his pipe.

Finally, the sky darkened, and the stars began to twinkle. The tiger removed his cold pipe from his mouth, and stared up at them. He switched his whiskers, listening to strange noises. Were the stars whispering messages across the sky? Or was someone laughing in the forest? He pricked up his ears. Yes! The noises were coming from the forest! Who would dare laugh at a creature as fine as he?

The tiger angrily jumped up, and his tail jerked him back down. Impatiently, he yanked on it. Much to his surprise, he discovered it was stuck in the creek, frozen solid in the ice. He gave a mighty roar, but its sound was barely heard above the laughter of the many smaller beasts in the forest. The three rabbits had outwitted him. Until the ice melted in the spring, they were free to roam the forest without fear.

*Since 1953 the Korean peninsula has been divided into the two nations of North Korea and South Korea. Old tales such as **The Tiger and the Three Wise Rabbits** help to maintain a common culture among all Koreans.*

Source: Carol J. Farley, *Korea: Land of the Morning Calm*. Minneapolis: Dillon Press, Inc., 1991.

Hand-Shadow Song

Traditional Indonesian Song, 1970

People in Indonesia possess a long, tradition of music, dance, drama, and shadow plays. In these plays, puppets are held up behind cloth screens and lit from behind, casting shadow figures onto the screen. Shadows have a lot of meaning in Indonesian culture and are featured in different kinds of theater. Many Indonesians believe that drama is a shadow of life. The "Hand-Shadow Song" is a favorite of Indonesian children. As the verses are sung, the hands are used to make shadows of the animals mentioned in the song. What other animals could you sing about in a hand-shadow song?

1.   Can you   see   the deer   He's munch - ing
2.   There's a   ti - ny mouse   He's talk - ing
3. The el - e - phant   you see   be - neath the

leaves   you hear: "Mil ke - te - mil mil ke - te -
to   his spouse: "Tji tjit tju - wit tji tjit tju -
bam - boo tree   "Nuk reng - gu - nuk nuk reng - gu -

mil," Be   qui - et   or he'll dis - ap - pear._____
wit, Is   there some   cheese a - round this   house?"_____
nuk," Does that sound strange to you and   me?_____

Source: William I. Kaufman, *UNICEF Book of Children's Songs*. Harrisburg, PA: Stackpole Books, 1970.

Tank, the Water Buffalo

by Huynh Quang Nhuong, 1982

Huynh Quang Nhuong (hwin kwong nyùəng) was born in Mytho, a small village in the central highlands of Vietnam. His village consisted of 50 houses made of bamboo frames and covered with coconut leaves. The village was bordered on one side by a dense forest and by a river on the other. Beyond the river lay endless rows of rice fields and a chain of high mountains. Wild animals were a part of everyday life in Mytho. In the following story, Huynh describes his childhood and a very special water buffalo named Tank. In what ways is Tank important to Huynh, his family, and his neighbors?

My family had land on which we grew rice. During July to January, the rainy season, the rice field was flooded, and only water buffaloes could be used to till the soil.

We owned three water buffaloes, one male and two females. One day our male died of old age. My father decided to look for the ideal water buffalo to replace him: a bull that was both a hard worker and a good fighter. Fighting ability was important because tigers raided the herd near the edge of the jungle. Buffaloes born and raised among mountain tribes had the reputation of being excellent fighters, but they were often too fierce, violent, and impatient to handle. On the other hand, buffaloes born and raised in the lowlands were patient and obedient, but they did not make good fighters, for they lived in an area where fierce **predators** did not exist. Neither type of buffalo would meet my father's needs.

However, it was possible to have the ideal buffalo if a young bull had a fierce father from the mountains and a patient mother from the lowlands. This unusual mixture occurred if a fierce

182

mountain bull wandered down to the lowlands and met a female which would bear its offspring. The owner of the female might not know that he had a mixed-blood calf until the calf grew older and the thickness of its coat indicated the mountain origin of its father. So sometimes a farmer who had more buffaloes than he needed would unwittingly sell a valuable mixed-blood calf.

My father, by a combination of luck and patience, discovered a mixed-blood buffalo at the ranch of a buffalo merchant in a town far below the river and bought it at a good price.

I was six years old when my father brought the new calf home. He let me give the young buffalo food and water, and sometimes he allowed me to pat its shoulders. But he told me never to approach it when I was alone, for calves were unpredictable. Although they usually obeyed everybody taller than they were, they did not obey small children and sometimes might hurt them.

I listened to my father, but I trusted our calf. I knew he and I would become great friends.

Our calf grew into a handsome and powerful buffalo. He not only became the head of our small herd, but also became the head of all the herds in our **hamlet** after many ferocious and successful fights with the other males. We named him "Tank," because when he hit another male during a fight, he struck as heavily as a tank.

One day a young bull from a nearby hamlet trespassed on Tank's territory and challenged his authority. Tank roared a few times to warn the intruder, but the other buffalo was determined to fight. When we heard Tank's roars we knew that there was trouble in the field. Everyone in the hamlet rushed to a hill to watch the fight. We could not prevent it, so we stayed on high ground to protect ourselves; for a defeated buffalo would often run to humans to be rescued and, in its panic, trample them.

Tank left his herd and faced the **arrogant** intruder. The other buffaloes stopped eating and waited. Suddenly the two bulls charged and ran into each other head on. I heard a mighty thud. Both buffaloes fell back. My heart was pounding. It was the first time any of us had ever seen Tank fall back. Tank was the pride of the hamlet, and we would be very ashamed if he lost the fight; or worse, if Tank were killed, some of our female buffaloes might follow the victorious bull home to the other hamlet, and it would be very hard to bring them back.

The two buffaloes recovered from the powerful collision and ran at each other again. This time they locked horns and tried to twist and break each other's necks. Next, each pushed the other and tried to overturn him. At first the intruder **sustained** Tank's push very well. But then, little by little, he began to lose ground. Tank pushed him farther and farther backward. Unfortunately for the other buffalo, who had fought quite well so far, there was a deep trench behind him. When his two hind legs fell into the trench, the animal was helpless. Tank's sharpened horns hit first his neck, then his shoulders; but unlike other

predators: animals that eat other animals

hamlet: small village

arrogant: proud

sustained: withstood

183

buffaloes, this one did not call for help.

My father felt sorry for the bull, and he asked my cousin, whom Tank loved the best, to try to stop Tank from killing him. My cousin rushed to Tank's side and called his name. Tank, furious because he was hurt himself, nevertheless listened to my cousin and let him lead him away. The defeated intruder was rescued from the trench and set free, and we never saw or heard from him again.

Tank became so famous that people from far away brought females to breed with him. Buffalo thieves also considered him a prize. One day it rained very hard and Tank did not come home. The next morning we went to look for him. We asked a friend who had a hound dog to help us. My father, my cousin and I, and a few well-armed friends followed the hound and found Tank near a river crossing about fifteen kilometers [9 m] from home, tied to the root of a tree.

When we untied Tank, he was very happy and licked everybody who had come to rescue him. But we were puzzled. There was blood scattered all around, but Tank himself was unharmed. And why, if thieves had taken Tank so far away from our home, had they finally left him there?

Weeks later these questions were answered. At a local wedding we heard a drunken man tell the story of how he had been hurt by Tank during his attempt to steal him. First, he and two **accomplices** had spent many days observing the clothes and mannerisms of my cousin, who took care of Tank and his herd. Then, helped by the pouring rain, which prevented Tank from seeing him clearly, and wearing the same clothes and whistling the same song my cousin did, he approached Tank in the field. When he was close enough he seized the rope that passed through the buffalo's nose. Tank was helpless. If he resisted, the rope would hurt his sensitive nose badly. With the help of his two accomplices, the thief led Tank away. When they reached the river crossing, he loosened the rope so Tank could drink some water. But instead of drinking, Tank hit him with his horns, gashing the man's leg from his knee to the upper thigh. Since the man could not walk, the other thieves had to carry him and leave Tank behind. They knew that we would soon be on their trail with a hound dog. But before they left, they managed to tie Tank's rope to the root of a tree so the angered buffalo couldn't attack them again.

When the thief finished his story, one of the wedding guests asked him why he had not killed Tank, since Tank had hurt him so badly. The thief answered that to kill a buffalo, under any circumstances, would bring bad luck. Besides, he admired Tank too much to kill him. He said that if they had succeeded in stealing Tank, they would have been able to sell him for ten times the price of any ordinary buffalo. Then he added that sometimes he still came to our hamlet just to have a look at the magnificent bull. No other bull was intelligent enough to fool him, a man of many years' experience as a buffalo thief. When asked if he would attempt to steal Tank again, he said no, because this time he would be risking his life for sure. He was right. My father had

accomplices: partners in wrongdoing

removed the rope passing through Tank's nose, just in case anyone tried to steal Tank again.

To our surprise, we learned we did not need the rope to command Tank. He continued to till the soil and guard the herd. We commanded Tank orally now. He quickly learned the meaning of "Left," "Right," and "Stop," and did exactly what my cousin wanted while working in the field. When my cousin put crops on his back and said, "Go," he would walk straight home by himself. And at home after we had unloaded the crops and said, "Go," he would return to the field.

Other buffaloes might be able to do the same job, but not as well as Tank. Most of them could not resist the green grass that bordered the path leading home. When they lingered to eat, they would be late for their tasks. Or sometimes on their way to the field they would see a female buffalo and would stay around and forget everything. But Tank was so exact about his work that one day an angry housewife said she wished that her husband would be as dependable as Tank.

My cousin also trained Tank to fight jungle cats. He made a stuffed tiger with straw and old linen, and **simulated** a tiger attack from different angles. He taught Tank to roll over, for without this trick a buffalo was helpless if a tiger or a panther jumped on its back. But a well-trained buffalo could make a tiger jump away by rolling over, or crush it under its weight. And every morning, my cousin attached a razor-sharp knife to each of Tank's horns before he let him go to the pasture on the edge of the jungle.

simulated: pretended to make

One afternoon all the buffaloes began roaring. Everyone rushed toward the pasture. Hunters blew their hunting horns, and hunting dogs raced out of houses to follow their masters. When we reached the pasture we saw all the adult buffaloes forming a circle to protect their young, and Tank apart from them, fighting with a huge tiger. As we approached, the tiger quit the fight and limped back into the jungle. We examined Tank and found blood on his horns. There was blood scattered all around the ground too, but it was the tiger that had been badly hurt, not Tank. Tank had only a few scratches on his neck.

After this tangle with the tiger, Tank never had to till the soil again. Other inhabitants of the hamlet told my father that if his two other buffaloes were not enough to till the land he owned, they would send theirs to help. Tank's only responsibility now was to guard the hamlet's herd during the dry season.

Huynh Quang Nhuong has written many stories describing his childhood in Vietnam. You can read some of these in his book, The Land I Lost. *Huynh graduated from Saigon University and was later drafted into the South Vietnamese army. He was paralyzed by a bullet during the Vietnam War, and in 1969 he came to live in the United States. For a description of life in Vietnam during the Vietnam War, read the* *next document on pages 186-188.*

Source: Huynh Quang Nhuong, *The Land I Lost: Adventures of a Boy in Vietnam.* New York: J. B. Lippincott Junior Books, 1982.

The War Years in Vietnam

by Le Ly Hayslip, 1989

As the story on pages 182-185 showed, Vietnam is a beautiful land of forests, rice fields, rivers, and mountains. Long, bitter wars, however, have scarred the land and the lives of its people during much of this century. The longest conflict, between North Vietnam and South Vietnam, lasted from the 1950s until 1975. For many of those years, the United States fought in this war on the side of South Vietnam. Le Ly Hayslip was only 12 years old when American soldiers first entered her small village in Vietnam. Because opposing armies competed in the countryside for people's loyalties, Le Ly Hayslip found herself both tortured by the South Vietnamese and sentenced to death by the North Vietnamese. In the excerpt below from her book When Heaven and Earth Changed Places, *Le Ly Hayslip recalls her wartime experiences. What lessons do you think she learned from her father?*

*O*nce, when I was the only child at home, my mother went to [the city of] Da Nang to visit Uncle Nhu, and my father had to take care of me. I woke up from my nap in the empty house and cried for my mother. My father came in from the yard and reassured me, but I was still cranky and continued crying. Finally, he gave me a rice cookie to shut me up. Needless to say, this was a tactic my mother never used.

The next afternoon I woke up and although I was not feeling cranky, I thought a rice cookie might be nice. I cried a fake cry and my father came running in.

"What's this?" he asked, making a worried face. "Little Bay Ly doesn't want a cookie?"

I was confused again.

"Look under your pillow," he said with a smile.

I twisted around and saw that, while I was sleeping, he had placed a rice cookie under my pillow. We both laughed and he picked me up like a sack of rice and carried me outside while I gobbled the cookie.

In the yard, he plunked me down under a tree and told me some stories. After that, he got some scraps of wood and showed me how to make things: a doorstep for my mother and a toy duck for me. . . . My father showed me the mystery of hammers and explained the customs of our people.

His knowledge of the Vietnamese went back to the Chinese Wars in ancient times. I learned how one of my distant ancestors, a woman named Phung Thi Chinh, led Vietnamese fighters against the **Han**. In one battle, even though she was pregnant and surrounded by Chinese, she delivered the baby, tied it to her back, and cut her way to safety wielding a sword in each hand. I was amazed at this warrior's bravery and impressed that I was her **descendant**. Even more, I was amazed and impressed by my father's pride in her accomplishments . . . and his belief that I was worthy of her example. . . .

Never again did I cry after my nap. Phung Thi women were too strong for that. Besides, I was my father's daughter and we had many things to do together. . . .

The next day, I took some water out to him in the fields. My mother was due home any time and I used every opportunity to step outside and watch for her. My father stopped working, drank gratefully, then took my hand and led me to the top of a nearby hill. It had a good view of the village and the land beyond it, almost to the ocean. I thought he was going to show me my mother coming back, but he had something else in mind.

He said, "Bay Ly, you see all this here? This is the Vietnam we have been talking about. You understand that a country is more than a lot of dirt, rivers, and forests, don't you?"

I said, "Yes, I understand." After all, we had learned in school that one's country is as sacred as a father's grave.

"Good. You know, some of these lands are battlefields where your brothers and cousins are fighting. They may never come back. Even your sisters have all left home in search of a better life. You are the only one left in my house. If the enemy comes back, you must be both a daughter and a son. I told you how the Chinese used to rule our land. People in this village had to risk their lives diving in the ocean just to find pearls for the Chinese emperor's gown. They had to risk tigers and snakes in the jungle just to find herbs for his table. Their payment for this hardship was a bowl of rice and another day of life. That is why. . . Phung Thi Chinh fought so hard to expel the Chinese. When the French came, it was the same old story. Your mother and I were taken to Da Nang to build a runway for their airplanes. We labored from sunup to sundown and well after dark. . . . Our reward was a bowl of rice and another day of life. Freedom is never a gift, Bay Ly. It must be won and won again. Do you understand?"

I said that I did. . . .

"Hey." He poked me in the ribs. "Are you getting hungry for lunch?"

"No. I want to learn how to take care of the farm. What happens

Han: an ancient Chinese dynasty

descendant: relative

if the soldiers come back? What did you and Mother do when the soldiers came?"

My father squatted on the dusty hilltop and wiped the sweat from his forehead. "The first thing I did was to tell myself that it was my duty to survive—to take care of my family and my farm. That is a tricky job in wartime. It's as hard as being a soldier. . . . You may remember the night I sent you and your brothers and sisters away with your mother to Da Nang."

"You didn't go with us!" My voice still held the horror of the night I thought I had lost my father.

"Right! I stayed near the village—right on this hill—to keep an eye on the enemy and on our house. If they really wanted to destroy the village, I would save some of our things so that we could start over. Sure enough, that was their plan.

"The real problem was to keep things safe and avoid being captured. Their patrols were everywhere. Sometimes I went so deep in the forest that I worried about getting lost, but all I had to do was follow the smoke from the burning huts and I could find my way back.

"Once, I was trapped between two patrols that had camped on both sides of a river. I had to wait in the water for two days before one of them moved on. When I got out, my skin was **shriveled** like an old melon. I was so cold I could hardly move. From the waist down, my body was black with **leeches**. But it was worth all the pain. When your mother came back, we still had some furniture and tools to cultivate the earth. Many people lost everything. Yes, we were very lucky."

My father put his arms around me. "My brother Huong—your uncle Huong—had three sons and four daughters. Of his four daughters, only one is still alive. Of his three sons, two went north to **Hanoi** and one went south to **Saigon**. Huong's house is very empty." . . .

My father drew me out to arm's length and looked me squarely in the eye. "Now, Bay Ly, do you understand what your job is?"

I squared my shoulders and put on a soldier's face. "My job is to **avenge** my family. To protect my farm by killing the enemy. I must become a woman warrior like Phung Thi Chinh!"

My father laughed and pulled me close. "No, little peach blossom. Your job is to stay alive—to keep an eye on things and keep the village safe. . . . Most of all, it is to live in peace and tend the shrine of our **ancestors**. Do these things well, Bay Ly, and you will be worth more than any soldier who ever took up a sword."

shriveled: wrinkled

leeches: worms that suck blood

Hanoi: the capital of North Vietnam at the time

Saigon: the capital of South Vietnam at the time

avenge: seek revenge for

ancestors: family members who lived long ago

Le Ly Hayslip survived the Vietnam War and fled to the United States with her children in 1970. Five years later the war finally ended with the victory of the North Vietnamese. Le Ly Hayslip returned to her homeland in 1986 and had a reunion with her mother and other family members. She now lives in California, where she founded the East Meets West Foundation, a charitable relief and world peace group.

Source: Le Ly Hayslip with Jay Wurts, *When Heaven and Earth Changed Places.* New York: Doubleday, 1989.

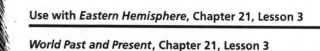

Life in a Cambodian "Reeducation" Camp

by Pin Yathay, 1987

When Pol Pot and his army, the Khmer Rouge (kə mer′ rüzh), came to power in Cambodia in 1975, they began a brutal reign of terror. More than 1 million Cambodians died over the next four years, due to starvation and mass killings. When Pol Pot's forces took over Phnom Penh (pə nom′ pen), the Cambodian capital, residents were forced to leave their homes in the city and resettle in large, rural camps. Among those rounded up and forced into a camp were an engineer named Pin Yathay, his wife Any, and their three children, Staud, Nawath, and Sudath. In the following excerpt from his memoir, Pin Yathay describes the hunger and harsh conditions of the Cambodian camps. What do you think helps people survive in difficult times?

Towards sunset, it began to rain, as usual in the rainy season. We were ordered to stop where we were. The downpour became heavier. There was no shelter. We covered the children with our jackets, and tried to rest on our soaked mats. Staud was crying, though Nawath and Sudath, toughened by months of hard living, squatted . . . silent and uncomplaining. Soon the ground was **awash**. Mud **dribbled** between our feet and soaked our bags. Water trickled down inside our clothes. Old and young alike huddled together, beaten and miserable.

awash: flooded
dribbled: dripped

189

I looked around. In the dying light and the rain, the mass of people around us were **undifferentiated** shadows, moving little, speaking little, eating rice distributed . . . two days before. There was no service or community organization to take care of the sick. No one complained. We were all **paralyzed** by fear of the Khmer Rouge, who stood around in groups of two or three, unmoving in the rain and the gloom.

Next morning, **rations** were distributed. The two Khmer Rouge in charge of the distribution stood under a thatched roof, one calling out names through a microphone, the other plunging a tin into a large sack of rice and measuring out the ration for each. As I received my ration—a half-measure of a condensed-milk tin, 4 ounces [113 g] of rice per person per day—the soldier said, as he was going to each of us in turn: "Wait for **Angkar's** decisions! Don't go anywhere!" . . .

With each column under the command of two soldiers, we marched off along a trail. After a mile [1.6 km] or so, the Khmer Rouge began to **allot** plots of land in the forest, pointing out trees about 20 yards [18 m] apart to act as markers. Here, in **virgin** forest, we were to construct huts. "You have to stay here," one of the black-uniformed young soldiers said, "Forever." . . .

We had never been in such a terrible situation as this. Before, we had always stayed in houses raised on **piles**, traditional houses protected from the damp. Our hut, set in the shade, would always be wet. It certainly was then. Even before dark, it began to rain again. Soon, the carpet of leaves and the mats over them were **impregnated** with water. We **wallowed** in a **bog**, freezing and worn out. Staud was now permanently sick. The other two children just stood or squatted sadly, watching us. As we huddled round the fire, Any and I looked at each other without speaking, and wept. No one spoke. Tears were the only words we needed, tears not so much for ourselves as for the children. . . .

Work started on the fourth day, by which time our houses were ready. The first task was to clear the forest, chopping trees and dragging them aside. Veal Vong, as our camp was called, was right in the middle of uncut jungle. There were no existing rice fields anywhere nearby. We had to create our own. The pattern was much the same as before— wake up at six a.m., a break for food between noon and one p.m., work until six p.m. However, for the first time, we were supervised by armed guards during our working hours. . . .

It was not long before the dying started. Even in the first week, I saw several people carrying **corpses** down the trail. . . .

In 1979 Vietnam invaded Cambodia and drove the Khmer Rouge from power. Pin Yathay survived the years of terror in Cambodia but one more of his children died in the camps. As he and his wife tried to escape through the forest, Any died too. Yathay has since remarried and moved to the Philippines, but he is still attempting to locate the son he left behind.

Source: Pin Yathay, *Stay Alive My Son*. New York: The Free Press, 1987.

Margin glossary:

undifferentiated: unclear

paralyzed: frozen

rations: food shares

Angkar's: the new government's

allot: assign
virgin: untouched

piles: stilts

impregnated: filled
wallowed: sat uncomfortably
bog: swamp

corpses: dead bodies

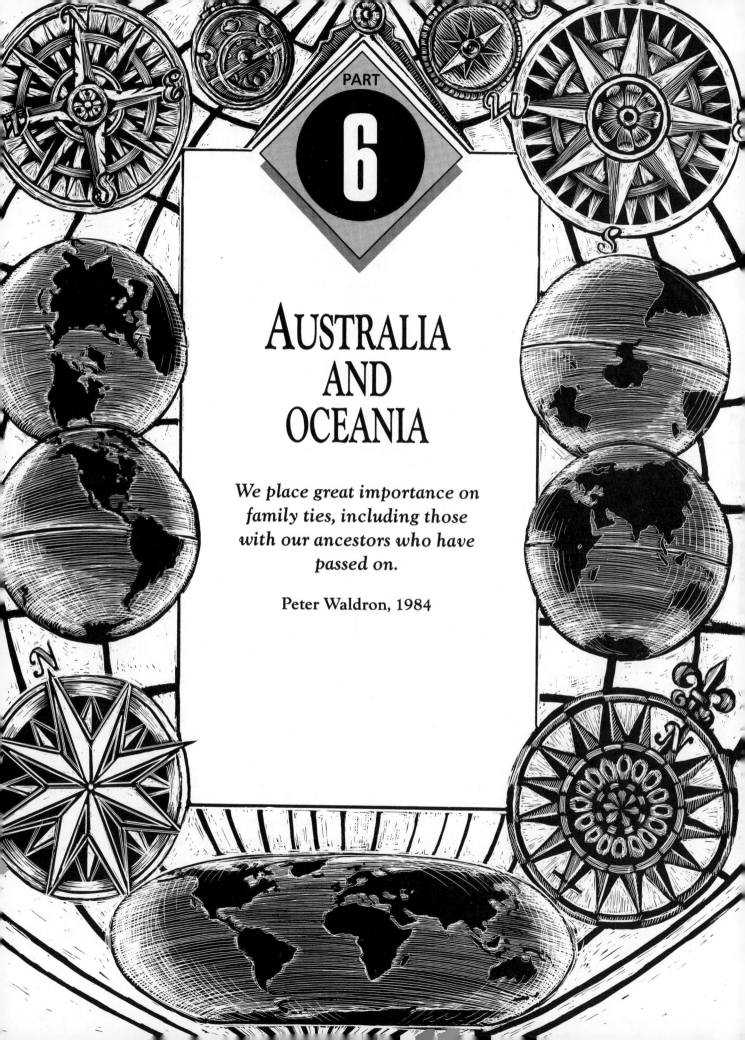

PART

6

AUSTRALIA AND OCEANIA

We place great importance on family ties, including those with our ancestors who have passed on.

Peter Waldron, 1984

THE GREAT BARRIER REEF

by Elspeth Huxley, 1967

Along the northeast coast of Australia lies one of the most amazing natural wonders in the world—the Great Barrier Reef. This reef, or underwater ridge of rocks, stretches more than 1,250 miles (2,010 km) and is filled with an endless variety of colorful coral and beautiful fish. In the following selection, Elspeth Huxley, an English travel writer who was born in Kenya, describes walking on the Great Barrier Reef and swimming in its waters. In what ways does Huxley compare the underwater marvels she sees to other objects found in nature? How does she help you to picture its beauty in your mind's eye?

There are some things that are simply too much for the imagination, like the Milky Way, eternity and the dimensions of the universe. The Great Barrier Reef is another. The basic facts are plain. It is a chain of more than 3,000 islands, some mere specks a few hundred yards across, but others much larger. . . .

[The Australian coast] was [explored] in 1770 by Captain James Cook, who sailed about two-thirds of the way along it, hugging the coast, before [his ship] struck a reef, and he realized that he had come upon one of the great natural phenomena of the world. Two centuries later, there are still islands that are uncharted and unexplored—indeed, there may be islands that did not exist when Captain Cook arrived, for the reef is largely made of coral, and coral is made by tiny animals called polyps, and polyps are continually at work in numbers quite impossible for the mind to grasp— continuously getting born, living, dying and making new coral. The reef is in a state of continual creation. . . .

Twice a day, at low tide, the custom [for us] was to walk about on the reef and observe what had been uncovered. The going is not easy; you stumble into rock pools, stub your feet on branching corals and feel the coral crunching and sometimes giving way under your feet. The sun is blistering, except when low tide happens to coincide with early morning or late afternoon, and the glare is blinding. An hour or so of this is tiring, but fatigue and discomfort are forgotten as you peer at the astonishing world underfoot. . . . In a few square yards you can see a greater variety of shapes and patterns than the boldest artist could dream of, and there are thousands of square miles of this. No two . . . branches, no two twigs, or **cavities**, or caves in miniature, or thumb-sized mountain ranges, are alike. And all this has been created by these **myriads** of tiny polyps. Why, you ask, in heaven's name, why? All this beauty and **inventiveness** of design cannot be necessary for mere survival. . . .

cavities: holes

myriads: great numbers

inventiveness: originality

192

On this particular stretch of reef there are 180 different species of polyp, and each not only shapes its coral skeleton to a different pattern and colour but has a different habit. . . . Small clusters of what appear to be green grapes quiver beneath a gently lapping tide; clumps of brilliant scarlet cactus blooms are one inch high; there is a bunch of bright **mauve** fingers. There is an extraordinary one—but they are all extraordinary—that looks exactly like a beaded purse studded with pearls and flung down on a table with the contents making bulges and hollows; the cinnamon-brown beads are sewn thickly on to green satin. Staghorn or antler corals may be blue, **heliotrope**, purple, pink, yellow, green or lavender . . . or lemon, or any combination of these. They branch into **protuberances** which make them look, as their name implies, like the **proliferating** horns of elks or reindeer. So-called brain corals, looking like lumps of brain flung down in the water, are everywhere; and mushroom corals, which are also correctly named; and dome-shaped **porites** which may be twenty feet in diameter; clusters of violet spikes that look like petrified **buddleias**. . . .

The reef ends abruptly and drops seventy or eighty feet into the ocean bed, and presumably, in places, to the full 180 feet which is the coral habitat. To explore this region you need to go skin diving, but even by swimming about with goggles you can see a good deal. So we hired a boat and set out well before dawn. . . .

As soon as the boat is over the reef's edge, a world of sheer fantasy unfolds. Enormous, terrifying caverns yawn below you and their walls are **honeycombed** with caves. So clear is the water that it seems to sharpen rather than to cloud your vision, so that every stone and shell and clam and coral can be seen in its glowing colours on the white sand. Then comes an abrupt end to the shelf, and down the eye is led to depths where light can never penetrate and eyes are sightless. Here are great clumps of [coral that look like] elephant's ears, huge elkhorns, pincushions, ledges, and what look like enormous pancakes stacked layer on layer.

Anything could lurk down there. Fish dart and gleam and vanish into caves. There are . . . large parrot fish with peacock-blue scales and yellow stripes, fish bandaged in black and white with golden tails, flat yellow boxfish, surgeonfish trailing behind them . . . like a scalpel, big creatures [like] sharks and stingrays and octopi—goodness knows what else, all **preying on** others and being preyed upon from birth till death, world without end. And all in these brilliant colours and with no eye to see and enjoy them.

You could drift above that secret, silent world all day.

The Great Barrier Reef is the largest coral reef in the world. Perhaps some day you will visit Australia and explore this great natural wonder for yourself!

Source: Elspeth Huxley, *Their Shining Eldorado: A Journey Through Australia*. New York: William Morrow & Company, Inc., 1967.

mauve: purplish

heliotrope: reddish purple

protuberances: things that stick out

proliferating: rapidly growing

porites: rounded types of coral

buddleias: type of trees with violet flowers

honeycombed: made into a checkered pattern

preying on: killing for food

Aboriginal Dreamtime

Aborigine Stories Retold by Charles P. Mountford, 1965

The first people to reach Australia arrived thousands of years ago by boat from Southeast Asia. These people, known as Aborigines, spread out across the continent and developed many different cultures. Despite these cultural differences, Aborigines shared many similar ideas about the origins of the world. One of these was the "Dreamtime," a period long ago in which giant, partly human creatures roamed the land. When Dreamtime ended, Aborigine stories describe how these creatures formed most of the features of the world, such as mountain ranges, rivers, and animals. Below are two Aborigine stories about Dreamtime. As you read them, think about other stories about the origin of the world that you read in this Anthology. In what ways are these stories similar and different? What do these Australian stories suggest about the values and ideas of the Aborigines?

Mirram and Wareen the Hunters

In the long distant Dreamtime, Mirram and Wareen were mighty hunters and the closest of friends. But although they roamed the country together and shared the food they caught, they had their likes and dislikes, just as men have today.

At night, Wareen liked a roof over his head, and always made a shelter for himself, but Mirram preferred the freedom of the open spaces and camped under the stars.

All went well until one night a sudden downpour of rain put out Mirram's fire. Cold, wet, and feeling sorry for himself, he thought how warm and dry Wareen must be. As the rain grew heavier and the wind bent the trees and bushes, Mirram ran to Wareen for shelter until the storm had passed. But Wareen was in a bad mood and told Mirram that he was not going to share his comfort with someone who was too lazy to build a shelter of his own.

Surprised, and then enraged at his friend's harsh attitude, Mirram picked up a large stone and threw it at Wareen. It hit him on the head, crushing his forehead quite flat. Roaring with pain, Wareen hurled a spear, which lodged deep in Mirram's spine.

Wareen, with his flattened forehead, changed into the **Wombat**, forever destined to live in a deep, dark hole. Mirram, with Wareen's spear now grown into a long thick tail, became the Kangaroo, who still follows his ancestor's love for the open plains.

These two creatures are still unfriendly, and do their best to avoid each other.

wombat: Australian mammal resembling a small bear

Tiddalik the Flood-Maker

Tiddalik, the largest frog ever known, awoke one morning with an unquenchable thirst. He started to drink, and he drank until there was no fresh water left in the world. The creatures everywhere were soon dying and the trees were shedding their leaves because of the lack of moisture. It seemed that very soon Tiddalik the frog would be the only one alive.

The animals could not think of a way out of their terrible plight, until a wise old wombat suggested that if Tiddalik could be made to laugh, all the imprisoned water would flow out of his mouth.

So everyone gathered by the giant frog's resting-place. For a long time they tried to make him laugh, but in vain. The **kookaburra** told his funniest stories, so good that he could not help laughing at them himself; the kangaroo jumped over the **emu**; and the blanket lizard waddled up and down on two legs making his stomach **protrude**; but the frog's face remained blank and indifferent.

kookaburra: Australian bird

emu: large Australian bird

protrude: stick out

Then, when the animals were in despair, the eel, Nabunum, driven from his favourite creek by the drought, slithered up to the unresponsive frog, and began to dance. He started with slow, graceful movements, but as the dance became faster he wriggled and twisted himself into the most **grotesque** and comical shapes, until suddenly Tiddalik's eyes lit up and he burst out laughing. And as he laughed, the water gushed from his mouth and flowed away to **replenish** the lakes, the swamps, and the rivers.

grotesque: unnatural

replenish: fill up

Aborigines have lived on the continent of Australia for thousands of years. When European settlers began arriving in Australia in the late 1700s, however, many Aborigines were forced off their lands. Throughout Australia's history, Aborigines have often been denied many of the rights and opportunities that are enjoyed by other Australians. In recent years, though, new laws have been passed by the government, protecting the civil rights of Australia's 200,000 Aborigines and providing them with greater economic opportunity. For a description of one of the earliest encounters between Europeans and the Aborigines, read the next document on pages 196-197.

Source: Charles P. Mountford, *The Dreamtime*. Australia: Rigby Limited, 1965.

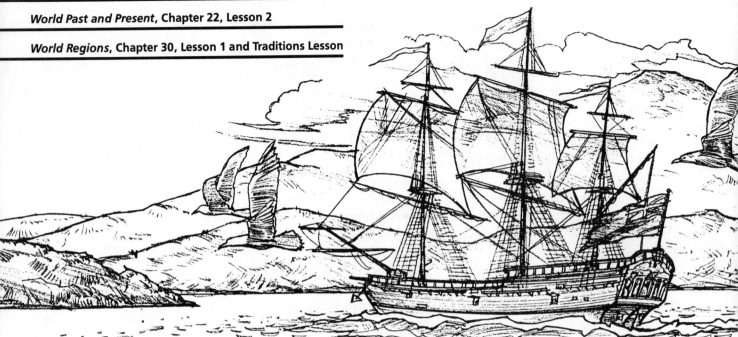

Captain Cook's Journal

by James Cook, 1770

In 1768 a British sea captain named James Cook set out on an expedition to find a giant continent that many Europeans believed existed in the Southern Hemisphere. In the course of his three-year journey, Captain Cook explored many islands, such as Tahiti, New Zealand, and Tasmania. He also explored the eastern coast of Australia. In a journal that he kept of his voyage, Cook described the great coral reefs, the beautiful fish and animals, and the Aborigines who inhabited the land. Below is an excerpt from Captain Cook's journal. What are some of the skills and traits of the Aborigines that impressed him? Why do you think the Aborigines had little interest in trading with Captain Cook and his crew?

Land animals are scarce, so far as we know [they are limited] to a very few species. . . . The sort which is in the greatest plenty is the kangaroo. . . , so called by the Natives; we saw a good many of them [as they were] eating. Here [in Australia] are likewise lizards, snakes, scorpions, . . . etc., but not in any [large numbers]. Tame animals they have none but dogs, and of these we saw but one, and therefore [they] must be very scarce. . . .

The land **fowls** are **bustards**, eagles, hawks, crows, such as we have in England, **cockatoos** of 2 sorts, white and brown, very beautiful birds of the parrot kind, . . . pigeons, doves, quails, and several sorts of smaller birds. The sea is . . . well stocked with fish of various sorts. . . . Here are also upon the shoals and reefs great

fowls: birds
bustards: Australian birds
cockatoos: a type of parrot

numbers of the finest green turtle in the world, and in the river and salt creeks are some alligators.

The Natives of this country are of a middle **stature**, [with] straight bodies and slender limbs; their hair [is] mostly black [and] they all wear it cut short; their beards, which are generally black, they likewise [keep] short. . . . Their features are far from being disagreeable, and their voices are soft and **tunable**.

I do not look upon them to be a warlike people; on the contrary, I think them a **timorous** and inoffensive race, no ways inclined to cruelty, neither are they very numerous. They live in small parties along by the sea coast, the banks of lakes, rivers, creeks, etc. They seem to have no fixed **habitation**, but move about from place to place in search of food. . . . They have wooden fish **gigs**, with 2, 3, or 4 prongs, each very **ingeniously** made, with which they strike fish. We have also seen them strike both fish and birds with their darts. With these they likewise kill other animals; they have also wooden **harpoons** for striking turtles, but of these I believe they get but few, except at the seasons [the turtles] come ashore to lay [eggs]. . . .

From what I have said of the natives of **New Holland** they may appear to some to be the most **wretched** people upon earth; but in reality they are far more happy than we Europeans, being wholly unacquainted not only with the **superfluous**, but with the necessary conveniences so much sought after in Europe; they are happy in not knowing the use of them. They live in a **tranquility** which is [based on the equal treatment of all members in their society]. The earth and sea of their own accord furnish them with all things necessary for life. They **covet** not magnificent houses, household-stuff, etc.; they live in a warm and fine climate, and enjoy every wholesome air, so that they have very little need of clothing; and this they seem to be fully sensible of, for many to whom we gave cloth, etc., left it carelessly upon the sea beach and in the woods, as a thing they had no manner of use for; in short, they seemed to set no value upon anything we gave them, nor would they ever part with anything of their own for any one article we could offer them. This, in my opinion, argues that they think themselves provided with all the necessarys of life, and that they have no **superfluities**.

stature: height

tunable: melodic, attractive

timorous: shy

habitation: home

gigs: pronged spears
ingeniously: cleverly

harpoons: long spears

New Holland: early name for Australia, which was claimed by Holland, or the Netherlands
wretched: miserable
superfluous: luxurious, wasteful
tranquillity: state of peace
covet: want

superfluities: unneeded possessions

Captain James Cook claimed eastern Australia for Great Britain in 1770. During his voyages Cook mapped many islands in the Pacific Ocean and explored the coast of North America from Oregon to Alaska. He was killed in Hawaii in 1789. One year earlier, in 1788, the first English colonists—many of them convicts—began arriving in Australia, and thousands of free settlers came in the 1800s.

Source: *Captain Cook's Journal During His First Voyage Round the World.* London: Elliot Stock, 1893.

The Road from Coorain

by Jill Ker Conway, 1989

People once said that "Australia rides on the sheep's back." This is because Australia, with its vast plains and large, open fields, is an ideal place to raise sheep. Since the early 1800s the wool industry has been an important part of Australia's economy. But life on a sheep farm has never been easy. Jill Ker Conway grew up in southeastern Australia on a sheep farm named Coorain, an Aboriginal word which means windy place. In the following excerpt from her autobiography, Conway describes her childhood on Coorain in the 1940s. What are some of the challenges she finds in raising sheep?

The first terrible dust storm arrived boiling out of the central Australian desert. One **sweltering** late afternoon in March, I walked out to collect wood for the stove. Glancing toward the west, I saw a terrifying sight. A vast boiling cloud was mounting in the sky, black and . . . yellow at the heart, varying shades of **ocher** red at the edges. Where I stood, the air was utterly still, but the **writhing** cloud was approaching silently and with great speed. Suddenly I noticed that there were no birds to be seen or heard. All had taken shelter. I called my mother. We watched helplessly. Always one for action, she turned swiftly, went indoors, and began to close windows. Outside, I collected the buckets, rakes, shovels, and other implements that could blow away or smash a window if hurled against one by the boiling wind. Within the hour, my father arrived home. He and my mother sat on the back step, not in their usual restful contemplation, but silenced instead by dread.

sweltering: very hot

ocher: reddish- or brownish-yellow color

writhing: twisting

A dust storm usually lasts days, blotting out the sun, launching **banshee** winds day and night. It is dangerous to stray far from shelter, because the sand and grit lodge in one's eyes, and a visibility often reduced to a few feet can make one completely **disoriented**. Animals which become exhausted and lie down are often sanded over and smothered. There is nothing anyone can do but stay inside, waiting for the calm after the storm. Inside, it is stifling. Every window must be closed against the dust, which seeps **relentlessly** through the slightest crack. Meals are gritty and sleep **elusive**. Rising in the morning, one sees a perfect outline of one's body, an afterimage of white where the dust has not collected on the sheets.

banshee: howling

disoriented: confused

relentlessly: without stopping

elusive: difficult

As the winds **seared** our land, they took away the dry **herbage**, piled it against the fences, and then slowly began to **silt** over the debris. It was three days before we could venture out, days of almost **unendurable** tension. . . .

seared: scorched
herbage: plants
silt: spill dirt

unendurable: unbearable

When we emerged, there were several feet of sand piled up against the windbreak to my mother's garden, the contours of new sandhills were beginning to form in places where the dust **eddied** and collected. There was no question that there were also many more bare patches where the remains of dry grass and herbage had lifted and blown away.

eddied: swirled

It was always a miracle to me that animals could endure so much. . . .

Feeding the sheep was hard work. Feed **troughs** made of metal could not be considered [for use] because the drifting sand would quickly cover them. If the weaker sheep were to get their nourishment, the . . . feeding troughs must be large so that every animal would have its chance at the grain. So we settled on burlap troughs hung on wire— light enough for the wind to blow beneath when empty, cheap enough to produce in hundred-foot lengths. . . .

troughs: bins

When we began our feeding program in the troughs placed by major watering places, the sheep seemed only slowly to discover the grain. Within a few weeks the hungry animals would stampede at the sight of anyone carrying bags of wheat, and someone had to be sent as a decoy to draw them off in search of a small supply of grain while the major ration was being poured into the troughs. Since I could carry only twenty pounds at a fast run, I was the decoy while the men carried forty-and fifty-pound bags on their shoulders to empty into the feeding troughs. At first the sheep were **ravenous** but **measured** in following the decoy. Soon they would race so hard toward the grain that they would send the decoy flying unless he or she outraced them. Then they would pause, **wheel** on catching the scent of the ration in the troughs, and stampede back toward the food. . . .

ravenous: very hungry
measured: restrained

wheel: turn around

Our principal enemies as we carried out this daily process were the pink **cockatoos** and crows, which tore the burlap to pieces in search of the grains of wheat left behind. Soon the mending of the troughs was a daily task, a task made miserable by the blowflies, the blistering sun, the blowing sand, and the stench of the bodies of the sheep for whom the wheat had arrived too late.

cockatoos: Australian parrots

Jill Ker Conway spent her childhood raising sheep on Coorain. She later became a historian, college professor, and president of Smith College in Northampton, Massachusetts. You can find out more about her childhood and life in Australia by reading her autobiography, The Road from Coorain. *Sheep farming continues to be an important industry in Australia, and today the country that "rides on the sheep's back" produces about one third of the world's wool.*

Source: Jill Ker Conway, *The Road from Coorain*. New York: Random House, Inc., 1989.

A *Maori* Warden

by Peter Waldron, 1984

Around the 8th century, a Polynesian people called the Maoris arrived by boat on the islands that are known today as New Zealand. The Maoris settled these islands in Oceania and lived in villages near the sea, where they hunted, fished, and farmed the land. When Europeans came to settle in New Zealand in the 1800s, conflicts broke out between the newcomers and the Maoris. Although the Europeans won control, the Maoris survived and continued to live in New Zealand. Today the culture of many Maoris is a mixture of both traditional and modern ways. One Maori tradition that has survived is the hongi, *the Maori form of greeting in which two people press their noses together. Peter Waldron is a Maori warden who lives in South Auckland. His father was a Maori and his mother was a Pakeha, the Maori word meaning "white." In the following excerpt from an oral history, Waldron describes his life as a member of two different cultures. What are some of the Maori values and beliefs that shape his life?*

*T*he Maori warden movement **evolved** from a desire to promote law and order within the Maori community in a way that was acceptable to their culture. It was also part of a repeated effort by Maoris to control their own destiny. Our Maori society has traditionally been a **communal** one, with authority being exercised by the tribal elders. Offenders were dealt with by people who knew and cared for them, and were respected by them. Maori wardens are not policemen. The only power they have is the respect, called *Mana*, that their community has for them. It is a voluntary job, but it is considered a great honor to be elected as a warden. We work within our community to promote law and order by treating the causes of disorder, rather than by disciplining offenders.

There are 290,000 Maoris in New Zealand. Over the years most have settled in the cities. . . . Maori values are retained within our homes. We place great importance on family ties, including those with our ancestors who have passed on. We are . . . close . . . to the earth and nature. . . . Different families have traditionally held special skills, as **orators**, healers, or planters. These skills are handed down through generations, and held with great pride by the families.

The place where Maoris feel their culture the strongest is on a *Marae*. Each community has its own *Marae*—an area of land containing

evolved: developed

communal: close-knit, based on sharing

orators: public speakers

200

a meeting house. A *Marae* is a sacred place; there are many traditions to be observed by locals and visitors, but there is also a strong sense of belonging for all Maoris. Some *Maraes* are simple buildings, others richly decorated with carvings. The traditions are more important than the surroundings. *Maraes* are used for meetings, weddings and all social occasions, but priority is always given to a *Tangi*.

We believe that when one of our people dies, their spirit rests in the body for three days before making the journey to their spiritual homeland. During this time the person lies in rest at the *Marae*, and is kept company by loved ones. It's a time for grieving, but it's also a time to express many other emotions, to tell stories, and to come to terms with the loss. A *Tangi* is a very moving experience; it brings out our feelings as Maoris, and as a community of caring people; it is our way of saying goodbye to a loved one, within our own traditions and culture. Many people will stay for the three days, living at the *Marae*. Banquets will be prepared for these guests, often cooked in a *hangi*. The food is wrapped in leaves and buried in the ground on hot stones. Nothing tastes quite as good as meat and vegetables from a *hangi*.

Our children have grown up now, and we have nine grandchildren. We all live and work in a *Pakeha* world. The old Maori lifestyle was doomed by the **onslaught** of the *Pakeha* technology, but Maoris are becoming more and more aware of the spiritual values of their culture. They see that these values can be **transplanted** into a *Pakeha* environment. There is a **regeneration** of Maoridom, which is being seen in a more positive light by both Maori and *Pakeha*. I see our culture as playing an increasingly important role in New Zealand society in future years.

onslaught: arrival

transplanted: moved

regeneration: spiritual renewal

About 1 in 12 New Zealanders is a Maori. Thanks to people like Peter Waldron, Maori culture has survived and continues to be an important part of life in New Zealand.

Source: John Ball, *We Live in New Zealand*. New York: The Bookwright Press, 1984.

The Banner of Freedom

by Sauni I. Kuresa, 1948

About 1,600 miles (2,575 km) northeast of New Zealand lies a small group of islands known as Western Samoa. These beautiful islands are surrounded by coral reefs and are covered with forests. The islands are home to about 150,000 people. In 1962 Western Samoa gained its independence from New Zealand and adopted The Banner of Freedom by Sauni I. Kuresa as its national anthem. How does this song express the importance of freedom and liberty to the people of Western Samoa?

Sa - moa, tu - la'i ma si - si ia lau fu'-a, lou

pa - le le - a; Sa - moa, tu - la'i ma

si - si ia lau fu'-a, lou pa - le le - a; {Va- / Pu-

ai i na fe - tū o loo ua a - gia-gi - a ai; Le
le_____ ma Tu - mu - a, I - tu 'au ma A - la - taua, A -

fa - ai-lo - ga lea o Ie - su na ma - liu ai mo Sa -
i - ga i le Tai ma le Vaa o Fono - ti, Mā - lō Tau -

202

moa Oi! Sa - moa e, u - u ma - u lau
tai! Oi! Ma - lie toa ma Tu - pu - a, Le

pu - le ia fa - a - va - va - u.}
Ma - lo ia fa - a - va - va - u.}
'Au - a e te

fe - fe, o le Atua lo ta fa'a vae___ O lo - ta

Sa'o lo - to - ga, Sa - moa, tu - la'i, ia

a - gia - gia lau Fu' - a lou pa - le le - a.

Samoa, arise and raise your banner that is your crown.

Oh! see and behold the stars on the waving banner
They are a sign that Samoa is able to lead.

Oh! Samoa hold fast
Your freedom for ever.

Do not be afraid; as you are founded on God;
Our treasured precious liberty.
Samoa, arise and wave
Your banner that is your crown.

Source: T. M. Cartledge, W. L. Reed, Martin Shaw, and Henry Coleman, eds., *National Anthems of the World*. New York: Arco Publishing Company, Inc., 1978.

Easter Island

by Thor Heyerdahl, 1989

Historians studying the past often find themselves trying to solve mysteries. For many years one of the world's greatest mysteries lay on a tiny Polynesian island in the Pacific Ocean. This island is more than 1,500 miles (2,400 km) from any other inhabited place. It is named Easter Island. Thousands of years ago, people settled there and developed a unique culture that included a written language and remarkable buildings.

When Europeans first reached Easter Island in 1722, they were amazed by what they saw. They found hundreds of gigantic stone statues standing on cliffs and hillsides overlooking the Pacific Ocean. Some of these statues—which consisted of heads, crowns, and bodies without the legs—were as tall as a four-story building! Near these statues lay wooden tablets, carved with hieroglyphics. Where, the Europeans wondered, did these statues come from? How were these statues—some weighing as much as 50 tons (45,000 kg)—moved into their standing positions?

The Europeans also noticed some of the people on the island moving around the statues, raising and lowering their arms, as if in prayer. Where had the people on Easter Island originally come from?

European explorers and missionaries who visited the island in the 1700s and 1800s asked the islanders these questions. The islanders told them that their ancestors had carved these statues and that the statues had walked to different parts of the island. But the Europeans dismissed these answers as myths and legends.

In 1955 an anthropologist from Norway named Thor Heyerdahl (hī ûr däl') visited Easter Island to try to find the answers to these mysteries. As you read his account of this trip, notice the skills and cooperation that the Easter Islanders demonstrated in order to carve a moai *(mō' i)—their word for statue. What does Heyerdahl think of the islanders' explanations of how the* moai *moved?*

The mayor [of Easter Island] was sitting on the floor, chipping away at a [statue of a] bird-man figure, when I entered his modest village home. He was known as by far the best sculptor on the island. . . . He was an amazing character. His brain was as sharp as his face, and he was always prepared to find a solution to any problem.

Did he know how his ancestors carved and raised the big *moai*? Of course. If he knew, was he willing to show me? Yes, how big did I wish the *moai* to be? If it was to be big, he would need help from some of the [other] men. . . . When I asked him why, if he knew, he had not revealed his secret to all those who had asked the same question before me, he answered calmly, "Nobody asked *me*."

In my subsequent dealings with the Easter Islanders I was to understand that this reply was **symptomatic** of the local character. They don't give away anything precious unless you ask for it directly. And anything hidden and not known to others is a treasure. . . .

symptomatic: typical

One night all the members of the expedition were wakened in their tents by the strangest choral singing any of us had ever heard— beautifully harmonized, but almost eerie and totally unlike any music we knew. It was the mayor and his family, who had come to perform an ancient ceremony essential to the success of their enterprise the following day, when they proposed to demonstrate how the work in the quarry was done. A child danced in a paper bird-man mask. Early next morning the mayor and his closest relatives had collected a large number of the stone pickaxes that had lain strewn about the quarry ever since the day work suddenly stopped. They held the picks in their hands, and when the points wore down they sharpened them again simply by chipping off pieces with another stone axe of the same kind. The name for these tools on Easter Island was *toki*, and *toki* is also the ancient word for stone axe among the aboriginal population of North Chile.

After three days' work, the outline of a statue had begun to take shape. . . . No tools were used except the hard [stone] *toki* and water bottles made of **gourds**. The workers constantly sprayed the surface with water to soften up the rock, the interior of which was very hard. . . .

gourds: hollowed-out shells of a type of fruit

contour: shape

By the third day, we began to see the complete **contour** of the *moai*. We did not have enough time to see them finish the carving, but calculated that it would take about a year for a medium-sized *moai*. There had to be elbowroom between the sculptors, who stood side by side, which meant that the number of men who could work on each statue at one time was very limited. . . .

When I asked the successful mayor how the statues had been moved the long distance from the quarries, he answered, with natural conviction, "The *moai* walked."

These people had been giving that same answer to the same question ever since the first missionaries had asked it. I did not, of course, take the answer seriously. . . . [Perhaps the *moai* had been dragged, I said.]

"This was not the way it was done," said the islanders.

Leonardo was the name of one of those who argued that the stones had walked in an upright position. It sounded so meaningless that I would long since have forgotten the episode had I not written it down in my own book on the expedition at the time.

"But, Leonardo," I said, "how could they walk when they had only heads and bodies and no legs?"

"They wriggled along like this," said Leonardo, and gave a demonstration by edging himself along the rock with feet together and stiff knees.

Upon learning that the word toki—meaning "stone axe"—had the same meaning among both the people of Easter Island and those in northern Chile, Thor Heyerdahl was provided with an important clue. Perhaps the first settlers on Easter Island had come from South America. This theory gained further support when the statues on Easter Island were found to be similar to ancient carvings done by the inhabitants of Peru, who lived hundreds of years before the Incan Empire flourished. These discoveries provided one answer to the questions surrounding the origins of the people of Easter Island. Some anthropologists reject Heyerdahl's theory. They believe that the island's original inhabitants, instead of being South American, were Polynesian sailors from the west.

By watching carefully, Heyerdahl also learned how the people of Easter Island carved the moai. *But what did the islanders mean when they said that the* moai *had walked? Like the missionaries who had come before him, Heyerdahl dismissed their explanation. Then, in the 1980s, an engineer from Czechoslovakia named Pavel Pavel believed he understood what the islanders meant. In 1986 Heyerdahl returned to Easter Island with Pavel. In the account below, Heyerdahl describes what happened.*

It was a great day with an air of suspense and nervous anticipation among the islanders when all was ready for Pavel Pavel to show us how a *moai* could walk. None of the elders doubted that their ancestors had formerly made the statues perform. . . . Old Leonardo was as sure now as he had been thirty years before: the legless stone busts had walked by wriggling forward from side to side. And again he showed us the motion, with the soles of his feet put together, before we had told him or anybody else about the experiment we were to conduct. . . .

Leonardo's sister Elodia . . . sang in a low voice a **monotonous** song in a jerky tempo that matched Leonardo's movements. While she sang an old text and tune she obviously knew by heart, her brother made a string figure like a cat's cradle, which he swung in time to the song. This was repeated during the actual experiment as a kind of magical **invocation**.

monotonous: repetitive

invocation: prayer

The islanders refused to help Pavel until they had observed the ancient custom of baking a pig and sweet potatoes in an **umu** earth oven. . . .

umu: islanders' name for an oven

Pavel had indeed worked out the **ingenious** technique by which the statues were moved—the same technique that we use ourselves to "walk" a heavy refrigerator or a stone too big to carry unaided. . . . All that was needed were four ropes. Two were attached to the top of the statue and used to pull it to each side alternately, while the other two were fastened down at the base and alternately pulled forward. As one team pulled on the top rope to make the statue tilt to the right, the other team pulled the left-hand side of the base forward before the giant tipped back again. The teams then changed sides, causing the **colossus** to waddle along like a drunken man. The technique required great precision and intensive training, but was incredibly effective when the waddling became rhythmic. We reckoned that a well-drilled team of fifteen men could make a twenty-ton [18,000 kg] statue "walk" at least an average of [one] hundred yards [90 m] a day. . . .

ingenious: clever

colossus: gigantic statue

We all felt a chill down our backs when we saw the sight that must have been so familiar to the early ancestors of the people around us. A stone colossus of an estimated ten tons [9,000 kg] "walking" like a dog on a leash. . . . After the successful performance, we all embraced a beaming Pavel Pavel. And Leonardo and Elodia willingly accepted part of the honor. We could all read from Leonardo's face that he had known the truth the whole time: it was the song he and Elodia had sung that had made the *moai* move.

The statue had indeed walked. I could find no better word for it in any European language. I suddenly had an idea. The Easter Island verb for "walk" is *haere*. But when the *moai* started to move, the old islanders used the verb *neke-neke*. I looked this up in [a] dictionary of the Easter Island language, and read: "*neke-neke*: to inch forward by moving the body, due to disabled legs or the absence thereof."

What other language in the world would have a special word for walking without legs? . . .

The technical problems behind the great stone giants were solved. The mysteries that had [long puzzled] visitors and . . . scientists . . . existed no more. The **genesis** of the blind giants dotting the slopes . . . was known, and how they walked. . . . The way each of these incredible feats had been accomplished with help from neither machinery or outer space—all these former puzzles now had their answers.

genesis: origin

One big question emerged: Why had nobody but the islanders themselves taken their ancestral traditions seriously? They would have given us all these answers. I confessed to my two friends that the value of the local oral history was, in a sense, one of the strangest discoveries we had made. A hundred years ago the Easter Islanders had answered all the questions that were put to the elders among them. We from the outside world had recorded what they told us, and saved the answers as primitive fairy-tales. . . .

Thor Heyerdahl believed that he had solved many mysteries during his stays on Easter Island in 1955 and 1986. He concluded that South Americans had traveled great distances across the Pacific Ocean long before Europeans had begun exploring the seas. Heyerdahl learned how the giant statues were made and how they "walked." But he could not solve every mystery. The carved hieroglyphics on wooden tablets on Easter Island have not yet been translated.

Perhaps Heyerdahl's major discovery was understanding the importance of the stories and oral histories handed down by people for hundreds of years. As you have learned, many types of documents can teach us about cultures and civilizations throughout the world. Newspapers, hot off the morning presses, and stone monuments thousand of years old—as well as songs, poems, tales, speeches, oral histories, and other types of documents—all provide clues about the world around you. By learning to understand these many sources of information, you can gain a better understanding of the world and prepare for the challenges of tomorrow.

Source: Thor Heyerdahl, *Easter Island: The Mystery Solved*. New York: Random House, Inc., 1980.

(continued from copyright page)

"Ode to an Artichoke" by Pablo Neruda from THE YELLOW CANARY WHOSE EYE IS SO BLACK edited and translated by Cheli Duran. Copyright © 1977 by Cheli Duran Ryan. Used with permission of Macmillan Publishing Company. "Oda a la alcachofa" from ODAS ELEMENTALES by Pablo Neruda. C Editorial Losada, S. A. 1958. Used by permission of Agencia Literaria Carmen Balcells, S. A.

"Road to Peace" from the speech by Haidar Abdel-Shafi recorded by Associated Press, as it appeared in The New York Times, November 1, 1991 issue. Reprinted by permission of Associated Press.

"The Banner of Freedom" Words and Music by Sauni I. Kuresa, arr. by Henry Coleman from NATIONAL ANTHEMS OF THE WORLD edited by T.M. Cartledge and W.L. Reed. Copyright © 1978, 1975, 1969 by Blandford Press Ltd. Used with permission of Cassell PLC.

"A Message to the Troops" from WORD OF A PRINCE by Maria Perry. Copyright © 1990 by Maria Perry. Used by permission of Boydell & Brewer.

"Guantanamera Guajira Guantanamera. Original lyrics and music by Jose Fernandez Dias (Joseito Fernandez). Music adaptation by Hector Angulo, Pete Seeger & Julian Orbon, Lyric adaptation by Julian Orbon. Based on a poem by José Martí. Copyright © 1963, 1966 by Fall River Music, Inc., New York. All rights reserved. Used by permission.

"The Great Barrier Reef" from THEIR SHINING ELDORADO: A JOURNEY THROUGH AUSTRALIA by Elspeth Huxley. Copyright © 1967 by Elspeth Huxley. Reprinted by permission of Chatto & Windus Ltd.

"Building the Transcontinental Railroad" by Wong Hau-hon from CHINESE AMERICANS: Realities and Myths Anthology edited by Joe Huang and Sharon Quan Wong. Copyright pending 1977. All rights reserved. Published by Association of Chinese Teachers.

"Amandla! Amandla!" from the speech APARTHEID HAS NO FUTURE Africa is Ours by Nelson Mandela from VITAL SPEECHES OF THE DAY vol. LVI, number 10, March 1, 1990. Used with permission of VITAL SPEECHES OF THE DAY.

"A Tale of Disappearance" from TALES OF DISAPPEARANCE & SURVIVAL IN ARGENTINA by Alicia Partnoy. Copyright 1986 by Alicia Partnoy. All rights reserved. Reprinted by permission of Cleis Press.

"The Sayings of Confucius" from SOURCES OF CHINESE TRADITION I by William Theodore de Bary. Copyright © 1965 Columbia University Press, New York. Used with permission of the publisher.

"From Mouse to Bat" from THE BIRD WHO CLEANS THE WORLD by Victor Montejo. Copyright © 1991 by Victor Montejo. Translation Copyright © 1991 by Wallace Kaufman. All rights reserved. Reprinted by permission of Curbstone Press.

"The War Years in Vietnam" from WHEN HEAVEN AND EARTH CHANGED PLACES by Le Ly Hayslip. Copyright © 1989 by Le Ly Hayslip and Charles Jay Wurts. Reprinted by permission of Doubleday, a division of Bantam Doubleday Dell Publishing Group, Inc.

Excerpt from THE DIARY OF ANNE FRANK: THE CRITICAL EDITION by Anne Frank. Copyright © 1986 by Anne Frank-Fonds, Basle/Switzerland, for all text of Anne Frank. Used with permission of Doubleday, a division of Bantam Doubleday Dell Publishing Group, Inc.

Excerpt from THE DARK CHILD by Camara Laye. Copyright 1954 by Camara Laye. Used with permission of Farrar, Straus & Giroux, Inc.

"Child of The Americas" by Aurora Levins Morales from GETTING HOME ALIVE by Aurora Levins Morales and Rosario Morales, published by Firebrand Books, Ithaca, NY. Copyright © 1986 by Aurora Levins Morales. Used with permission of the publisher.

"A Voice for Women's Rights" from WOMEN IN CANADIAN POLITICS edited by Jean Cochrane. Copyright © 1977 Fitzhenry & Whiteside Limited, Toronto. Used with permission of Fitzhenry & Whiteside Limited.

"The Vision that I See" from Ch. 10 "Nkrumah the Orator" from KWAME NKRUMAH: FROM CRADLE TO GRAVE by Bankole Timothy. Copyright © 1981 by Bankole Timothy. Used with permission of the Gavin Press Limited.

"In the Streets of Accra" by Andrew Amankwa Opoku from VOICES OF GHANA. Ministry of Information and Broadcasting, Ghana, 1958.

Excerpt from "The People Yes. . ." from THE COMPLETE POEMS OF CARL SANDBURG. Copyright © 1936 by Harcourt Brace Jovanovich, copyright © 1964 by Carl Sandburg. Reprinted by permission of Harcourt Brace Jovanovich.

Excerpts from "The Frost Giant" and "Moon and Sun" from IN THE BEGINNING: CREATION STORIES FROM AROUND THE WORLD told by Virginia Hamilton. Copyright © 1988 by Virginia Hamilton. Reprinted by permission of Harcourt Brace Jovanovich, Inc.

Excerpt from "The American Dream" from A TESTMENT OF HOPE The Essential Writings of Martin Luther King, Jr. edited by James Melvin Washington. Copyright © 1986 by Coretta Scott King, Executrix of the Estate of Martin Luther King, Jr. Reprinted by permission of Joan Daves Agency. Recorded by permission of Estate of Martin Luther King, Jr.

Excerpt from ON THE WAY HOME by Laura Ingalls Wilder. Copyright © 1962 by Roger Lea MacBride. Reprinted by permission of HarperCollins Publishers.

Adaptation of "The Canoe in the Rapids" from THE TALKING CAT AND OTHER STORIES OF FRENCH CANADA by Natalie Savage Carlson. Copyright © 1952 by Natalie Savage Carlson. Reprinted by permission of HarperCollins Publishers.

"Tank, The Water Buffalo" from THE LAND I LOST by Huynh Quang Nhuong. Text copyright © 1982 by Huynh Quang Nhuong. Illustrations Copyright © 1982 by VoDinh Mai. Reprinted by permission of HarperCollins Publishers.

"Precepts" from The Mahabharata from POEMS FROM INDIA selected by Daisy Aldan. Copyright © 1969 by Daisy Aldan. Published by Thomas Y. Crowell Company.

"Stopping by Woods on a Snowy Evening" from THE POETRY OF ROBERT FROST edited by Edward Connery Lathem. Copyright 1923, © 1969 by Holt, Rinehart and Winston. Copyright 1951 by Robert Frost. Used by permission of Henry Holt and Company, Inc.

"An Immigrant to the United States" from MEXICAN VOICES/AMERICAN DREAMS by Marilyn P. Davis. Copyright © 1990 by Marilyn P. Davis. Reprinted by permission of Henry Holt and Company, Inc.

"Famine in Ethiopia" by Roberta Oster from IN THESE TIMES (Jan. 29, 1992, vol. 16, no. 10). Reprinted by permission of the publisher.

"My Return to South Africa" by Dennis Brutus from IN THESE TIMES (Nov. 6, 1991, vol. 15, no. 41). Reprinted by permission of the publisher.

Excerpt from ALL QUIET ON THE WESTERN FRONT by Erich Maria Remarque. "Im Westen Nichts Neues", copyright 1928 by Ullstein A.G.; Copyright renewed © 1956 by Erich Maria Remarque. "All Quiet on the Western Front", copyright 1929, 1930 by Little, Brown and Company; Copyright renewed © 1957, 1958 by Erich Maria Remarque. All Rights Reserved. Reprinted by permission of the Estate of Erich Maria Remarque.

Excerpt from "Mirram and Wareen the Hunters" and "Tiddalik the Flood-Maker" from THE DREAMTIME Australian Aboriginal Myths in Paintings by Ainslie Roberts with text by Charles P. Mountford. Copyright © 1965 Ainslie Roberts and Charles P. Mountford. Reprinted by permission of the Estate of Bessie Ilma Mountford.

Excerpt from "Maruch" from FOCUS ON MEXICO by Louis B. Casagrande and Sylvia A. Johnson. Copyright 1986 by Lerner Publications Company, Minneapolis MN. Used with permission. All rights reserved.

"The Coach of Time" by Alexander Pushkin from A SECOND BOOK OF RUSSIAN VERSE translated and edited by C.M. Bowra. Used with permission of Macmillan Publishers Ltd.

Excerpt from JI-NONGO-NONGO MEANS RIDDLES by Verna Aardema. Text copyright © 1978 by Verna Aardema. Reprinted by permission of Four Wind Press.

"The Aeneid" from THE AENEID FOR BOYS AND GIRLS retold by Alfred J. Church. Copyright © 1962 by Macmillan Publishing Company. Reprinted by permission of Macmillan Publishing Company.

"Life in a Cambodian 'Reeducation Camp' " from STAY ALIVE MY SON by Pin Yathay. Copyright © 1987 by Pin Yathay. Reprinted by permission of the Free Press, a Division of Macmillan, Inc. By permission also of I.B. Tauris & Co. Ltd.

THE GOLD COIN by Alma Flor Ada. Text copyright © 1991 by Alma Flor Ada. Reprinted by permission of Atheneum Publishers, an imprint of Macmillan Publishing Company.

"The Tiger and the Three Wise Rabbits" from KOREA: LAND OF THE MORNING CALM by Carol Farley. Copyright © 1991 by Dillon Press. Reprinted with the permission of Dillon Press, an Imprint of Macmillan Publishing Company.

"The Splendors of Hangzhou" from CHINESE CIVILIZATION AND SOCIETY by Patricia Buckley Ebrey. Copyright © 1981 by The Free Press. Reprinted with the permission of The Free Press, a Division of Macmillan, Inc.

"The Iliad" from THE CHILDREN'S HOMER: THE ADVENTURES OF ODYSSEUS AND THE TALE OF TROY by Padraic Colum. Copyright © 1918 by Macmillan Publishing Company; copyright renewed 1946 by Padraic Colum and Willy Pogany. Reprinted by permission of Macmillan Publishing Company.

"Kokoom" (The Origin of the Moon) from A FOLKLORE SAMPLER FROM THE MARITIMES edited by Herbert Halpert. Copyright © 1982 by Memorial University of Newfoundland, Department of Folklore. Reprinted by permission of the Director of Canadian Studies, Mount Allison University.

"Icy Reaches of the North" by Thomas O'Neill from CANADA'S INCREDIBLE COASTS. Copyright © by National Geographic Society. Reprinted by permission of National Geographic Society.

"Leave Us in Peace" from the address by President Oscar Arias Sánchez of Costa Rica upon receiving the Nobel Peace Prize from The New York Times, December 11, 1987 issue. Copyright © 1987 by The Nobel Foundation. Used with permission of The Nobel Foundation.

"When the Atomic Bomb Fell" from CHILDREN OF THE A-BOMB edited by Dr. Arata Osada. Copyright © 1959 and 1963 by Dr. Arata Osada. Reprinted by permission of Peter Owen Publishers, London.

"Test of Friendship" from THE DANCING PALM TREE and other Nigerian folktales by Barbara Walker. Text copyright © 1968 by Barbara Walker. Published by Texas Tech University Press, 1990. Reprinted by permission of Parents Magazine Press. The author is not responsible for the illustrations.

"Canada at 100" by Chief Dan George from TOUCH THE EARTH by T.C. McLuhan. Copyright © 1971 by T.C. McLuhan. Used with permission of the publisher, Dutton, an imprint of New American Library, a division of Penguin Books USA Inc.

"Sur le Pont d'Avignon" from AROUND THE WORLD IN SONG by Dorothy Gordon. Copyright © 1930, 1932 by E.P. Dutton & Co., Inc. Used with permission of Penguin USA.

"The Story of the Flood" from THE EPIC OF GILGAMESH translated by N.K. Sandars. Copyright © N.K. Sandars, 1960, 1964, 1972. Reprinted by permission of Penguin Books Ltd.

Excerpt from CHILD OF THE DARK by Carolina Maria de Jesus, translated by David St. Clair. Translation copyright © 1962 by E.P. Dutton & Co., Inc., New York and Souvenir Press, Ltd., London. Used with permission of the publisher, Dutton, an imprint of New American Library, a division of Penguin Books USA Inc. Used with permission of Souvenir Press.

"Praying at the Western Wall" from GAVRIEL AND JEMAL by Brent Ashabranner. Copyright © 1984 by Brent Ashabranner. Reprinted by permission of G.P. Putnam's Sons.

"Fighting for Freedom" from THIS GILDED AFRICAN: TOUSSAINT L'OUVERTURE by Wenda Parkinson. Copyright © 1979 by Wenda Parkinson. Used with permission of Quartet Books Ltd.

Excerpt from EASTER ISLAND: The Mystery Solved by Thor Heyerdahl. Copyright © 1989 by Thor Heyerdahl. Reprinted by permission of Random House, Inc.

Excerpt from THE ROAD FROM COORAIN by Jill Conway. Copyright © 1989 by Jill Conway. Reprinted by permission of Alfred A. Knopf.

"New Year's Address" from OPEN LETTERS: SELECTED WRITINGS 1965-1990 by Václav Havel. Copyright © 1991 by A.G. Brain. Preface/translation copyright © 1985, 1988, 1991 by Paul Wilson. Reprinted by permission of Alfred A. Knopf, Inc.

Excerpt from THE TALE OF GENJI by Murasaki Shikibu, trans. by Edward Seidensticker. Copyright © 1975 by Edward Seidensticker. Reprinted by permission of Alfred A. Knopf, Inc.

"Road to Peace" from the speech by Yitzhak Shamir from The New York Times, November 1, 1991 issue. Copyright © 1991 by Reuters. Reprinted by permission.

Excerpt from "Farewell Address" by Mikhail Gorbachev from The New York Times December 26, 1991 issue. Used with permission of Reuters.

"Song for the Dance of Young Girls" from PEOPLE OF THE SMALL ARROW by J.H. Driberg, originally published by Payson and Clarke Ltd. in 1930. Used with permission of Routledge and Kegan Paul Ltd.

"The Man Who Shared His Hut" from FACING MOUNT KENYA by Jomo Kenyatta. First published 1938 by Martin Secker & Warburg Ltd. Used with permission of R.I.B. Library, Reed Book Services, Rushden, England.

Excerpt from "The Ringdove" in KALILA WA DIMNA: FABLES FROM A FOURTEENTH CENTURY ARABIC MANUSCRIPT, by Esin Atil. Published by Smithsonian Press, copyright 1981 by Smithsonian Institution. Out of print.

"A Queen's Promise" from "Obelisk Inscriptions" from ANCIENT EGYPTIAN LITERATURE, THREE VOLUMES translated by Miriam Lichtheim. Copyright © 1973-1980 Regents of the University of California. Reprinted by permission of University of California Press.

"The Lakota and Nature" from LAND OF THE SPOTTED EAGLE by Luther Standing Bear. Copyright 1933 by Luther Standing Bear, renewal copyright 1960 by May Jones. Reprinted by permission of University of Nebraska Press.

"Why India Must Be Free" from GANDHI IN INDIA In His Own Words edited by Martin Green. Copyright © 1987 by the Navajivan Trust. Reprinted by permission of University Press of New England.

"The Glory of the Incas" from The Incas of Pedro de Cieza de Leon edited by Victor Wolfgang von Hagen. Copyright © 1959 by the University of Oklahoma Press. Reprinted by permission of University of Oklahoma Press.

"Notebooks from the Renaissance" from SELECTIONS FROM THE NOTEBOOKS OF LEONARDO DA VINCI edited with commentaries by Irma A. Richter. Published by Oxford University Press, 1952. Reprinted by permission of Oxford University Press.

"Working in the Mines" from VICTORIAN WOMEN: A Documentary Account of Women's Lives in Nineteenth-Century England, France, and the United States edited by Erna Olafson Hellerstein, Leslie Parker Hume and Karen M. Offen. Copyright © 1981 by the Board of Trustees of the Loland Standford Junior University.

"The Lumber Camp Song" from CANADA'S STORY IN SONG edited by Edith Fowke and Alan Mills. Used by permission of Edith Fowke.

"Yellow Submarine" Words and Music by John Lennon and Paul McCartney. © Copyright 1966 NORTHERN SONGS. All Rights Controlled and Administered by MCA MUSIC PUBLISHING, A Division of MCA INC., 1755 Broadway, New York, NY 10019 under license from NORTHERN SONGS. International Copyright Secured. All Rights Reserved.

"Fall Rain, Fall Rain" Joseph Shabalala. Courtesy of Full Keel Music Company o/b/o Gallo Music Publishers. All rights reserved. Used by permission.

"Mountains in Israel" Music by H. Coopersmith; Words by T.E. Sampter. From THE SONGS WE SING, selected and edited by Harry Coopersmith. Copyright 1950 by The United Synagogue of America. Utilized with permission of the publisher, The United Synagogue Commission of Jewish Education.

"Saving the Rainforest" from p. 193 from THE FATE OF THE FOREST Developers, Destroyers and Defenders of the Amazon by Susanna Hecht and Alexander Cockburn. Copyright © 1989 by Susanna Hecht and Alexander Cockburn. First published by Verso, 1989. Reprinted by permission of Verso/NLB, London and New York.

"Separation" by Sherko Bekas. Copyright © Sherko Bekas. Used with permission of Zian Halmat for the author.

"Hand-Shadow Song" from UNICEF BOOK OF CHILDREN'S SONGS by William I. Kaufman. Copyright © 1970 by William I. Kaufman. Published by Stackpole Books, Harrisburg, Pa.

"A Pilgrimage to Mecca" from WE LIVE IN SAUDI ARABIA by Abdul Latif Al Hoad. Copyright © 1982 by Wayland (Publishers) Ltd. Reprinted by permission of Franklin Watts, Inc., New York.

"A Maori Warden" from WE LIVE IN NEW ZEALAND by John Ball. Copyright © 1982 by Wayland (Publishers) Ltd. Reprinted by permission of Franklin Watts, Inc., New York.

"Life of a Hindu Priest" from WE LIVE IN INDIA by Veenu Sandal. Copyright © 1981 by Wayland (Publishers) Ltd. Reprinted by permission of Franklin Watts, Inc., New York.

"Becoming a Buddhist Master" from WE LIVE IN MALAYSIA AND SINGAPORE by Jessie Wee. Copyright © 1984 by Wayland (Publishers) Ltd. Reprinted by permission of Franklin Watts, Inc., New York.

"Governing Japan Today" from WE LIVE IN JAPAN by Kazuhide Kawamata. Copyright © 1984 by Wayland (Publishers) Ltd. Reprinted by permission of Franklin Watts, Inc., New York.

"A Craftsman in Bethlehem" from WE LIVE IN ISRAEL by Gemma Levine. Copyright © 1981 by Wayland (Publishers) Ltd. Reprinted by permission of Franklin Watts, Inc., New York.

"Poems for Peace" from MY SHALOM MY PEACE Paintings and Poems by Jewish and Arab Children. First published in Hebrew under the title Hashalom Sheli © 1974 by the American Israel Publishing Co. Ltd., and Sonol, Israel Ltd. English translation copyright © 1975 by Sabra Books, Tel Aviv.

"Letter from Jamaica" from SELECTED WRITINGS OF BOLIVAR compiled by Vicente Lecuna, edited by Harold A. Bierck, Jr., translated by Lewis Bertrand. Volume One 1810-1822. Second edition published by the Bolivarian Society of Venezuela. Published by The Colonial Press Inc.

"This Scepter'd Isle from Richard II" from THE ANNOTATED SHAKESPEARE edited by A.L. Rowse.